Marina Svetlova

A Tribute

Michael Limoli

authorHOUSE®

AuthorHouse™
1663 Liberty Drive
Bloomington, IN 47403
www.authorhouse.com
Phone: 1 (800) 839-8640

Cover photograph
Marina Svetlova in Don Quixote
Photo: Maurice Seymour, courtesy of Ron Seymour

Published by AuthorHouse 03/06/2019

ISBN: 978-1-5462-7673-9 (sc)
ISBN: 978-1-5462-7672-2 (e)

Library of Congress Control Number: 2019900589

Print information available on the last page.

CONTENTS

ACKNOWLEDGMENTS

I wish to express my deepest gratitude and most sincere appreciation to the curator of photographs for the Indiana University Archives, Bradley D. Cook, and his associate Hannah Keeney. They were enormously helpful in arranging access for me to the Svetlova Collection at the B. Wells Library in Bloomington, Indiana. Their knowledgeable guidance was most appreciated as I perused the treasure trove of personal and professional materials that Marina had donated to the library.

I will forever be indebted to Madeline Schrock, managing editor of *Dance Magazine*, *Dance Spirit*, *Dance Theatre*, *Pointe*, and *Dance Retailer News* (Dance Media LLC), for granting me permission to include passages that were previously published by *Dance Magazine*.

I am sincerely appreciative of the generosity afforded to me by the Metropolitan Opera Guild. They were most helpful in locating and providing me with photographs that showcased the artistic expertise of Mariana Svetlova during her years as prima ballerina of the Metropolitan Opera Ballet Company.

Norton Owen and his associate Patsy Gay offered expert assistance and constructive advice concerning the procuration of precious photographs, most of which are housed in their own archives at Jacob's Pillow in Beckett, Massachusetts.

The Australian National Library of Sydney, Australia, was most cooperative in complying with my requests for photographical materials. I wish to express my sincere gratitude for the cooperation offered to me by Mike Thomas in assisting me to locate photos found in the archives of the State Library of Victoria, Australia.

Ryan Stoker of the Reference Librarian Information Services at the National Library of Australia, Melbourne, was particularly effective in guiding me through the process of obtaining photos and permission for their use in this book.

I am grateful for the assistance given to me by David Rosado and Andrea Felder as I sought permission to publish photos from the collection of photographs at New York's Museum of Modern Art.

I owe a dept of gratitude to the New York Public Library, most especially to the Library for the Performing Arts at Lincoln Center, New York City. The breadth of the writings, recordings, and photographs in the Jerome Robbins Dance Collection, which I had the privilege of examining, was certainly among the most extensive and inclusive of the world's greatest repositories of research materials for the understanding and appreciation pf the discipline of the dance.

Assistant curator Dale Stinchcomb of the Harvard Theatre Collection at the Houghton Library at Harvard University, Cambridge, was most helpful in procuring permission to incorporate into this book a photo of Marina Svetlova, taken by the late John Linquist.

It is impossible to find the words to adequately express my sense of gratitude for the cooperation and generous assistance provided by Ron Seymour, the heir of the estate of the esteemed artist Maurice

Seymour, who blessed the world with a divine legacy of beautiful photographs of many of the world's most beloved ballet stars.

I was granted permission to quote from Kathrine Sorley Walker's book *De Basil's Ballet Russes,* by David Leonard, managing director of Dance Books Ltd.

I am thankful for the friendly encouragement and thoughtful advice provided to me by Larry Kelley concerning the legacy of our mutual friend, Marina Svetlova. It is friends like Larry who help keep the memories alive.

I am most appreciative of the helpful input I received from the Indiana Society of Arts and Letters and the Vermont Center for the Arts as I researched the many facets of the career of one of the most influential ballerinas of the twentieth century. Completion of this book was tremendously assisted by my wife, Denise Warner Limoli, former featured dancer with American Ballet Theatre. She was also a friend of Marina and extremely helpful in the selection of photographs to be included in this book.

Elizabeth Diggans and Eloise Giegerich, assistant editor of *Opera News,* have been most generous and helpful in supplying me with some rare and beautiful pictures. Marina Svetlova would have been proud of and touched by their cooperation.

INTRODUCTION

This book does not in any way pretend to be a ballet history book, nor is it a veritable biography. Rather, it is a celebration of the life and accomplishments of a giving and caring woman whose hard work and careful planning culminated in the creation of a career of magnificent proportions. Marina Svetlova became one of the world's most celebrated and ubiquitous ballerinas. In the course of my book, it is my goal mainly to offer some insight into the professional accomplishments of a highly complicated woman who devoted her entire life and never-ending energy to the advancement of an artistic discipline of which she was most fond—that of the dance.

Most of the authors and critics cited throughout my book refer to her as Marina Svetlova. Initially, as one of her students, I was among those who addressed her as "Madame." As the years passed, I went on to become an accompanist for classes she taught. As a solo dancer, I performed with her and eventually became an employee at the Svetlova Dance Center. We became close colleagues and good friends, but for the sake of consistency and to avoid confusion, I have chosen to address her personally as "Marina," although in professional contexts, I refer to her under her stage name of "Marina Svetlova."

I present a sampling of commentaries and critiques written by several of her contemporaries. I have included similarly sounding quotations for the purpose of demonstrating that there existed extensive concurrence concerning the exceptional quality of Madame's work. The enthusiasm and even adulation for her activities in the arts was widespread and not limited only to a number of select, supportive critics and fans. These writings allude to some of the political machinations at work in the ballet world in the early twentieth century, as well as some of the curious social mores that were prevalent when Marina Svetlova was becoming a major player. I examine her interactions with a host of personalities—dancers, ballet companies, choreographers, critics, musicians, and students alike. I have added some of my own interpretations, as if being seen through the looking glass, because I had not yet been born by the time Marina Svetlova embarked upon dance engagements and company affiliations that catapulted her to the zenith of her incredible performing career.

I first met Marina in the spring of 1969, and that date marks the turning point in this book, after which I offer a firsthand account of the aspects of her career to which I was privy. Eventually, we came to realize that we had much in common. We had been artistic associates of many of the same artists, especially from the Metropolitan Opera, and had even studied under some of the same ballet teachers.

My book also provides a glimpse into the workings of a ballet class taught by Marina Svetlova. Initially, I was one of her ballet students. I then became a piano accompanist for some of her classes. Next, I became a performing dancer in certain of her productions and taught at the Svetlova Dance Center in Dorset, Vermont. Ultimately, I danced alongside her in performances presented by the Indiana University Ballet Theatre. Therefore, I became the person who probably knew her in the largest number of diverse artistic circumstances. As witnessed by her undying enthusiasm and seemingly endless energy for producing and supporting excellence in the world of performance art, the impact of Marina's accomplishments cannot be overstated. Foremost among her contributions to the world of the arts was certainly her career as a major performing artist in the dance world. She became known internationally as a prima ballerina—from New York City to Dallas, from Sydney to Honolulu. The impact of her performance career is evidenced by the huge number of adoring fans who enthusiastically attended her performances. Additionally, her penchant for organizing and promoting activities in the other performing arts, such as music and theatre, afforded her the opportunity to acquire some of the necessary tools for assembling her own performance troupe, running her own dance center, and becoming chairperson at one of the country's major college dance departments.

Although Marina Svetlova was extremely professional and earnest about her work, she possessed a devilish sense of humor and enjoyed the making of a good joke or the grabbing of a quick chuckle. My old Russian friend, dancer, and choreographer Zachery Solov (who occasionally taught at the Svetlova Dance Center) told me that he once said to Madame, "As time goes by, Marina, your Russian accent is getting more and more pronounced." He continued his anecdote by telling me that her response was delivered with an even more exaggerated accent, and she asserted that it was "very, very good for business."

She had a tendency not to not take herself too seriously, particularly while working with me during the planning and writing of this book. During these collaborative moments, I sensed that her mind-set was such that it afforded me license to incorporate moments of fun into this missive. For example, my somewhat intense chapter on what allows a dancer to be acknowledged as a true ballerina is soon followed by a lighthearted chapter devoted to the definition, description, and identification of a verifiable (some would have it a "certifiable") balletomane. This juxtaposition of serious propositions with more lighthearted considerations illustrates one of Madame's favorite "old Russian" expressions. She would refer to this opportunity for simultaneously addressing multiple issues—like shooting two squirrels with one rock—which is certainly one of my intentions with this book.

Courtesy of Marina Svetlova

CHAPTER I

Yvette

The Beginning of the Dance Life of Marina Svetlova

Leon Harris wrote a book entitled *Yvette*, an irresistible introduction to the rigorous, glamourous, and private world of ballerinas-to-be. One friend of the author endorsed this book by opining that "ballet belongs to the child within us." He felt that a child's being has not yet become hindered by the inhibitions exhibited by adults, as they are inclined to forfeit the physical freedom they once embraced during their early formative years. When is the pure quest for an ideal expressed with such gracious defiance of gravity? He goes a step further in his description of the unique freedom a child finds while engaging in the special world of ballet. A child unknowingly finds a mean whereby he or she can express in motion what later one attempts to say in words. In a society of children, the impossible is still possible, and one is permitted to enter a fairy-tale world and trained to speak to the emotion within us.

The shortest and least experienced in her class at the Paris Opera Ballet School, Yvette realizes that she must work especially hard to pass her examinations, which would then allow her to become a *petit rat* (little rat) in the famous school. The competition among the girls in her class was fierce, and owing to her age and diminutive size, Yvette received the nickname "Flea."

Yvette is a biographical fairy tale based on the early years of ballet training of a young girl who went on to enjoy a life as a world-renowned ballerina. Its protagonist is—you guessed it—a young Yvette von Hartmann, who was born in Paris on May 3, 1922, and eventually resided in Bloomington, Indiana, until she departed this world on February 11, 2009. The author of *Yvette* was her adoring husband. I knew him as a sophisticated, well-educated professional who was in love with the woman and enthralled by the story of the making of a prima ballerina, Marina Svetlova.

Name

"What's in a name?" asked Dame Ninette de Valois as she acknowledged a closing-night ovation for her company. She was referring to the fact that recently, the Sadler's Wells Ballet had changed its name to the Royal Ballet. She was delighted that at performances, the new name had made no difference in the enthusiastic response awarded her company. Could Valois have been thinking of the words written by William Shakespeare in his *Romeo and Juliet?*

What's in a name? That which we call a rose by any other name would smell as sweet.

Lovers of the arts were of the opinion that Americans may have had some painters and composers, but it seemed that dancers were yet to come. Little did they know that most, if not all, of the American dancers who had already assimilated into the Russian ballet were obliged to change their names from Peterson to Petrovsky. Patrick Kay became first Patrikieff and then Anton Dolin. Hilda Munnings was Sokolova, Alice Marks, Markova. The early American public was trained to expect a *Russian* ballet. And so Russian American dancing teachers instructed their pupils to attempt to be Russian dancers or at least try to give that impression. During the tours of the de Basil Russian Ballet across the United States, auditions were held in many cities to acquire new members for the troupe. Not a few Americans had been chosen to appear with the Russians. Yet of necessity, the printed program had to reflect the mores of the time and display the names of "Russian" dancers. Shirley Bridges of Rochester, New York, appeared under the sobriquet Adrianova. Nina Radova was Vivian Smith of Cleveland; Kyra Strakova was known in St. Louis as Patty Thrall. Marcel Leplat of Seattle became the excellent mime Marc Platoff. The dancers appearing with David Lichine in his ballet *Protée*, labeled Lerina, Sabinova, and Denisova (by any chance, Leroy, Sabin, and Denis?) were trained by June Roper, a dancing teacher of Vancouver.

For years, there has been a slight discrepancy concerning Marina's original name. Some sources claimed that her family name was Hartman, sometimes spelled "Hartmann." Others insisted that her original name was Yvette von Hartmann. Her married names included Parsons, Harris, and Haigue. Marina's father's name was Max von Hartmann, and her mother's was Tamara Andreyev.

To add to the confusion, during Marina's dance competition days, her mother wanted the young girl to use the first name Tamara (her name at that time was still Yvette). Although her mother originally did not wish for her daughter to become a professional dancer (one is reminded of the book *No Daughter of Mine Is Going to Be a Dancer!* written by Sharry Traver Underwood in 2012). Marina told me that her mother had herself wished to have been a ballet dancer. Therefore, she had her daughter assume the first name of Tamara during the earliest of Marina's dance competition days.

Marina also informed me that her professional name, Svetlova, was modeled after the name of the husband of Trefilova, with whom she had studied for several years. The name of the man, a renowned and esteemed arts critic at that time, was Svetlov. He once said, "Talent is an all-embarrassing spirit, it is contented with seven notes, seven primary colors and five positions in dancing; with these it will perform marvels in art, such marvels as will remain young when the present generation, and those that follow it, are in their graves."

Marina is a favorite Russian name, found in many Russian folktales and made renowned by the Mussorgsky opera *Boris Godounov*. Since Russianization was the vogue for ballerinas of that time, why not adopt the name Marina? Another prominent Russian ballet dancer, Igor Eglevsky, named his daughter Marina. However, as demonstrated on several official dance competition documents, Marina Svetlova early on went by the name of Tamara-Yvette Hartmann.

Here is another example of the association of names. The first of the famous young Ballet Russes dancers, known as "baby ballerinas," was Tamara Toumanova, who was also a classmate of Marina's in the Parisian ballet schools, especially Preobrojenska's. At any rate, in a relaxed moment, Marina confided in me that her real name was Yvette—not Tamara, not Marina. (Although "Marina Svetlova" had the ring of an authentic Russian name, I always have found the name Yvette to be more beautiful than Marina or Tamara.)

Courtesy of Ron Seymour

CHAPTER 2

Ballet Pedagogy

Marina Svetlova, Trained by a "Galaxy of Leading Teachers" in Paris[1]

Marina Svetlova began dancing in Paris at the age of eight, and she was definitely in the right place at the right time. Early in the twentieth century, Paris was blessed with an inordinate number of extraordinary ballet pedagogues, many of whom had been admired ballerinas with the Russian Imperial Ballet. Marina Svetlova was anxious to avail herself of the opportunity to study with each of the eminent pedagogues, so she explored all of the studios. When I approached Marina to share with me her recollections of the respective personalities and approaches to teaching of the pedagogues of those with whom she had studied, and to reflect upon the individual strengths of each of the various teachers, I expected to hear her talk about the three most widely known: Lubov Egorova, Mathilde Kchessinska, and Olga Preobrajenska. The latter of these three, Olga Preobrajenska, is the one mentioned most frequently in ballet histories and archives, and she has achieved the recognition as a teacher of extraordinary expertise. Most of the important ballet dancers of the twentieth century were students of Preobrajenska at one time or another. As it turned out, much to my surprise, Marina told me that although she had studied with these three esteemed ballet pedagogues, she felt that the most outstanding teacher among the ballerinas from the Russian Imperial Ballet tradition who had settled in Paris was a fourth pedagogue *exemplaire*, Vera Trefilova. I was familiar with the trio above, but for me, Trefilova was a new commodity. Apparently, all four of these former dancers of the Russian Imperial Ballet had been extraordinary ballerinas in their own right. After emigrating from Russia, Trefilova had "opened a studio where she brought such well-known dancers as Nina Vybroubova and Marina Svetlova."[2]

It was from Trefilova that Svetlova early on acquired a love of and ambition for performing. It could be said that Marina became a protégée of Trefilova, who took Marina around town to enter her in various international dance competitions. Much to the delight of both of them, Marina frequently won top prizes. The Federation Internationale de Danse Championnat du Monde de la Danse awarded Marina the Premiere Prix avec Medaille d'Or pour la Danse Pure Classique in 1931. Marina went on to have the unprecedented distinction of being awarded this prize also in 1932 and 1933. She was the only dancer ever to have been awarded this prize for three consecutive years. In addition to Lydia Loupokova, other Trefilova students included Mary Skeaping and James Selva.

Lubov Egorova

Although ballet history has not dwelt upon the fact, I was pleased to learn that there were also significant male ballet teachers in Paris in the early twentieth century. Marina had the fortunate opportunity to study with a few of them. One of these men, an esteemed dancer as well as teacher, was Alexander Kovsky, who apparently took Marina under his wing. Another pedagogue was Anatol Vilzak. He remained one of Marina's favorite ballet teachers, and she continued to study with him after they had each relocated to New York City.

Anatole Vilzak

Anatole Vilzak was one of those ballet teachers beloved by many dancers of the time. He came from Lithuania near the end of the nineteenth century and was a pupil of Michel Fokine. He had been a dancer in the Maryinsky Ballet in St. Petersburg before becoming the quintessential danseur noble in Diaghilev's Ballets Russes. He was a frequent partner of several of the leading ballerinas of the day, including Mathilde Kchessinska and Olga Spessivtseva. He received much acclaim for having originated certain roles in ballets created by Nijinska, the sister of the superstar Vaslav Nijinska. These ballets included *les Biches* (1924) to the music of Francis Poulenc, and *Les Facheux* (1924) to the music of William Walton.

Vilzak, as was Marina, was among the ranks of the many major dancers and choreographers who gained considerable artistic recognition in a ballet company directed by Ida Rubinstein. In her company, Vilzak was premier danseur, and he created roles in ballets such as Ravel's *Bolero* (1928). In that company, he was also in the first productions of certain Nijinska ballets, such as *Les Nocees de Psyche e de l'Amour* and *Baiser de la Fee* (1928). Eventually, he immigrated to America with his wife, ballerina Ludmilla Schollar. In the US, he danced for Balanchine's American Ballet and also danced in the Ballet of the Metropolitan Opera. He taught at several schools across the United States, including those of the Ballets Russes, American Ballet Theatre, the San Francisco Ballet, and the

Washington Ballet. In 1940, he opened his own school on New York's West Fifty-Fourth Street, where he enjoyed success for several years. Vilzak remained one of Marina's favorite teachers throughout her performing career.

Alexander Govsky

Alexander Govsky, along with Vilsak, was one of the prominent male ballet teachers active in Paris during Marina's early years as an aspiring young dancer. Govsky is perhaps best known as a choreographer and regisseur. Born in Russia near the end of the nineteenth century, he became ballet master of the Bolshoi Ballet. He is credited with having improved the quality of the Maryinsky Ballet in St. Petersburg, but he is best remembered for his restaging of several of the great ballets of Marius Petipa, including *Swan Lake, Don Quixote,* and *Nutcracker.* Marina was one of his favorite students.

Edward Caton

Where does one begin when it comes to a Caton? He was one of the leading dancers in Pavlova's company, then the Mordkin Ballet company, and later the American Ballet Theatre, where he also became a ballet master. After his retirement from being a performing dancer, Caton became a teacher with the Pennsylvania Ballet company and the Washington Ballet in Washington, DC. In New York City, he taught in the school of the Ballet Russe de Monte Carlo. Ultimately, as a dancer, he cultivated a rather powerful presence in character parts, and his intensity on stage in these dramatic roles was hard to ignore. He also became a ballet teacher who had acquired an inimitable stature in the world of ballet.

Marina was outspoken concerning her respect for Edward Caton, as was I. Our love and respect for Caton was one of the several aspects of life in the ballet world that Marina and I had in common. She considered him to have had an enormous influence on her progress toward perfecting her ballet technique. He was one of the most respected ballet teachers of his day. I became one of his protégé, and he often gave me private classes.

During my early years as a ballet dancer, Caton's instruction in ballet was among the most rigorous and the most productive I had experienced. Many of the prominent dancers from that era studied with Caton. I have never heard a negative statement about the quality of his teaching. In fact, Melissa Hayden, a prominent ballerina with NYCB, told me that she had never danced better than when she was at American Ballet Theatre, working with Caton. Once when I was having dinner with a number of dancers, one of them asked me what had made Caton the exceptional teacher that he was known to have been. I tried to describe his method, and I remarked that "Caton was dedicated to his students …"

"He was strict, but you got better," remarked the illustrious Ballet Russe ballerina Eleanor d'Antuono, who finished my sentence. She, too, went on to say that when Caton taught and coached her at ABT, he brought out the very best in her. Caton had also had some success as a choreographer. His most celebrated composition was *Sebastien*, which was greatly admired in performances of Lawrence Rhodes with New York's Harkness Ballet company.

Although Mr. Caton is temperamental, he is one of the most popular choreographers with the dancers. He is imaginative and sympathetic and never fails to make amends for his outbursts, which seem to come from pent-up nervous energy rather than ill-humor.[3]

The Svetlova Ballet Class

In all the twenty-five or so years that I worked with Marina, I would be hard-pressed to remember a class that she missed that she had been scheduled to teach. Her classes began precisely at the prescribed hour. She was always punctual and totally reliable.

Until she was in her seventies, Marina always donned a pair of leotard and tights in which to teach. She usually wore a pair of waist-to-ankle, woolen leg warmers over her tights. As do many professional dancers, she occasionally wore a pair of old pointe shoes with the shanks removed, instead of ballet slippers. When teaching children, usually she wore pink ballet slippers, and on occasion, she wore pink ballet teaching shoes with a low heal at rehearsals or when she was not planning to demonstrate during a class. When she entered the classroom, no special reverential response was required or anticipated. She expected her students to be stretching and warming up as preparation for the class. Marina always did her own short warmup by facing the barre and stretching out her Achilles tendons. She then clasped her fingers behind her back and stretched her arms and obliques by lifting her arms over her head and then bending from side to side. Before commencing the instruction, she would address the class with a casual and friendly greeting, and then class would begin.

She usually started the class directly with an uncomplicated grand plie exercise. Her class then followed a fairly predictable, standard progression of exercises at the barre, from small to larger movement. Usually, at the barre, her combinations were not extremely complicated, but she was adamant that the students should execute the exercises precisely in the manner in which she had prescribed. She often completed the exercises on the first side while facing the class. After one time through, she would circulate around the class, offering precise, personal corrections. I rarely saw her sit down while teaching a class. She had a few favorite responses to the unacceptable execution of certain exercises on the part of the students. For example, especially during a battement tendu exercise, for instance, were there any students prone to moving their hips while executing the combination, she would admonish the students by urging them to maintain their hips in a stationary placement. Were it that the correction was not successfully demonstrated by the students, she would admonish them by saying, "I don't want to see any hoochie-koochie going on," and she would show how she saw some students moving their hips from side to side while completing the combination. She was adamant about not raising the hip of the working leg as the leg was being raised. Another pet peeve of hers was when students would fake the turnout of the legs. No turning out of your feet past the point at which you were able to accomplish the procedure with the entire leg was allowed. She was not overly dramatic at the barre and generally gave the impression that she considered herself and her students all to be dancers engaged in the learning process. Although she was rather strict, I never once saw her lose her temper and shout at any student.

One idiosyncrasy of Marina's class occurred when she would demonstrate a stretching exercise at the barre, familiar to most experienced ballet dancers. While standing in fifth position, she would have the dancers execute a demi-plié on the inside leg while sliding a stretched outside leg back and into a deep fourth position. While most teachers refer to this movement as a stretch or a "lunge," Marina would say, "plunge." I always laughed to myself about what seemed to me to be an amusing choice of words. In all my years in the ballet studio, as dancer or dance accompanist, I had never heard another teacher describe the movement in those terms. This is an example of how she sometimes employed a personalized vocabulary to make the classroom situation less formal.

An example of one of the more unusual teaching concepts espoused by Marina at the barre was when she would have the dancers hold on to the barre with the outside arm, not the usual arm closest to the barre. I have witnessed this approach only one other time in my career in ballet, when I was accompanying a class being taught by a former dancer of the French Opera Ballet. The first time I experienced this phenomenon as a dancer in Marina's class, I thought to myself that it was the most ridiculous thing I had ever experienced as a ballet dancer, and I was secretly rather judgmental and somewhat resistant. However, somehow, seemingly miraculously, when the class moved on to the center part of the class, I found myself uncommonly on top of my game, particularly when it came to pirouettes. I cannot with all confidence credit this unorthodox teaching method of placing the "wrong" hand on the barre with having had a remarkably positive effect on my center work that day. It may simply have been coincidental, but it was definitely unexpected. I have no idea what the results might have been were this unusual approach to the placement of the outside hand on the barre to be used frequently or even regularly.

When the class left the barre and relocated themselves to the center of the studio, her combinations became more complex, and the movement displayed a greater degree of intricacy. One aspect of her teaching of the center work that I admired was that she did not always begin the center work from a traditional starting point. The emphasis was more on building a secure technique than becoming involved with attempting to decipher intricate choreography, although she demanded precision and polish.

Apropos the use of proper ballet terminology, Marina was extremely articulate. She did not describe any ballet maneuver in a colloquial nomenclature. Her French was precise and descriptive. She was one of a few ballet teachers among the hundreds with whom I have worked, for example, who employed the appropriate French ballet term *racusi* rather than "run to back the back of the studio around" when instructing the class to circle back upstage and to take their respective position before the repetition of a given combination. One other unique use of terminology she employed occasionally was when she was describing the execution of a *bouree suivee sur les pointes*. She would encourage the girls to employ a more rapid oscillation with the toes by saying, "Pietinez, pietinez." This practice Marina had to use correct French terminology helped to promote an awareness and appreciation for proper ballet terminology.

Another source of inspiration in Marina's ballet class was that she was one of the most musical ballet teachers with whom I have worked (Denise Warner falling into the same category). Marina was a natural. She had a good ear and could recognize quality and outstanding performance. She was a good friend of the famous pianist Claudio Arrau, which might have contributed to the development of her discerning ear for music. She was always certain of the style of music she wanted and needed. She and I played this little unspoken game. As the accompanist for Marina's classes, I would diddle a bit at the piano, while waiting for the dancers to transition from exercises at the barre to combinations in the center. With Marina, I would occasionally bring a new little piece and mark through it. She would often come to the piano and say, "Let's use that," and she would spontaneously construct a combination to that composition. She was creative as well as adventuresome. Although her barre routine generally progressed in a predictable order, her center part of the class did not always follow a predictable progression of movement that one might have expected. Frequently, she would not begin with an Adagio or a battement tendu combination, as is the case with most ballet teachers. For example, she was not averse to beginning the center part of a class with a light or fluid little waltz. For this reason, her classes were unpredictable but comprehensive.

Marina was insistent on promoting a disciplined musical awareness. She wasn't fanatical or overly ostentatious, but she expected musical precision. When it came to music, Marina was a natural. She once confided to me that she had never had any training in music. I sometimes wondered if her facility with incorporating an enviable musical sensitivity with her sometimes intricate dance movement was a result of having been a close friend and neighbor of the world-class pianist Claudio Arrau.

In spite of her Russian name, Marina's class was not what one would consider a totally Russian class. Although most of her early instruction in ballet was delivered by Russian teachers, Marina's background was a bit more cosmopolitan. She called upon her experience with the various schools of ballet training with which she had been associated. Her method of ballet instruction seemed to represent an amalgamation of the style of training that was representative of the Paris Opera Ballet, where she also had been a young student, and the Russian syllabus to which she had been exposed as a young student in Paris. Her classes reflected a sensitive composite of these various styles. She was strict but adaptable. There was never a sense that the class was Marina's performance.

She predictably ended class with a traditional reverence.

Marina was often selected to be master teacher at various dance conventions and performance venues. Along with guesting in Fort Worth, Dallas, and New Orleans, for example, she was invited to Puerto Rico, to Mexico, and to Massachusetts's Jacobs Pillow to give serious instruction in ballet. Svetlova went on to design the curriculum for many dance schools throughout America and Central America.

Performance Warm-Up Class

In my impression, Marina's strong suit was her construction of the typically short warm-up class preceding a performance—especially when she too was about to perform. It seemed to be her truly inspired teaching moment. When she and I were dancing in the same performance, I realized one truly inspired aspect of her performance preparation. Her pacing was not that of a usual ballet class. She would spontaneously deliver a sharp, quick combination immediately following a long, slow, and stretched-out exercise. At first, it took me completely by surprise. It was a short, compressed warm-up class, and eventually one could see and respect the type of calculated warm-up that had come to be part and parcel for a dancer who had learned how to quickly prepare for a performance after years of touring, one-night stands, and often several performances in one day, often during a long series of one-night stands.

CHAPTER 3

Baby Ballerinas

One of the most enduring publicity catch phrases in ballet history is *the baby ballerinas*. Haskell, who may have invented it, says that before the London Alhambra season the company was known as the 'Babies' Ballet', the principals being anywhere between thirteen and seventeen years in age. Once coined, whoever the coiner, it was too vivid to die ... a trio of divinities on stage who revert outside the theatre into unsophisticated, chaperoned schoolgirls with shoulder-length hair, innocent of make-up, wearing childish clothes and ankle socks.[1]

Baby ballerinas were not young girls who provided inspiration for the subsequent television show, *Dance Moms*.

> The Monte Carlo Ballet was substantially the late Diaghilev ballet, except for the apparition of the much-heralded new baby stars: Toumonova, Riabouchinska, and Baronova. It delighted the Diaghilev audiences who feared that with him, his ballet was dead.[2]

Dancers who received the distinction of having been awarded such a privileged position within a company were few, but they all shared in the accompanying publicity. After entering the Original Ballet Russe, Svetlova quickly was acknowledged as one of the young starlets. Unlike other developments in the ballet world in the early twentieth century, most ballet lovers were comfortable with the distinction and the deference being bestowed upon these young darlings.

> The glade, in which the Sylphs are ... is well known to followers of the ballet ... it may hold a content of other-worldliness, as it does when Baraonova, Toumanova and Riabouschinska appear in it under Colonel de Basil's direction.[3]

> Diaghilev had often gone the rounds of the dancing schools of London and Paris in search of talent while it was young. Colonel de Basil too went the rounds – and collected his company while it was even younger.[4]

To this day, there exists some controversy about to whom should be bestowed the honor of having "discovered" the *babies*. Some ballet history books credit Balanchine with the genius of having "fathered" them. Certainly, he saw in them unique choreographic material. Initially, it was with the Blum/de Basil Ballet Russe de Monte Carlo company that he began to mold their talents. However, some credit de Basil for their discovery. Truth to be told, it would seem to have been de Basil with one of his Ballet Russe companies who championed their full potential. Owing to the great confusion surrounding the authenticity of who owned and who ran each of the Ballet Russe companies throughout the 1930s, each director and ballet master wanted to lay claim to the victory of having found, recognized, molded, and promoted the phenomenon of the first three babies.

> De Basil it will be remembered, then created the 'baby ballerina' troup:
> Toumanova, Riabouchinska, Baronova and of course, Svetlova.[5]

The celebrity accorded the baby ballerina was not only peculiar to the days of the Ballet Russe. For decades, ballet audiences have remained enthralled with the charm of these child stars and maintained an endearing regard for them, on and off stage.

> Wonder children, indeed, these three 'baby ballerinas', who in their brilliant teenage
> years could command panegyrics.[6]

From the very onset, Col. de Basil took some big gambles. The young girls whose ages ranged from fourteen to eighteen were to become his headliners. He felt that the public would warm up to these wunderkind after they had proven themselves, and from that point on, the fans would come to the ballet primarily to see the famous young starlets.

> The trio promised to be inspiring choreographic material for Balanchine, and for
> Blum and de Basil, an assurance that their company had a new image to offer.[7]

As was to have been expected, as audiences became more and more infatuated with the youngsters, parents of other young dancers envisioned their child as being due a slice of the pie:

> It is said that a ballerina is born, and like a princess, can never rise from the ranks.
> Yet every mother assumes that her dancing daughter is bred for it, and it is true that
> a child appearing as a prodigy has some advantage …[8]

Although it does depend somewhat on the unique circumstances (e.g., location, type of dancer, history of appearances, and relative success of young dancers in that company), the public in general is very sympathetic to youth in performance and publicity.

> The 'baby ballerinas' publicity campaign is legendary … they were often referred to
> collectively as 'the young girls' because of their extreme youth.[9]

One can perhaps recall the captivating performance of a very young Judy Garland when she appeared in *The Wizard of* Oz. Not only was her voice kissed by an angel, but she could convey a childlike sincerity that won the hearts of a loving audience.

I doubt that the infatuation with youth in the performing arts will ever disappear. The fascination with and love for the child prodigy will endure. From the days of the precocious composer Wolfgang Amadeus Mozart to the era of the gifted young violinist, Joshua Bell, youthful accomplishments in the arts foster a love affair between the young performers and their fans. Another example of this phenomenon can be witnessed with the genius entertainer Michael Jackson. His early fame was achieved when he appeared as the young soloist with the Jackson Five—youth reigns.

When it comes to the baby ballerinas, their immense international notoriety was accomplished through de Basil's Ballet Russe.

Baby Ballerinas Became Superstars

In the thirties, at the height of the personality cult, ballet dancers entered the star system. This included the baby ballerinas who were featured daily in social columns and in illustrated magazines from London to Bombay, from New York to Buenos Aires. The public's fascination with their careers and their individual antics was reflected in the international press and in movie house newsreels.

Previously, one looked to the more established, older, more experienced dancers to mesmerize the audiences. It was Karsavina, Trefilova, and Dudinskaya whose reputations for being the foremost interpreters of the classics were the exulted divinity. Their positions in their respective companies were not to be questioned, but they were being challenged.

> This policy of featuring extreme youth was as firm as it was novel. Child dancers in themselves were nothing new, but they had never been the dominant theme of a company ... Blum and de Basil approved, knowing that instead of limping along as a poor descendant of Diaghilev their company should find its own personality, and de Basil, ... must have recognized immediately what excellent publicity such a policy would attract.[10]

Certainly it is difficult, if at all possible, to estimate whether or not the affection directors displayed toward these young stars was based exclusively on their success at the box office. One would like to think that audiences and directors alike remained aware that these young dancing stars were also children:

> It was the little girls in whom Blum and de Basil were putting their faith. Both felt a proprietary fatherly interest in their school girl stars ... de Basil also recognized how valuable the 'baby ballerinas' were in terms of publicity ... He would make much of them and the sentimental appeal of their youth to the press and public with an eye to pulling in audiences ... He launched a succession of them over the years[11]

By way of summary, one could look to the eminent impresario Sol Hurok:

Once the pattern had been set, it continued. Dancers were regularly engaged in their mid-teens. [12]

Humanity's obsession with youth is as old as time itself and has virtually never disappeared. Witness the excursions of Ponce de Leon in his eternal search for the fountain of youth. Then there was Tazio in Thomas Mann's *Death in Venice.*

It was not long before Marina was cast in the same roles as each of the original three babies. She also received comparable praise from the critics. Here is some biographical information to illustrate the line of succession into which Svetlova entered after she became recognized as one of the gifted young girls.

Tamara Toumonova

Sol Hurok was a friend of Toumonova and had watched her growth as a dancer from the years when she was a young student to the days when she became a superstar. He felt that it was more than her talents as a dancer that catapulted her into the headlines and the imaginations of many a fan.

> She was born in a box-car in Siberia, while her parents were escaping into China from the Russian Revolution, is a tale too often told … Toumonova's whole life, career, and story have been … the thrice-familiar tale of the White-Russian *emigree* … hers is extremely sentimental. Sentiment and sentimentality play a big part in Tamara's life.[13]

Tatiana Riabouchinska

Riaboushinska was called by some critics "the most unusual dancer of her generation." Her natural style of dancing was considered to be light in spirit. However, she was considered to be somewhat deficient when it came to technical prowess. She was considered to represent a style of dancing that came to be known as "lyrical dance." Riabouchinska cast a captivating spell on much of her audience. She had long, luscious blond hair that awarded her a special allure. She was quite a versatile dancer and appeared in films and musical comedies. She danced with most of the major companies of the time, including Balanchine's les Ballets 1933. She eventually became the wife of the handsome dancer David Lichine, and they became a glamorous Hollywood pinup couple.

Riabouchinska was born in Leningrad in 1917. Her father was a banker for the czar, and her entire family was put under house arrest by the revolutionists. Obviously, it was incumbent upon her family to flee Russia. They joined the roster of the White Russians and relocated to the Russian colony in Paris, France. She was brought to the Original Ballet Russe by the choreographer to perform in some of his major works, such as *Cotillon,* choreography by George Balanchine, the George Balanchine Trust.

Irina Baronova

From the first days of the ballet renaissance in 1933, a round-faced, long-legged adolescent was acclaimed by the press and public. It has been conceded that Irina Baronova was a great dancer; her greatness is undisputed. In his 1934 bestseller, Arnold Haskell devoted a whole chapter to the fifteen-year-old, whom he singled out as "the ideal dancer of today." John Martin, who is not easily won over, wrote in the *New York Times* in October 1935 about the increasing loveliness of Irina Baronova, the richly endowed young artist who had begun to sense her own potentialities. He felt that no other dancer of the day could hold a candle to her for the purity of her classical style. Lincoln Kirstein, who is reluctant to praise those who he considered to be a member of the clan of the "overpublicized Russians," wrote in June 1936: Baronova has become a ballerina, almost a *ballerina assoluta* in two years.

An esteemed dancer from the Ballet Russe days and an outstanding pedagogue with whom I worked at the North Carolina School of the Arts, Duncan Noble, shared with me his opinion that of the original three babies, it was Baronova who "could really dance." He had partnered her in Ballet Russe de Monte Carlo and considered her to be the outstanding star among the three original baby ballerinas.

> At last the growing superstition that the dancer was only in her prime after thirty had gone forever.[14]

It was not long before Marina was cast in the same roles as each of the original three babies. She also received comparable praise from the critics.

A Group of Talented Young Dancers Also Emerged, Including Marina Svetlova[15]

The headliners of the de Basil's Original Ballet Russe were the three original baby ballerinas, Baronova, Riabouchinska, and Tumonova, and although they were considered to be the most brilliant ballerinas of the day, there were younger babies in the wings, so to speak, who were growing in notoriety. *Dance Magazine* had a regular column called "Dance in Review." After one appearance of the de Basil Original Ballet Russe in 1940, this magazine wrote that the company included a flock of young soloists whose names would shine brightly on the ballet horizon for years to come. Among those described were Alexandra Denisova, Genevieve Moulin, Tatiana Leskova, and Anna Volkava and Marina Svetlova.

Marina Svetlova, one of the Ballet's new group of starlets pictured here. Paris-born of Russian parents, Svetlova is a product of the Trefilova school in Paris and though only sixteen years old now, began her professional career five years ago.

Tatiana Leskova is also French-born of Russian parents, and studied in Paris in the Egorova school, beginning at the age of eleven. After about three years of appearances in Europe, she joined de Basil last year in London for the Australian tour.

Genevieve Moulin is that rarity, a French ballet dancer, and a product of the Egorova school. Sixteen years old now, she first appeared professionally with Egorova's Ballets de la Jeunesse and joined de Basil last year in London for the first time.

Alexandra Denisova, seventeen-ye old Vancouver girl, studied w June Roper and Egorova, joining Original Ballet Russe three years for the European and Austra seasons. Her principal roles in Graduation Ball and Pagan

DECEMBER 1940

Photo: Maurice Seymour, *Dance Magazine*, courtesy of Ron Seymour

Baronova and Tamara Toumonova alternated in the Mazurka and pas de deux ...
the Baronovites and the Toumanivites had their field days. Marina Svetlova danced
this part on one occasion and appeared to excellent advantage.[16]

Marina Svetlova

Born in Paris of Russian parents, the truly Russian temperament and natural joy in
dancing so characteristic of this race are in her happily blended ... I followed her
career closely until the moment supreme for every dancer when, as a full-fledged
ballerina ... Still in her teens, Marina Svetlova has received wide recognition for her
exceptional talent.[17]

The effect of Marina's early signs of exceptional stage presence was widely recognized. Her varied
gifts developed naturally, and close friends saw that Marina Svetlova had blossomed into a harmonious
being, a great dancer and a delightful personality. In an ode to ballerinas an early twentieth-century
poet described her as being akin to a soft rose petal:

O toi, don't le pied se pose ...
Songe habille de satin.[18]

Another of Svetlova's fans found her performances to be particularly outstanding because, for
him, her talents seemed to demonstrate a tremendous versatility:

Her inherent spirit of the dance ... a feeling of exquisite interpretations, delicate
precision in steps of the most intricate difficulty, unerring dramatic and musical
sense were immediately recognized. As a "baby ballerina' Svetlova was held in high
esteem.[19]

Serge Lifar, the famous dancer and director of the Grand Opera of Paris Opera, had this to say
about a young Marina Svetlova:

All her movements are inspired and her lines enticingly fluid.[20]

Marina Svetlova photo: Maurice Seymour, courtesy of Ron Seymour

> The Original Ballet Russe … returns. They present 7 premieres … and dancers include … the so-called baby ballerinas: Tatiana Leskova, Genevieve Moulin, Tatiana Stepanova, and Marina Svetlova.[21]

Marina's quick graduation from the category of baby ballerina to the level of ballerina and eventually prima ballerina was described by the dance expert Olga Maynard when she made the following observation:

> Svetlova is a strong technician, with a sharp, clean attack … she is in turn passionate, vivaciously comic and lyrical.[22]

Marina displayed her versatility in her portrayal of dramatic roles, such as the Divine Genius in Fokine's *Paganini* and Violetta in *Camille*. She also realized success in comic roles, such as one of the Junior Girl as well as the solo part for the Student found in Lichine's *Graduation Ball*. Her softer roles, as found in Fokines's *Les Sylphides* and *le Spectre de la Rose*, were also greatly admired. However, some journalists focused on one specific aspect of her dancing:

> De Basil has a grand bunch of newcomers … of the new girls, Svetlova has the best classical style.[23]

The following opinion points to the lasting impact of a baby ballerina. It is all about process. It began with a vision. It continued through publicity, coupled with the artistic growth of the young superstars. It becomes a reality through the support of the audience.

In spite of the fact that most patrons of the ballet agreed that it was the senior ballerinas from the Russian Imperial Ballet who had saved ballet after the disbanding of the Diaghilev Ballets Russes, "many fans felt that one must give credit to de Basil, who was fearless and far-sighted enough to realize that only by composing his company of these children and entrusting them to the guidance of experienced artists could ballet become a possibility … All honor to him."[24]

As an aside, who can forget the enchanting presence of the precocious child star, Shirley Temple? With "On the Good Ship, Lollipop," not only were viewers in awe of little girl-ness, but she also displayed enviable talents as a dancer. This attribute allowed her to hold her own against the formidable skills of the world-renowned dancer Bojangles. Who could ever forget the scene with the two of them tapping up and down the staircase in the movie *The Little Colonel*?

Granted, the babies needed to produce a product in order to grow up and became mature artists in their own right. However, I am not certain that those who discovered them and promoted them had actually thought beyond the spontaneous impact that these young darlings would have on the audiences of that time.

> The ballet world has long been of the opinion that no dancer becomes a *ballerina* until she is 30 … They also understand, who have seen a talented dancer change and gradually improve until suddenly she is altogether different from what she was before; she is gracious, modest, mature.[25]

Just as the ballet world was falling in love with their child stars, including Marina Svetlova, a similar event became prevalent in the world of music, especially with young singers—Deanna Durban, case in point. She was a very pretty girl with a beautiful, crystalline voice. The range of her voice was rather extensive, and her style was similar to that of an accomplished opera singer. Durban appeared in her first film at age fourteen and eventually became the top-salaried woman in America. (One might recall that the famous opera diva Maria Callas made her first documentable radio appearance at the age of fourteen, under the sobriquet "Nina Foresti," singing "Un Bel Di" from Puccini's *Madame Butterfly*.) Rare as it may be, here are two examples of child stars who went on to having immense, enviable success.

> The baby ballerinas of the first company have grown into young ladies in their early twenties. And are today the finest ballet dancers of our generation.[26]

The acceptance of the phenomenon of the child star was not always met with great enthusiasm. In point of fact, from certain camps, the growing popularity with which these babies were being showered was greeted with a little trepidation:

> Baronova is reported to have told a Daily News reporter: "I feel like a grandmother now that we have ten children in the ballet. They are aged from 14 to 17, and I tell you, I feel old."[27]

CHAPTER 4

Ballerina

Photo: Maurice Seymour, courtesy of Ron Seymour

"Ballet is woman."

The above statement was made by one of the indisputable dance geniuses of the twentieth century, George Balanchine. BALANCHINE is a trademark of the George Balanchine Trust. His opinion indicates his tremendous respect for the ballerina.

> *Ballerina* is the Italian word for a female dancer. All girls who dance professionally in Italy are, therefore, *ballerinas.*[1]

I must confess that I find myself referring to any female ballet dancer as a ballerina. Perhaps this is because I am Italian, but I suspect that is a habit of mine that has nothing to do with the level of accomplishment having been obtained by said dancer. Marie Taglioni, a heroine of the Romantic Age of ballet that began during the 1830s is the danseuse credited with having originated the elevation of the solo female dancer onto the tips of her toes. This innovation evoked an ethereal vision of a sylph flying into the stratosphere. It was this fantasy that captured the imagination of many a dance dreamer and propelled the danseuse into a position of preeminence among all dancers. The ballerina became a symbol of man's eternal struggle to reconcile his temporal exigencies with his supernatural aspirations.

~When entering into a discussion of ballerina-ism, prend-garde!~

An example of the controversy one will encounter is demonstrated by the assertion that the term "a plain ballerina" rings as an impossible contradiction.[2]

The *danceur* was often obliged to assume the identity of the everyman cavalier and to gallantly assist the ballerina of the moment in presenting herself to best advantage. However, he was not totally willing to go silently into that good night and abdicate his claim to royalty in the face of what was becoming the realm of the ballerina. Especially during the time of Diaghilev's Ballets Russes, male superstars continued to flex their balletic muscle and retain a modicum of celebrity, but it was the ballerina who had begun to enjoy increasing success in attracting enthusiastic audiences.

The public remembered the legacy of the Diaghilev Ballets Russes, during which the male dancer was the headliner. The ballet fans were accustomed to shouting out the names of their favorites, such as Dolin Massine and Lifar, from all corners of the auditorium.

Toumanova, Baronova, Danilova—Riabouchinska—these are the names that come drifting down to the stage under the de Basil aegis. Massine, Lichine, and Shabalevsky all have their following but now they have to share the plaudits with the *ballerine* of the company …[3]

In her book *Footnotes to the Ballet,* Caryl Brahms goes on to say that shortly after the reign of the Diaghilev Ballets Russes, "the new ballet public is supremely ballerina-conscious."[4]

From Pavlova to Svetlova

Anna Pavlova was among Marina's earliest dance idols and was the inspiration for the formation of the traveling Svetlova Dance Ensemble. It is fascinating to notice how Marina modeled her dance adventures after those of her idol. Marina eventually was described by experts and fans with many of the accolades previously bestowed upon her guru.

I cannot begin to explain where others more competent have failed, why, with no *corps de ballet* or décor to help, it affects me as it does; there has been, and will be, only one Pavlova. … Those who have never seen her can never understand the translation … She was the Goddess of Nature personified.[5]

Anna Pavlova, for whom Michel Fokine created his solo ballet, *The Dying Swan,* quickly became the ballet legend of the early twentieth century. This Fokine ballet for the solo ballerina soon became emblematic of the world's perception of what it means to be a ballerina. The balletomane became mesmerized. Through the extensive travels of her own concert group, Pavlova's name became nearly synonymous with that of the classical ballet.

> Pavlova was not a great virtuoso, but her personal quality made virtuosity of the simplest movements … For some aspects of ballet, there are not personal opinions but very definite standards. In judging whether a dancer is a good dancer such attributes as style, posture, bearing, line, musicality, the ability to create atmosphere are important. [6]

Eventually, Marina gained similar name recognition as that of Anna Pavlova, as described above.

> One of the most widely traveled and highly acclaimed ballerinas of the Twentieth Century, Miss Svetlova's name is synonymous with the classical ballet in a dozen countries.[7]

Svetlova is a *prima donna* in the grand manner.[8]

Marina Svetlova, courtesy of Ron Seymour

She epitomizes the Ballet in style and form.[9]

Marina's accomplishments as a ballerina were achieved through the combination and application of a collection of specific skills—some innate and others acquired—these being training, knowledge, experience, communication, respect, stamina, and versatility.

Training

One could be reminded that Marina studied with virtually all of the famous and important Russian ballet teachers who had settled in Paris early in the twentieth century. In this way, she strove to allow her training to reflect an amalgam of the various strong points of each of the well-respected pedagogues. In addition to a well-orchestrated balance among the instruction of these pedagogues, which Marina was already accomplishing, she studied at the Paris Opera, where she was able to assimilate the slightly lighter, perhaps more embellished style of the French school. Marina never stopped in the quest for improvement. When she came to the US, she sought out the best teachers that America had to offer.

Knowledge

Marina had a reverential appreciation for the accomplishments of her distinguished predecessor, Anna Pavlova. Marina performed some of the Pavlova roles, such as *The Dying Swan*, and also learned some of her favorite roles from their creator, Michel Fokine. For example, he personally coached Marina in solo roles from his *Paganini* and from his signature ballet, *Les Sylphides.* He also prepared her for performances of his *Dying Swan,* which Marina would on occasion find herself performing multiple times in the same day while on tour.

> Though every step comes to her as easily as breathing, she believes in the tradition that "unless you go forward you may slide back" ... Marina Svetlova studied under the great masters ... who developed in the youthful artist, alongside the classical basis, understanding and knowledge of modern rhythm and dance.[10]

Experience

Marina performed with many of the leading ballet companies of her time, both here and abroad, including the Ida Rubinstein company, the Original Ballet Russe, Ballet Theatre, the Ballet of the Metropolitan Opera, the Ballet of the New York City Opera, London Festival Ballet, Finish National Ballet, Irish National Ballet, Het Netherlands Ballet, and the Royal Swedish Ballet. These collaborations brought to Marina's teaching and choreography a great regard for ballet history and the lasting influence she felt it would have on students of all ages. Actually, she herself had played a leading role in the ongoing pathway of ballet tradition. In addition to Fokine, Marina worked with other important and influential choreographers of the twentieth century. Choreographer Leonide Massine had an influence on Marina throughout her career, beginning with having created a role for her in his ballet *Amphion,* which he made for the Ida Rubinstein Ballet company. With the Original Ballet Russe, her performances in his *les Presages* and *Choreartium* were met with great enthusiasm. Massine also created a new version of *Mlle. Angot* (1951) for her at the NYC Opera. Another choreographer with whom Marina worked was David Lichine. Before he created a role for Marina in his magnum opus *Graduation Bal,* she appeared to great acclaim with the Original Ballet Russe in performances of another of his ballets, *Protee.*

Communication

It was perhaps her uncanny gift for speaking to the audience through movement that was the most important characteristic of Marina's performances and made her a favorite among her fans. In addition to my reactions to her performances while I was an audience member, my observations as a fellow cast member provided me with ample opportunities to witness the commitment Marina had to conveying her truth about performing to her audiences.

She has *Ce je ne crois pas* of irresistible charm.[11]

Viennese Waltz · ·· Strauss

Marina Svetlova with Robert Roland.
Photo: Bruno of Hollywood, courtesy of the *Opera Metropolitan News.*

22

One characteristic of her technical prowess was displayed especially while performing pirouettes. She employed such a quick, sparkling use of the head coupled with an infectious smile whose sincerity was unmistakable. She was concentrating on engaging her audience at least as much as she was concerned with the execution of all the steps, and she was a dynamo of energy and stamina. Marina was highly skilled at pacing herself throughout a performance. She knew how and when to save of up energy and when to release a visceral power to propel a phrase to the ultimate climax. Her stage presence was especially captivating through her regal carriage of the body.

Respect

I told Marina how much I had enjoyed Samsova's dancing and in place of showing any sense of being challenged, Marina became somewhat animated and stated what a wonderful dancer Samsova was. Marina went on to elaborate on her statement of appreciation by describing how much she admired Samsova's talent for fluid movement and "dancing with her whole body." On another occasion, the name of Zizi Jeanmaire came up. I recounted how much I admired her dancing. Marina responded with a lively facial expression and stated emphatically, "Oh, yes, excellent dancer." Rather than talking about herself and her many accomplishments, Marina preferred listening to one tell of their own accomplishments in the arts and their personal development. She seemed to be sincerely interested in learning about how one arrived at a given point in time during the sojourn toward artistic excellence.

Stamina

Her performance schedule at the Metropolitan Opera was likewise gruesome. Along with many performances in a number of operas, Marina appeared on the programs of many of the Metropolitan Opera Galas. The number of cities in which Svetlova performed on tour with her own troupe, coupled with the number and variety of roles she commanded, sometimes all in one day, was extraordinary.

Adagio Classique   Liszt

Marina Svetlova and Robert Roland in *Adagio Classique.*
Photo: Bruno of Hollywood, courtesy of *Metropolitan Opera News.*

Versatility

Along with Marina's successes with the classical and romantic repertoire, Marina was also capable of and interested in performing choreography demonstrating contrasting styles. Her roles in Schwezoff's *Lutte Eternelle* as well as her participation in Balanchine's *Balustrade* were ventures into uncharted waters. At Ballet Theatre, Marina also worked with Anthony Tudor. Marina danced the French Ballerina role in his *Gala Performance,* which provided her with the opportunity to assume a tongue-in-cheek, almost comic role.

> In the variety field Svetlova made a debut in a three-month's run in Bournemouth In Herold Fielding's "The Big Show of 1958" and danced the Dying Swan twice a day. This Christmas (1959) found her dancing in her first pantomime, "Humpty Dumpty" at London's Palladium, and the show will continue (twice daily).[12]

Here is a sampling of the many ballets in which she performed solo roles with major ballet companies around the world. The list reflects the scope of her proficiency with the portrayals of divergent roles. I have included reviews written by critics and fans who witnessed Marina's performances in these ballets.

Here is a list of choreographers and their respective creations in which Svetlova appeared to great distinction:

David Lichine

Graduation Ball

> Svetlova's power as a mime came to the fore in the role of a *pig-tail school girl.* She was bouncing with vitality, amusing and unsophisticated and made a small dance convey much. [13]

On another occasion, a critic pointed out that:

She imbued the part with airy grace, playful nonchalance, and a delightful spirit of coquetry. [14]

Protee

> Svetlova was alluring to the eye and brilliantly efficient in some intricate and technically difficult steps.[15]

Marius Petipa

Aurora's Wedding (Sleeping Beauty)

Here is a sampling of reviews that Marina received for her many appearance in the role of Aurora:

> As Princess Aurora, Svetlova was superb. The precision of every movement, the purity of every arabesque gave an amazing poise and fluidity to her style. [16]

> Marina Svetlova received repeated applause for her exquisite interpretation, her grace, her charm and her youthful slenderness. [17]

> An item of great interest was Marina Svetlova's dancing in *Aurora. The technique is certainly there but at the same time there is a delicacy of movement, a refinement in every detail that conceal every trace of effort.* [18]

Le Spectre de la Rose

> Marina Svetlova danced this part with the warmth and tenderness, which are characteristic of this young and brilliant dancer.[19]

> Svetlova's appealing personality and the pure classicism of her dancing were perfectly suited for this romantic part. [20]

Michel Fokine

Paganini

Although this ballet may not have been one of Marina's signature roles, here are some examples of press releases that illustrate the impact produced by Marina's performances in this ballet:

> There is no praise too high for *Miss Svetlova's* interpretation of a most demanding role. Only complete understanding of her part could bring forth such ardent artistry.[21]

> *Paganini* is excellent theater throughout … Alexandra Denisova and Marina Svetlova who alternate in the role of the Divine Genius possess an extraordinary technique, a fluency of movement and a poetic quality so necessary in this part. Of the two, Svetlova is the more romantic one …[22]

> Svetlova a young dancer in the Pavlova tradition danced the *Divine Genius,* imbued with such an unerring musical sense, she preserved a rhythm in the toes that was enchanting and the like of which was never seen before.[23]

Les Sylphides

I have saved mention of Marina's performances in Fokine's *Les Sylphides* because aside from a few of her many assignments with New York's Metropolitan Opera, *Les Sylphides* could be considered Marina's signature ballet.

In Svetlova's dancing we saw that graceful lyrical quality which we associate with the idea of *Sylphides*.[24]

An example of the importance this ballet had in the development of Marina's career, in performances of *Les Sylphides* with the Original Ballet Russe, she found herself alternating to high acclaim in solo roles with each of the three original baby ballerinas, Baronova, Riabouchenska, and Toumonova.

Original Ballet Russe, Aug. 23, Watergate, Washington D. C. Mgt. Fortune Gallo

The first bill presented included: *Les Sylphides* with Marina Svetlova, Tatiana Riabouchinska, Anna Volkava and Roman Jasinsky in the solo parts … Marina Svetlova gave a fine performance in the Mazurka and Pas de Deux.[25]

All around the world, Marina danced each of the solo ballerina roles in this ballet. Audiences saw in her performances a special affinity for both the composer and this choreographer.

She captured the subtle spirit of Chopin's music and welded it with skill to Fokine's choreographer.[26]

Sensational reviews abound from various countries of the world regarding her performances in both of these ballets, but I have chosen to place more emphasis on Marina's experience with performing various solo roles in *Les Sylphides* because it was Marina who invited me to appear as the solo danceur in performances of this ballet she was preparing for in the US and abroad.

Roman Jasinsky (center), Marina Svetlova (center), and artists of the company in *Les Sylphides,* the Original Ballet Russe Australian tour, His Majesty's Theatre, Melbourne, 1940, author: Hugh P. Hall, PIC/11102/913 LOC ALBUM 1111/22, courtesy: National Library of Australia.

Svetlova and Jasinsky in the *Valse* are the most spiritually beautiful.[27]

Marina Svetlova in *Les Sylphides* photo: Valente, New York, courtesy of the Metropolitan Opera Association

The appreciation for Marina's exceptional performances in this *Les Sylphides* were recorded around the world.

> Svetlova danced with admirable buoyancy and while gliding through the air creating the effect so much desired in *Les Sylphides* of not trying to rise but of being too light to remain on the ground.[28]

> ~A ballerina is not a ballerina is not a ballerina!~

> There was a great distinction to the title ballerina. For instance, while dancers of other ranks, soloists, corphees, corps, danced their parts, or in the corps, a ballerina danced a ballet.[29]

For many ballet aficionados, it was—and still is—the captivating aura produced on stage by the ballerina that most completely captures the imagination and even adulation of a loving audience. The ballerina often manages to inspire an ardent, even rapturous devotion. My translation of the words of the famous French writer Jean Cocteau help to illustrate the spell that can be cast over an audience by a truly great ballerina. In the following sentiment, he is describing an entrance of the star ballerina in the ballet *Swan Lake*. Beginning with the Diaghilev Ballets Russes, Vera Nemchinova was recognized as one of the great ballerinas of the era, and she was a guest ballerina with several of the ballet companies active in the post-Diaghilev days. She was a guest ballerina with the de Basil Original Ballet Russe contemporaneously with Marina. In fact, Marina credited Nemchinova for helping to advance her own career with the de Basil company.

The entrance of Nemchinova was proprement truly sublime. From the moment that this *petit dame* leaves the wings of the theatre and arrives on stage, my heart either beats faster, or stops beating at all.[30]

A passionate audience member is on occasion wafted into a state of indulgence wherein he believes that the ballerina is dancing only for him. At any rate, she should be powerful without being self-conscious—expressive without being self-indulgent. Sound like a tall order? Bring on the pointe shoes!

Some writers about ballet and ballet dancers felt that the title "ballerina" was too frequently bantered about without being given due scrutiny.

The word ballerina is now being used very widely and indiscriminately. Anyone who dances a little solo in a ballet is often referred to by the audience and in the press as ballerina. This was not so in the Imperial Theatre. The title ballerina was the highest rank a dancer could achieve, and it carried a very definite significance.[31]

Some ballet scholars describe the difficulties presented to a dancer who strives to become recognized as a veritable ballerina.

It is easier by far to become a Cabinet Minister or a captain of industry than a great dancer.[32]

The consummate ballerina is the dancer who has the ability to make her performance a two-way road. The ratio of participation between audience and ballerina is not necessarily a fifty-fifty proposition, but a true ballerina should draw the spectator into the conversation.

In classic ballet the … ballerina of a company is its central dynamo; she sets the style, she exemplifies it at its most completely expressive. It is through watching her that the audience understands the style of a piece, and the style creates the poetic illusion in which the drama becomes real.[33]

When we consider only the basic essentials, what makes Markova different from Fonteyn and Ulanova different from Plisetskaya? It is the personal element, the character and temperament of each individual, expressed through the highest achievement of technical skill.[34]

Just when is it appropriate to use the word "ballerina" when describing the display of balletic prowess?

The mistake that is always made by the opponents of ballet dancing … arises. from the fact that they have never seen a first class ballerina … There is nothing great about the *pirouette* itself … yet it can be made great by a great exucant, and from an abstract point of view it is a thing of intense beauty …[35]

One ballet director offers a somewhat poetic reckoning when it comes to assigning to a dancer the title ballerina. When considering reviving *Les Sylphides*, Alex Martin of the Cleveland Ballet Center stated that he remembered Diaghilev's comment on this ballet: there are no soloists; they are all ballerinas.[36]

By way of comparison, one journalist observes that few dancers achieve the distinction of being officially recognized as a ballerina. Once the title has been bestowed, the dancer, having received the honor, has arrived at a highly coveted cultural plateau.

> Actually, even in Russia, the home of the ballet the *ballerina* was a rarity. It was as definite and as official a rank as that of a General." [37]

Alexandra Danilova, who was one of the star ballerinas with most of the Ballet Russe companies, beginning with that of Diaghilev, got in one of her delightful quips when she offered up her assessment of the power and responsibility that accompanies being recognized as a true ballerina when she professed, "In my little world of ballet, I'm a five-star general."[38]

This discussion of the nomenclature employed to designate the respective level of recognition awarded a given dancer, such as corps de ballet, soloist, or ballerina, reminds me of the time I read an article asserting that Balanchine rejected the concept of ranks within the company. He eschewed the notion that a select few of his dancers be awarded the distinction of the title of ballerina. He called his corps de ballet his "Milky Way" and lovingly referred to his ballerinas as "jewels" in his ballet of the same name.

Who were the shining stars in the Milky Way? First comes Suzanne Farrell, who in her time with the New York City Ballet Company almost instantaneously became Balanchine's most profound inspiration. She was the quintessential personification of a veritable porcelain doll. This image was arresting and worked wonderfully to her advantage. In Diamonds from *Jewels,* for instance, her presence was incomparable. Balanchine had his other jewels for certain. Some of the other stars in Balanchine's constellation included Patricia McBride, Violette Verdi, and Mimi Paul, each with their individual luster.

> The ballet dancer is the perfect example of the balance between the individual and the group. Her whole aim is to shine as a star, a *ballerina assoluta,* yet she subordinates herself to the whole, the ballet.[39]

The imminent ballet critic Anatole Chujoy also observed that the ballerina was not only a name being granted to a distinguished dancer; the dancer was treated with an obvious deference—noblesse oblige. He believed that a ballerina was granted a supreme position in the social/artistic community that not even the director of the Imperial Theatre could dismiss. He observed that not even the omnipotent Imperial Court held the power to elevate a dancer to the exalted rank if she did not possess all the qualities of a ballerina. He believed that in addition to a strong technique, a ballerina must possess a combination of a number of other qualifications. Preeminent among these attributes is a ballerina's personality. It may be cold as steel, aloof, high above our little worlds, or it may be of a radiant warmth, in which all poor mortals are allowed to bask. Chujoy observed that her disposition may be cold or warm but must remain lofty, always majestic, always out of our reach. He opined that when a ballerina gets to be more than a symbol to us, she ceases to be the incarnate spirit of whatever we wish her to be. She runs the risk of becoming one of us, which destroys the illusion it is her job to create and uphold.

Other dance writers and dance fans apply a slightly less philosophical approach. This faction of dance lovers place the prerequisites of gaining the designation ballerina in a noticeably different order.

> The very first consideration is physical beauty, face as well as body, the perfection of the instrument … *Ballet dancing is the maximum exploitation of physical beauty in motion.* [40]

In my lifetime, there have been exceptional dancers who were not at all pretty. Of course, it is certainly an added dividend to have a beautiful face and body, such as the distinguished Italian ballerina Carla Fracci, but cognoscenti are considering the whole package—the ability to convey a sincere emotional message and the skills with which to convincingly depict a character in a gripping drama, such as the wonderful Brazilian ballerina Marcia Haydee.

> A ballerina is not only a superacrobat with extra publicity. She is also an artist whose performance shows you the heart of a ballet. She sets the tone …[41]

Does the impact of the role of the ballerina differ from ballet to ballet, or role to role? In opera, there are compositions that rely upon and revolve around the presence of the prima donna. The success of a production of Verdi's *La Traviata* rests primarily upon the presence of a superb Violetta, whereas a veritable prima donna can sing "Rossina" in Rossini's *Il Barbiare di Siviglia* and is not obliged to carry the show. Also, who could envision a successful *Lucia de Lammermour* without a true prima donna in the title role? Some operas such as Mozart's *Impressario* sport a cast of not one but two prima donna sopranos, similar to *Giselle*, which presents three ballerina roles, Giselle and Myrtha and girl in Peasant pas de Deux, which are often each danced by reigning ballerinas in a company. Then there are operas such as Puccini's *Gianni Schichi* that are basically an ensemble show (although the prima donna does sing the major aria, "O Mio Babbino Caro").

> She projects not only her own role, but the entire world of fantasy in which that role becomes dramatic, in which every body and everything on stage can play a part.[42]

For the sake of logic (which is an oxymoron when it comes to discussing ballerinas), the audience might prioritize its performance values and its artistic expectations. Most criteria for conferring upon a female dancer the title ballerina are totally arbitrary, based on one's own taste (and sometimes intelligence). Along with the individual talents possessed innately or through extensive training by each candidate, there are several external parameters apart from the dancing that could influence one's perception as to whether or not a dancer should be considered a true ballerina.

> A ballerina exists, not to demonstrate ideas of art, but herself: instrument and personality.[43]

Here are some tangential elements that can influence one's opinion when attempting to analyze and categorize the degree to which an aspiring dancer accomplishes her goal of being accepted as true ballerina of a given company:

I.   Audience. Does the size of the audience play a role when considering whether or not the ballerina has stimulated an interest in the performance and inspired such attendance? Was the size of the audience a reflection of the popularity of the ballerina scheduled to perform that night? What was the audience's reaction? Was it receptive? Were there moments of enthusiastic applause? Sometimes the most telling moments that reflect the success of a ballerina are to be found in the moments of silence. Does the ballerina remain vital when she is not the central protagonist in the spectacle? Does the audience respond with silence after a variation by the ballerina?

II. Company. Did the size of the company affect the impact of the dancing of the ballerina? What was the artistic identity of the company? Did it primarily reflect the style of a certain choreographer?

III. Training. Various schools of training exist in the ballet world. Was the syllabus under which the ballerina was trained compatible with that of the company? Did she stand out? Did she blend in? For example, was it a success when a Balanchine-trained ballerina was asked to perform in a Tudor ballet? Did a dancer trained in the Bournonville syllabus seem alien to a company steeped in a Russian inclination? Did she fit in or seem aloof? Was it her fault?

IV. Choreography. Was the ballerina asked to perform choreography that was indigenously flattering? Did the choreography make the ballerina look graceful or awkward? Was it imaginative? Did it have form and direction? Did the ballerina seem to be on the same page as the choreographer?

> The power of the presence of the ballerina on stage is such that "The other dancers can add to it but cannot go counter to it, and so her quality is of crucial importance to them. Indeed, company, ballerina, and chief choreographer need to have a sort of affinity, an unconscious confidence in one another if they are to become completely effective.[44]

V.   Music. Was the music to which she was asked to dance supportive of the choreography? What was the level of performance of music? Was it live or taped? Was it too loud? Was it a piece of music that is well known and well liked? Did the music overwhelm the dancing, or did the audience so enjoy the music that it assumed that the ballet was a masterpiece and that the ballerina was exceptional?

VI. Impact. Perhaps the most telling paradigm with which one might assess the stature of a ballerina is the impact. How long did the performance of the ballerina stay in your mind? Momentarily? After exiting the theatre? For days? For weeks? For years?

For me, one proving ground for the lasting effect of a true ballerina is when during a performance, you wish that that moment could be suspended in time and her dancing never would never stop. When I watched Svetlova dance, the degree of exhilaration she exhibited on stage was captivating. She had a unique talent for communicating with her audience.

I am reminded of the time I attended an opera performance at l'Opera in Paris, France. The opera was *Die Frau Ohne Schatten* (performed as *La Femme sans Ombre*). The conductor was Karl Boehm, and the lead soprano and the role of the Empress was assumed by a singer with whom I was totally unacquainted, the Norwegian soprano Ingrid Bjorner (who became a great favorite of mine). Christa Ludwig was the Dyer's Wife, Walter Barry was Barak, and Ruth Hesse was the Nurse. For me, it was a night in the theatre that I wished would never end. Everything seemed like perfection, and I longed for the moment to be suspended in time. Forget the blares of the car horns by which I would soon be assaulted upon leaving the theatre. I was already in heaven. I have had many glorious evenings at the ballet as well. When I saw Sally Wilson as Hagar in Tudor's *Pillar of Fire,* there was a moment when I felt the wind had been knocked out of me. The first time I saw Cynthia Gregory in *Swan Lake* is indelibly inscribed upon my balletic sounding board. Allegra Kent astounded me in *Symphony in C, and* Suzanne Farrell electrified me in *Jewels.* However, perhaps the ultimate "please don't let the evening end" occurred when I saw Gelsey Kirkland in *Giselle.*

Gelsey Kirkland was primarily trained at the school of American Ballet and subsequently performed with the New York City Ballet. She mastered the speed, attack, and articulation of the Balanchine style, which became her trademark. I saw her in Balanchine's reworking of *Firebird,* which he had done for her, and I became a fan. Eventually, I saw her in *Dances at a Gathering,* and I was in love. When I attended a performance of *Giselle* danced by Kirkland and Baryshnikov, I became transfixed. She embodied the grace, composure, and versatility that were trademarks of Svetlova's performances.

Another ballerina who impressed me with her versatility was the international star ballerina Eva Evdokimova. Among many others, Cynthia Gregory of American Ballet Theatre was likewise impressive in roles of noticeably contrasting styles.

VII. VII. Ambiance: One should not overlook the enormous effect exerted on an audience member simply by the appearance of the theatre and the regalia associated with the moment. I am reminded of an experience I had when through the continuing education program at Empire State College, I was teaching a course in music appreciation. In the course of discussing the effect of music, opera, and ballet on their lives, it became apparent to me that most of the class had never attended a live performance anywhere, not to mention in a major performance venue. Many of the students lived in NYC, some in the environs of Lincoln Center, and had never attended a performance at Lincoln Center. I decided to remedy that blind spot, black hole if you will, and made the following assignment:

- Stay within your personal budget.
- Attend a performance presented at Lincoln Center, be it at the Met, Avery Fisher, or State Theatre.
- In preparation for the night out, get dressed up; wear something special from your wardrobe. Allow yourself to feel special.
- Make a dinner reservation for before or after the show at an upscale restaurant within your budget. Plan your schedule so that you do not feel rushed.
- If you must travel to the theatre, take a cab, not the subway.

The intensity of the responses to the experience were overwhelming:

"I live a few blocks from Lincoln Center. I have never attended a performance there. I was astonished by the quality of the performance."

"I walked into the Met, and I felt like I was in a castle. I had never experienced anything like it. It made me feel special."

"It was my first time. When can I go back?"

There are those who assert that stars are born, not made. I am not one of them. Children are born with certain attributes one might label as talents, but becoming a true ballerina requires more than the obvious gifts, both physical and musical. How frequently does a trained eye walk down the street and see a young girl standing there, waiting for the bus, with the extraordinary banana legs (the hyperextended legs that are often a gift to a girl dancing in the ballet world)? Shockingly, one might subsequently learn that this girl is not a dancer and has no such inclination. It takes more than being born a ballerina. On occasion, a quiet, even somewhat introverted individual can find a voice through dancing.

One can actually grow into the rank of ballerina because becoming a star involves bringing life experiences to the table. A child isn't born with a broken heart that might be useful in portraying the emotions in a Tudor ballet, for example, or has not yet tasted the potion of purity that one might hope to see in a Balanchine ballerina.

That is not to say that all ballets are pantomimes or even vehicles for projecting a gripping melodrama. One must be reminded that all ballets do not have a plot. Even in the most abstract or what some call neoclassic compositions, an accomplished ballerina will strive to maintain some appropriate dynamics among herself and the other dancers.

Svetlova and Fonteyn

Margot Fonteyn was a great friend of Marina Svetlova. For Fonteyn, Svetlova choreographed *The Faery Queen*, a ballet in which Svetlova herself danced. For me, Fonteyn was the center of the ballet universe: not flamboyant but always possessing a solid, modest commitment to the material. I also saw her do a somewhat modern piece with Nureyev, where she rose to the challenge. The ballet was very angular, and the setting and costumes were quite stark. Certainly not the type of ballet with which Fonteyn had become associated. I once saw her perform the role of Cinderella when she had already officially retired. It was mesmerizing the way she could transform a fifty-five-year-old woman into a beaming young maiden. I gasped at her first entrance. She was totally convincing. Fonteyn's movie of *Swan Lake* with Nureyev is perhaps the most moving portrayal of Tchaikovsky's Swan of our times.

About Fonteyn's command over one of her favorite roles, one journalist wrote:

> There were many times, especially in that final variation from *Sleeping Beauty,* when one wanted to weep for the sheer plenitude of her performance.[45]

Marina Svetlova and Rudolph Nureyev as seen in a 1960's montage from *Dance Magazine*

When asked about working with Margot Fonteyn, her most frequent partner, the wonderful Rudolf Nureyev responded by saying, "It was an enigma for me … I came from the Kirov School, the best school, and Margot didn't finish any school … she is supposed to have no technique, yet she did everything. She is supposed to have no school, and yet in many ways she was stronger than me."[46]

Nureyev went on to observe that he couldn't understand how it was done. To him, it seemed as though there was no visible technique bursting out of her, and yet she was doing things that were impossible by Russian standards. He praised her for being so precise and disciplined.

> Fonteyn's great musical gift was not simply to dance as if the music welled up from inside her. She did that, but she also rode the music like a champion surfer, sometimes holding back, sometimes anticipating, always buoyant, impelled by and always partaking of its primal energy.[47]

Nureyev, her most prominent partner observed that:

> Her performance was always above the waterline, you know—she never sank.[48]

Rudolf Nureyev and Margot Fonteyn
"Marguerite and Armand"
The Royal Ballet

Marina Svetlova

Prima Ballerina

Prima ballerinas are few and far between.[49]

Sylphides was received with warmth last night. Marina Svetlova commanded one of the greatest ovations yet received by any member of the company.[50]

Photo: Maurice Seymour, courtesy of Ron Seymour

"The last two weeks of the season Marina Svetlova will also
teach and dance, as our prima ballerina."[51]

Jacob's Pillow is Mount Olympus in the dance world, especially for American ballet dancers. For Marina to have been given the title prima ballerina from "Papa" Shawn was an incredible honor and represented the esteem in which Marina was held by the dance world at large.

Other well-known dancers have held the title prima ballerina of the Metropolitan Opera Ballet. One such is Melissa Hayden. The famous ballerina from NYC Ballet briefly was a guest prima ballerina at the Met. After Romanov's first season as director of ballet at the Metropolitan Opera Ballet, he had Ruthana Boris as his prima ballerina. When she left her position as prima ballerina, she was replaced by Marina Svetlova.

Another writer, Arnold Haskell, expressed the sometimes complicated life of a ballerina when he said that the entire goal of a ballerina is to shine as a star, and yet a ballerina assoluta subordinates herself to the whole ballet.

In 2011, Lorca Peress, the artistic director of NYC's MultiStages, the recipient of many grants and awards in dance, including a Manhattan Community Arts grant and Dramatist Guild Fund grant, and copresident of the League of Professional Theatre Women, was asked about what had inspired her to pursue her chosen career in dance. She responded, "I danced with Marina Svetlova, the prima ballerina of the Metropolitan Opera, and she was a gorgeous, gorgeous dancer."[52]

John Masefield and Edward Seago wrote an ode to the ballerina in a 1940–41 Ballet Russe de Monte Carlo souvenir booklet:

> But what are you to us, O radiant dancers …?
> You bring together all that makes men happy …
> The grace and elegance of gentle women …
> It needs but skill of toe …
> And by it men progress …

CHAPTER 5

Balletomania

Balletomania is a magnificent obsession.[1]

Balletomane is a term that is used—sometimes lovingly, sometimes derogatorily—to describe anyone who seems to be infatuated with most things having to do with ballet. The soubriquet is usually, but not exclusively, given to gentlemen who have become smitten with ardent adoration for their favorite ballerina, whom they regularly—sometimes vociferously—defend against any sort of adverse comment or criticism. Occasionally, a balletomane can become annoying, even obnoxious when trumpeting what he or she considers to be the indisputable superiority of their ballerina-select over the inferiority of the regrettable rivals to the throne. Beware to any critic, journalist, spectator, or fellow balletomane who unfortunately champions a rival ballerina.

> To-day, my best definition of a *balletomane* is, that he is a person who is sad, very sad, on the first night of a season, just because he realizes that it is only for a season, and that a first night implies a last night, most exciting and melancholy of events.[2]

Marina was occasionally inclined to be amused by the fanaticism exhibited by the arch ballet lover, even when she was the object of such extravagant praise. Here is one example of a writer who blends his own sense of humor into a piece that is intended to be a jubilant appreciation of the Marina mystique:

Variation

Marina Svetlova, prima ballerina of the Metropolitan Opera, is one of the reasons why classical ballet has not yet ossified completely. When the pasta-filled basso struts upstage and Marina Svetlova glides in, weary husbands who have been yearning for a cigar and slippers shake themselves awake and reach for the opera glasses—Ballerina Svetlova is a superbly rewarding sight.[3]

Photo: Maurice Seymour, courtesy Ron Seymour

Is there any more flattering accolade for a ballerina than to have one's dancing compared to a character out of a Shakespeare play? Presumably the following quip penned by an adoring fan references a character from Shakespeare's *Romeo and Juliet*. Furthermore, the character referred to is the Queen of Fairies who flows through the air while exerting fairy's magic on the earthbound, temporal folk below.

> Shakespeare's Queen Mab was no more gossamer-like than ballerina Marina Svetlova.
> The spirit of the dance is in the very tip of her toes yet there isn't a staccato in all her
> ecstasy to rob dancing of its grace. [4]

To enter into a discussion of ballerina-ism is akin to walking into an apiary without protective accoutrement. One needs an armory for self-protection and—de rigor—an arsenal of ammunition for selective counterattacks. One enters the lion's den, convinced that they are in possession of a sufficient amount of self-fortitude to ward off the challenges that will indubitably be hurled their way. One is expected to elaborately describe and defend the grandeur of their beloved dulcinea. It is helpful to brandish (or feign to) a sincere sense of patience and open-mindedness when humoring the protestations asserted by adversarial ballet lovers who wish to champion the perceived divine right of their own favorite ballerina to reign supreme. Certain arbiters of debate are not content with merely defending their home turf, so they assure themselves of their acumen in the art of persuasion. They plan to persuade the opposition to drop the devotion they manifest toward their favorite ballerina and "come on over." (These *cavalieri* are rarely the successful types.) Most of the devotes of a particular star are usually not willing to jump ship.

Balletomania was by way of being a definite polite career, alternative to the Army and Navy or Diplomacy. Such and such an émigré, wishing to account for his social worth, will tell you that his father was a great general, a great statesman or indifferently a great balletomane ...[5]

A perfect example of how arbitrary ballet fans can be when selecting their favorite among respective ballerinas is illustrated by a situation of which I became aware shortly after I began dancing. Shortly after Nathalie Makarova's arrival at American Ballet Theatre, the big scuttle was that a rivalry was smoldering among fans of Makarova and those of Cynthia Gregory. There ensued a clinical dissection of the relative merits and talents of these two ballerinas. Makarova was a beautiful product of the Kirov School. Her legs were perfectly shaped, somewhat hyperextended, and her feet were gorgeous from a balletic point of view. Her arms were lovely, and her physical proportions were perfection. Her carriage was that of the quintessential prima donna / prima ballerina—always intense and somewhat aloof. Cynthia, on the other hand, embodied the bold and audacious talent of a young American prodigy. She occasionally was not shy about allowing the audience to share in her innocent arrogance and sense of humor. The fans became divided into factions based on the major attributes of the two ballerinas: Makarova could jump, but Cynthia could turn. It was at first that simple. (As a balletomane in the making, I loved them both.)

> When we consider only the basic essentials, what makes Markova different from Fonteyn and Ulanova different from Plisetskaya? It is the personal element, the character and temperament of each individual, expressed through the highest achievement of technical skill.[6]

Marina was an endearing soul because she refused to take herself too seriously. Of course, as is the case with most celebrities, she appreciated the attention and admiration expressed by the press and her fans.

The revered dance scholar P. W. Manchester suggested that there exists a ranking system by which balletomanes may be observed. The initial level is the one in which a fan becomes awestruck and is ecstatic about everything they attend. The second level is when one has been attending the ballet for a few seasons and are looked down upon. The ultimate level occurs when one has acquired tolerance and is impervious to the fools making themselves appear ridiculous by shouting and carrying on for a particular favorite of theirs.

> Balletomania is one of the most virulent diseases extant.[7]

It would seem that some people are just born to the obsession. For certain types, it does not matter what the repertoire is. Others find their way to the feast stemming from their love or experience with one or a few of the components that combine to make a ballet composition.

> I may have become a *balletomane* from my very first contact with the ballet ... The impression made on me in 1887 by *La Bayadere,* that dear old ballet of romantic dreams and exotic fantasy, was so powerful that I actually fell ill with ecstasy ...[8]

Sometimes one must have patience and allow themselves to have some fun when confronted by a true balletomane. Yes, their outspoken and seemingly relentless support of any or all aspects of the ballet world can be somewhat off-putting, but they are sincere believers. Often they come across benign fanatics. What can I say? You gotta love 'em.

> No *balletomane* ever knew the meaning of restraint, and his infernal din is the dancer's main reward.[9]

It should be remembered that balletomania is not synonymous with hysteria. Degas, for example, was the consummate balletomane and demonstrated his passion for the ballet through his beguiling paintings; Cocteau through his inspiring pennings.

> Comparison plays a great role in the making of a balletomane.[10]

Competition is part of the human condition. Some prefer to call it survival of the fittest or even the process of natural selection.

> Some devotees virtually made ballet-going an addiction and never missed a performance. These fans were called the balletomanes and they were walking ballet encyclopedias, for they knew all the facts and figures about every dancer's career.[11]

At times, I am reminded of my father who was an ardent sportsman. I recall that as a child, I was astounded at his ability to have one sport game on the television and simultaneously listen to another game on the radio, which had been placed in close proximity to the television, thus allowing for the jumping from one game to the other as dictated by the encroachment of the commercial interruptions. Is there such a word as *sportsomania*?

> The name of *balletomane,* once given in derision, was becoming almost an hereditary dignity …[12]

Balletomanes were capable of high enthusiasm. It is often owing to them that ballet stars become box office draws:

> It is necessary to arrange for seats several weeks in advance [for] Simienova, the great Maryinsky ballerina … just as in the old days when the best seats were a coveted heritage privilege. Ballet originated at a Court, flourished under an Emperor, but balletomania is the privilege of no one class, and it is not the artificial exotic thing that some might think.[13]

Here is an observation that cannot help but encourage one to empathize, if not fall in love with, a balletomane:

The highly respected dance journalist Arnold Haskell, in his book, apltly titled *Balletomane* proclaimed that each dancer had her partisans, and fiercely devoted fans. He confessed that I all he wanted to do was to stand up on his chair and vociferously shout out in support of his favorite star dancer.,

Anthony Tudor choreographed a fun balletic farce, *Gala Performance,* a ballet in which Marina appeared with Ballet Theatre. It involved the pitting of a rivalry among three ballerinas based on their own stage personalities as well as the nationality and style that they were attempting to display. Along with their cavaliers, there was the Russian ballerina, the Italian ballerina, and the French ballerina (which was Marina's role). This ballet was conceived as a parody of the pitfalls of balletomania.

However, if ever there was a vehicle that more encapsulated the loving essence of balletomania-ism than Dolin's *Pas de Quatre,* I don't know what it is.

Pas de Quatre

The quintessential ballet to inspire the balletomane's exhilaration is a performance of the ballet *Pas de Quatre,* and Marina Svetlova held the distinction of having performed each of the respective variations of the four solo ballerinas. This ballet is a satire of the very phenomenon of uncontrolled adulation for one's favorite ballerina. Vocal display and rapturous applause is encouraged by the very mise-en-scène of the ballet. After each ballerina finished her respective solo, while she left the stage, she turned to the following ballerina and made a grand gesture as if to challenge her to attempt to surpass the performance of the solo she had just finished. There is a constant clamor of applause throughout the sarcastic gestures. Each claque of balletomanes attempts to out-cheer the fans offering an ovation to their favorite ballerina. The audience is ecstatic by the end of the spectacle, and the show can be quite amusing when well executed. The audience must be willing (and able) to buy in to the whole sport of the show. The stage is often strewn with a barrage of tossed flowers.

This ballet is performed widely by students, regional ballets, and even professional ballet companies. Since the inception of Dolin's concept of this ballet, certain personalities have become associated with the various roles. In early photos from this ballet, hardly one exists without the presence of Nathalie Krassovska (a.k.a. Nathalie Leslie or Nathalie Leslie-Krassovska). She was a frequent guest faculty member at the Svetlova Dance Center, and she became one of my good friends. She seems to have been the quintessential image of the romantic ballerina (as well as Fokine's neoromantic ballerina). Krassovska was most closely associated with the role of Grahn, although she performed Taglioni and occasionally Grissi. Krassovska became a good friend of mine, and not coincidentally, it was at Marina's Svetlova Dance Center that I met her when I was pianist for classes she taught. Taglioni was most often represented in photos by the presence of Alicia Markova, widely considered as the total embodiment of the essence of the romantic ballerina. Sometimes Danilova appeared as Taglioni. Other notable ballerinas who scored success in this ballet included Barbara Fallis, Meredith Baylis, and Mia Slavenska. Marina Svetlova held the distinction of having performed each of the variations of the four distinctive ballerinas.

> In those early days, it mattered little to me where I sat; but now I feel strongly that
> one should watch from different angles and distances … Comparison plays a great
> role in the making of a *balletomane.*[15]

Many ballet fans agree that watching the progress of young dancers and the prospects of their future development offers the greatest possible pleasure and interest—yet another phase in the composition of a balletomane.

> Followers of the ballet who have seen the *Les Sylphides* of Toumonova, Baronova and Riabouchinska, die at the death of each *variation*. 'I shall never see *Les Sylphides* danced in quite this way again.[16]

Some serious fans may prefer Baronova's *Valse* with her conveyance of the feeling of a heritage accepted. Or others may prefer Toumonova in the role because of her apparent perfection of line. One may sit amazed at Riabouchinska's imaginative *Prelud*e, or another fan may prefer Toumonova's interpretation with its content of the foreshadowing of an Eve who is soon to lack her Eden. But these are the signs of a perfection that crowns its own achievement in bestowing the illusion of choice and establishes the flower of the ballet in the happy position of one who lingers on the steps of the national Gallery: '"Now, shall I look at the Vermeer today, or go straight to the Michelangelo?"

I had my own tenure as balletomane. During a season of the New York City Ballet Company at Blossom Center near Cleveland, Ohio, I attended every performance of *Swan Lake*. I had to see the various Swan Queens (e.g., Melissa Haydn, Violette Verdi, Allegra Kent, Patricia McBride). I was avid—obsessed with seeing each ballerina do their thing. I knew nothing about each ballerina and little about *Swan Lake*, but I had been bitten by the ballet bug.

The Special World of Balletomania

An imaginary spectator asks another, "Are you a balletomane?"

"Well," he answers, "I like ballet, if that's what you mean. Just what is a balletomane?"

The balletomane-to-be can be astonished after seeing just one performance of a given ballet, or it may take repeated viewings. One usual character trait of a true balletomane is that he or she becomes convinced that they have just witnessed their favorite ballerina do a performance that no other current or former ballerina could ever come close to matching in its exquisiteness. Often the dyed-in-the-wool balletomane cannot tolerate the opinions expressed by a nonfanatic. Actually, if one fan says that his dearest would never be equaled in success and such a role, he is put at ease when his comrade says, "Don't be silly. Riabouchinska could never be excelled." Balletomanes are sometimes more aptly titled *balletomaniacs*!

One of the largest traps into which a balletomane falls is talking in hyperbole or absolutes. For instance, I recently heard a confessed balletomane declare that their beloved favorite ballerina was the "best Swan Queen of the twentieth century." This assertion was made in the year 2008. One cannot help but wonder if this balletomane had ever seen Margot Fonteyn or Nathalie Makarova or Cynthia Gregory. In addition, let's not forget about Tamara Karsavina.

Occasionally, exuberant balletomanes find pathways through verse to express their fanaticism for the ballerina creature.

The Russians have become balletomanes, even more ardent than the French, and more critical. In *Eugene Onegin,* which he dedicated to her, Poushkin wrote of Istomia, a dark-haired ballerina who captivated not only the pit but the salons of St. Petersburg:

On pit, stalls, boxes, brightly blaze…
The curtain now they slowly raise…
Forth from the crowd of nymphs
Istomina the nimbly-bounding…[17]

Balletomanes faithfully are in attendance at all opening nights. They avidly support a premiere of a new ballet but cast aspersions on a ballet set to new or substandard music. They act as though they were the designated regisseur of the company—the guardian of the veil and the keeper of the faith. To borrow lyrics from *Fiddler on the Roof*, "Tradition! Tradition!"

Helpful Hints to the Balletomane

When amid all the glamour of a ballet season's opening, you notice with great delight and no little satisfaction that your favorite ballerina took her curtain calls from a stage strewn with luxurious flowers. Maybe you thought the pretty things just grew there on their own. A quick call to a florist, possibly that of any other confirmed balletomane, will reveal the whole incredible carnage. One might ponder, what would we do without the florist, but what would the florist do without us? Not that flower sending is the chief symptom of balletomane poisoning, but it is certainly one of its first—and most chronic—manifestations. Generally speaking, floral extravagance is more fun and does the most good on opening nights and on the occasions of premiere performances of new ballets—particularly when one or more of said ballets has been designed to show off the particular talents of your favorite ballerina.

> If you progress to the point where you get written communications from your dancing friends, treasure them for your grandchildren … But don't get me wrong, I love the ballet. "Hello, florist? Make that another three dozen American beauties…"[18]

It might be well to give a quick once-over to the general mise-en-scène of balletomania. The innocent bystander notices that the "dahling" type flourishes at its ubiquitous best when the ballet performs at New York's Metropolitan Opera House. This ostentatious type holds forth in the first row and is usually dressed to kill, if not to blind or bewilder. Its favorite form of conversation is ballet gossip, with special emphasis on the company's sex life. This little group of enthusiasts habitually dashes backstage to impress the company with a few squeals of "Dahling, you were magnificent." For the less pretentious type, the whole ballet business is a life and death affair. An evening at the ballet for an authentic balletomane can also be ruined when any dancer's pirouettes go astray, and God save the queen should any of the performers take a spill! Life is not worth living if its favorite doesn't dance its favorite ballet. Fouettés, entrechats, arabesques, attitudes—they are all more important than the price of tea in China. This type flourishes all over the house, is often the most loyal to its dancing idols, and applauds vigorously, even hysterically, as these dancing goddesses make their entrances and complete their specialties.

> My knowledge of dancing grew with Alice's (Alicia Markova) increasing technique.
> I watched her constantly in class, analyzed her movements, learned with her … Here

at last was a definite, thrilling contact with the thing I loved best. Now I, too, could make my debut as a true *balletomane*.[19]

Here is an example of a true balletomane who imagines the sort of imagery that another balletomane might have penned about ballerinas of the nineteenth century, such as Taglioni or Elssler. The dreamer then updates these sentiments to describe a twentieth-century ballerina. He conjures up verses that might have been written to immortalize Marina Svetlova: "Her eyes, two pools of crystal clear mountain water, or the infinity of the sky changing in its moods from the misty grey of a veiled day to the shining glory of the Mediterranean firmament, the bluest of all blue. Lashes that lay a fluttering shadow on the tender satin of a peach-like skin … The little head crowned by a profusion of auburn hair …"

Marina Svetlova, courtesy of Ron Seymour

The above referenced poet goes on to muse about Marina when he describes her profusion of auburn hair cuddling a swanlike neck.

In a foreword to a souvenir program heralding an imminent appearance of Marina Svetlova and her touring ensemble, Olia Philippoff wrote:

> Still in her teens, Marina Svetlova has received wide recognition for her exceptional talent and critiques … her varied gifts developed naturally and Marina Svetlova blossomed into a harmonious being, a great dancer and a delightful personality.[20]

A Half Century of Balletomania

One pastime of a serious balletomane is to wander through a bookstore, regardless of the town or country, in search of books on ballet. Stumbling upon a treasure during one of these rambling excursions is akin to heaven on earth for the dyed-in-the-wool enthusiast. Some of these balletically possessed folk partake of this ritual from country to country. Many a hard-earned buck is expended on this idiosyncratic pastime. Many a balletic bookstore fanatic can even identify which country is most promising for the procuration of books or memorabilia from a given ballet style or particular ballet company. When one young ballet fan was asked if he had ever thought of seeking a job in the ballet world to help assuage his seemingly unquenchable appetite for all things having to do with ballet, his reply was that he felt freer without such a responsibility: "I'm content ... to stay a member of the audience ... we're a very important part of the performance. I'm very happy—each day really is an adventure."[21]

I once read about the objections harbored by many a balletomane. They become impatient with the abhorrent behavior displayed by audacious audiences. Although they may have on occasion succumb to the same temptations, it is difficult for some balletomanes to abide someone else's applause during a performance instead of after it! Then there are the neophytes who are overwhelmed by what seems to them to be an inordinate number of extraneous flowers! It seems as though a ballerina will gather roses to her bosom and pick bouquets off the floor until she is in danger of throwing her back out, and if she can't get the whole lot of them off the stage in one exit, she will make several trips. Certain observers contend that actresses occasionally get flowers, but they don't make a production out of receiving them. One fan who had recently returned to the fold described how he had had an alarming shock toward the beginning of the night at Col. De Basil's Ballet Russe de Monte Carlo at the Metropolitan Opera House. To this audience member, the whole thing was as Russian as it gets. And when the dancing began, he leaned backed and thought, *What a life!* He saw the entire evening to be the life of carefree, delicious luxury. Coincidentally, he found the ballet to be simply wonderful.

> Right after the dizzy, unreal opening I began to notice things in the theatre. ... as word got around in the nether world that the ballet had been reborn topside their numbers increased ...[22]

One seasoned ballet attendee remarked about what seemed to be a performance being offered up by the audience:

> What do you suppose makes audiences do such strange things? 'Some of them want to appear to be connoisseurs when they aren't ... "In other words, they try to act like balletomanes," we suggested. "That terrible word" said Dolin, "it sounds like a really dreadful disease, doesn't it?" [23]

I feel that balletomanes are members of one big family, contributing to the evening's entertainment. One balletomane in the making remarked after the premiere of Jules Perrot's *Esmeralda*, "Each time she spurned the earth ... we experienced a tendency to leave the soles of our boots; to each rattle of the tambourine we fell victims to a palpitation of the heart ... The representation of a modern tragedy leaves us in a state of thorough prostration, while the execution of a ballet is a good excuse for a three-day lunacy."[24]

National Artists Corporation from a 1940's publicity flyer

CHAPTER 6

Sleeping Beauty

Marina Svetlova as Princess Aurora, courtesy of Ron Seymour

She epitomizes the ballet in style and form.[1]

For many ballerinas, it is not having the leading role in *Giselle* or *Swan Lake* that is the ultimate dream come true. Rather, it is Princess Aurora in *Sleeping Beauty* that remains the coveted role. It was one of Svetlova's most celebrated creations.

There isn't a ballerina in the world who has not danced or does not want to dance

Princess Aurora …[2]

Most ballerinas are attracted to this ballet because of the stature and the challenges of the role of Aurora. The entire scope of this ballet is nearly unmatched in the entire classical ballet repertory. The Tchaikovsky music is also inimitable in its melodic splendor.

> *Princess Aurora* is a grand show, staged in the grand manner and performed In the grand style …[3]

Arnold Haskel, the distinguished ballet critic, confessed that his love for and fascination with ballet began with his attendance at the famous Diaghilev production of *The Sleeping Princess* at the Alhambra in London, 1921. He became smitten with ballet, and the rest is history. Interestingly enough, it was also this ballet that Pavlova credits as having inspired the beginning of her love for ballet. For Marina, the role of Aurora brought her tremendous international adulation. With de Basil, she started out as one of the solo fairies before assuming the role of Aurora, the prima donna in this ballet. In some performances of this ballet, Marina appeared in the role of Aurora, while Tatiana Riabouchinska, one of the three original baby ballerinas, danced in the Bluebird pas de deux.

> *Aurora's Wedding* gave the opportunity to appreciate the talent of a young and charming star, Marina Svetlova. She danced the difficult and dangerous pas de deux with a surprising elegance. She was as outstanding that she even stole the show from Riabouchinska and Jasinsky in the Blue Bird.[4]

Musicians often quarrel over the merits of the music when it comes to the assessment of the quality and value of the music scores of the respective ballets. However, when the discussion turns to *Sleeping Beauty*, there is universal agreement that its musical qualities exceed those even displayed in other Tchaikovsky ballets. It has been reported that Igor Stravinsky once proclaimed, "The convincing example of Tchaikovsky's great power is, beyond a doubt, the ballet of *The Sleeping Princess*."[5]

Vera Trefilova

The role of Princess Aurora was one Svetlova's most appreciated roles. Perhaps this should come as no surprise, for Svetlova's main and favorite teacher was Vera Trefilova, who was among the first and most successful ballerinas in the role of Aurora.

> During the season of 1921, *The Sleeping Princess* was presented at the Alhambra, the most important event since the coming of the Russians in 1909.[6]

Indeed, in his book *Balletomania,* Denby said that in his opinion, Trefilova exemplified the qualities of a true classical ballerina in training and temperament. He felt that her interpretation of the role was enlightening, inspirational, and full of meaning. He found her to be the ultimate in the creation of the role of Aurora and the ballerina with whom he will always associate with the role of Aurora. He rather poetically asserted that if Pavlova were the Poussin of the dance, Trefilova was the Ingres.

In the program there the names of two Russian *Prima ballerinas,* Vera Trefilova and Olga Spessiva (under her true name of Spessivtseva) … There is one point especially that each of these ballerinas have in common: she is *classical …*[7]

On the meaning of Classicism

Kchessinska, Trefiliova, Pavlova, Pavlova, Karsavina, Egorova, Preobrajenska, all have this one thing in common: they are 'classical' dancers, though in every other aspect they differ … Fortunately, the majority are now teaching and have formed the dancers of to-day in their image. Trefilova is the classical dancer *par excellence …* [8]

VERA TREFILOVA
Paris, 1925

Talent is an all-embracing spirit, it is contented with seven notes, seven primary colors and five positions in dancing; with these it will perform marvels in art, such marvels as will remain young when the present generation, and those that follow it, are in their graves. She passed her gifts for the portrayal on to her student, Marina Svetlova. [9]

Before Marina was given the leading role in de Basil's *Aurora's Wedding,* Marina's contribution to the success of the ballet did not go without notice. On one occasion, *Dance Magazine* reported that Svetlova, Leskova, and Panaiff had been extremely effective in the pas de trois.

The *Sleeping Princess* is a somewhat condensed version of the lengthy Petipa/Tchaikovsky ballet *Sleeping Beauty.* These modified versions of the original ballet appeared with various names: *Princess Aurora, Aurora's Wedding, Le Marriage d'Aurore,* and *La Belle aux Bois Dormante.* Performances of the original *Sleeping Beauty* became rather sporadic after its debut with the Maryinsky in 1890.

Aurora's Wedding: As Princess Aurora, Svetlova was superb. The precision of every movement, the purity of every arabesque gave an amazing poise and fluidity to her style.[10]

Along with acknowledging Svetlova's graceful lyricism, critics were also impressed by this ability to infuse her natural smoothness of execution with a sharp, aggressive attack. "Marina Svetlova surprised us by the grace and care with which she attacked her difficult part and brought it to the culminating point of the brilliant pas de deux."[11]

Marina Svetlova and Robert Roland in *Sleeping Beauty*.
Photo: Bruno of Hollywood, courtesy of the Metropolitan Opera Guild.

Marina Svetlova received repeated applause for her exquisite interpretation, her grace, her charm and her youthful slenderness.[12]

An item of great interest was Marina Svetlova's dancing in *Aurora*. The technique is certainly there but at the same time there is a delicacy of movement, a refinement in every detail that conceal every trace of effort.[13]

Margot Fonteyn

It is virtually impossible to discuss the ballet *Sleeping Beauty* and not mention the ballerina Margot Fonteyn. It was she who made the role her own and who made the ballet popular in the United States when she performed it at the Metropolitan Opera House in 1949. Before Fonteyn came to the United States to perform this ballet with London's Royal Ballet, Marina gained success with this ballet in other countries.

> Miss Svetlova, one of the rising stars in ballet, took the leading spot. The response she gained from the audience was warm and spontaneous.[14]

Fonteyn credits the role of Aurora for containing her fondest memories of her own performance career. Fonteyn also was part of Svetlova's life because it was Marina who choreographed Purcell's *Fairy Queen* especially for her.

Marina Svetlova and Olga Spessivtzeva

> Considered by many to be the true successor to Pavlova, Olga Spessivtseva (1895–1991) suffered one of the saddest lives of any twentieth century dancer.

> Immediately recognized both at the Imperial Ballet School in St. Petersburg and in the Maryinsky company as a singular talent, she quickly ascended to major roles such as Giselle (her most famous creation) and Odette-Odile. For a while she danced with Diaghilev's Ballets Russes.[15]

For a while, she danced with Diaghilev's Ballets Russes, and she toured with many companies through Europe and South America. In 1937, she suffered the first of her nervous breakdowns. She was hospitalized in in New York in 1943 and remained institutionalized until 1963, when friends, led by Anton Dolin, had her moved to the Tolstoy Farm in Rockland County, New York, where she lived quietly until her death at the age of ninety-six.

Something that Svetlova never talked openly about or even remotely hinted at was the intimate role she had played in the final years of the great Spessivtseva. This part of the Svetlova saga emphasizes the generosity within Marina's heart. Part of this reticence perhaps comes from the fact that Marina was a tough professional who had also witnessed misery. Marina had a penchant for solving situations, and I believe that Marina actually believed she could at least ease the pain. The immensely tragic episode of the plight of Spessivtseva is indelibly stamped on the hearts of all dancers who are aware of the story. Spessivtseva's talent has been described as having been completely harmonious, balanced, and consummate in its design. With regard to her art, we are dealing with a person who was so special and delicately individual that she deeply impressed the public with the features of her unique and original beauty. The permanent stamp of undying childhood lay in this artist. Ballet authorities of that time believed that Spessivtseva need only stand and then smile with her mouth and eyes, and an unexpected radiance poured forth. In addition, she was considered to have been a rare jewel of dramatic art in ballet. All agreed that her acting was classical in the best sense of the word, but most fans were astounded at her overall ability to carry with her the coming sound, the silent tangle of emotions just on the verge of unfolding, the anguish and anticipation of artistic inspiration and intellectual wonder. Hers was a spirit that wept children's tears.

She does not ignite the audience with the fire of her talent, but she extends over it the palpitating sheath of all these tears, as yet unborn but already tormenting her heart. Eternally young, she does not face the bitter fate of a flower past its bloom. And I pity anyone who has never seen this everlasting bud of beauty and talent.[16]

In June 1946, at the request of Anton Dolin, Marina Svetlova went to Italy be a guest star with productions he was presenting at the Rome Opera. She brought with her news that Olga Spessivtzeva had made a wonderful recovery after her tragic breakdown in NYC in the winter of 1940. Marina told them that during the past two years, Olga was considered to be cured. In June 1963, Marina Svetlova had just arrived back in New York from a US tour, and they were to dine together that evening. Dolin was thankful that Marina spoke not only English but French and Russian fluently. He phoned her, and Olga agreed to drive with them up to Rockland County, New York. Marina and Dolin took Olga into the house in the Russian community in Valley Cottage, where Dolin left her with Marina. Shortly thereafter, Marina came out and joined him in the dining room. There were tears in her eyes. Marina told Dolin how much it meant to Olga that she was home in her own room. She could not believe that she was in her own room. She said, "Sleep alone, alone and with privacy—not with twenty others? No, it cannot be true." A peace had transcended over her still lovely face. Dolin recounted how Olga's mother then arrived, carrying a small box, and Olga reacted like a happy young girl. She undid the box and took out the tissue paper in which her furs had been wrapped. First she put on her winter hat and coat. Then, her ermine wrap was placed around her shoulders. The small party told her that she looked like a prima ballerina. She smiled, laughed with joy, and took Marina's hand in dance position. Spessivtseva went on to say: "Merci mes amis merci a vous tous. Je suis tres heureuse. C'est ci calm, c'est ci bien ici. Merci, merci … She spoke to me on the telephone a few days ago: 'Dear Dolin, I thank you with all my heart for all you have done.' Dear wonderful Olga—it was destiny."[17]

CHAPTER 7

Guest Appearances

Alicia Markova minus recently removed appendix will retire to civilian life for some months and will be replaced in the Markova-Dolin Company by Tamara Toumanova. Marina Svetlova had been solicited but was unable to comply owing to other contractual commitments.[1]

Appearing as a guest artist can be a double-edged sword. It has its attractive qualities because the title "guest artist" connotes a certain deference to a dancer, giving them added notoriety in the vicinity in which they are to perform. It can also add luster to a specific show or to a season as a whole because it sends a signal that someone special is to appear with their own ensemble. There can also be a bit of reciprocity involved with the designation of guest artist. John Gilpin, a famous dancer with London's Festival Ballet, described one of the burdens often associated with being a guest artist. These appearances are frequently accompanied by obligations to keep the fans as well as the donors and sponsors happy: "Performances were squeezed in between socializing … After flying back to England we landed in London and then made our way to Oxford by train, where Marina and I dance the first ballet of the evening program."[2]

For approximately twenty-five years, Marina did much guest performing, especially after having left the de Basil's Original Ballet Russe in 1941. Along with increasing international recognition as a leading ballerina of the time and before securing professional representation in 1944, she became, as they say in sports, sort a free agent.

When Mme. Bronislava Nijinska produced her two ballets on the Jacob's Pillow Dance Festival, 1942, Marina Svetlova and Nina Youskevitch were the two prima ballerinas. "Marina Svetlova returns to dance at Jacob's Pillow again this summer (1943) after completing her California season with Ballet Theatre."[3] Owing to the fact that the Metropolitan Opera had only a nine-month season and that the Met did not require dancers for every performance, Marina had time to do guest performances in venues around the world.

At the half-way mark the ballet season in Montreal can be said to have been a successful one on the whole … of the recitals, Marina Svetlova from the Metropolitan Opera gave the best account of herself. [4]

The News Bureau at Indiana University Bloomington reported that Marina Svetlova was:

> One of the most widely traveled and highly acclaimed ballerinas of the Twentieth
> Century … Miss Svetlova's name is synonymous with the classical ballet in a dozen
> countries. [5]

It became a pattern with Marina to have a run of guest appearances from city to city, or even by continent hopping. One year, she appeared on television in Frankfurt, Germany, at the end of June. Within a week's time, she performed with a symphony orchestra in Italy, and later that same month, on August 30, 1958, she found herself performing in Manchester, Vermont, with her pianist, Theodor Haigue.

Marina danced with many of the greatest ballet companies all around the world. Not only were the locations of her performances extensive, but the scope of her repertoire was exceptional. She performed the prima ballerina roles in most of the standard ballet classics.

> Rave reviews have followed Marina Svetlova around the world … What precision,
> what art, what intelligence. It is something unbelievable.[6]

She was a guest artist with Het Netherlands Ballet, Holland. With this company, she danced in *Giselle,* partnered by Anton Dolin.

With the Royal Swedish Ballet in Stockholm, Sweden, Marina starred in *Swan Lake.*

In Helsinki, Finland, she performed the role of Princess Aurora in *Sleeping Beauty* with the Finish National Ballet.

At the Rome Opera House in Rome, Italy, Marina performed the role of the Sugar Plum Fairy in the *Nutcracker,* as well the role of Kitri in *Don Quixote.* While in Rome, Marina also danced in a ballet called *Les Petits Riens,* which was created especially for her by Boris Romanoff.

With the Irish National Ballet in Cork and in Dublin, Ireland, (October 1, 1958) she performed leading roles in *La Fille mal Guardee* and the role of the Sugar Plum Fairy in the *Nutcracker.*

Marina performed the role of Swanilda in *Coppelia* at the Teatro Colon in Buenos Aires, Argentina on July 4, 1962.

In England, Marina was also a guest artist with the Cosmopolitan Ballet (originally the International Ballet). With this company, she starred in performances of *Giselle, Copellia*, and *Swan Lake.*

Above: in *Giselle*, Act I

Ballet Today, March 1960

Following an Israeli tour and guest appearances with the Rome Opera Ballet, Marina Svetlova joined the Festival Ballet for its London season, July 9 through September 12. She made her debut in *Swan Lake* and appeared subsequently in *Nutcracker* and *Les Sylphides.*

> Marina Svetlova, who had a successful debut with the Dolin Festival Ballet when she danced *Swan Lake,* flew to make a guest appearance with the Toronto Symphony Orchestra.[7]

Dancing with the Festival Ballet of London enabled Svetlova to strengthen her friendship with Krassovska. Little did the two of them know that they would both end up directing ballet companies in Texas.

> Dallas Civic Ballet performed the 2nd Act *Nutcracker* and Dallas Civic Opera presented the 2nd Act of *Tosca* at a joint concert. Nathalie Krassovska and Marina Svetlova alternated as the Sugar Plum Fairy.[8]

Festival Ballet was a young company. Compared to the Royal Ballet and the Bolshoi and the Kirov, its dancers were young and dynamic. Youth and freshness were its hallmarks, and there was an abundance of energy and from everyone remotely connected with the formation of the new company. In many ways, Festival Ballet was my favorite English Ballet company, and Marina's guest appearances with Festival Ballet also proved to be extremely fruitful for her from a professional point of view.

It afforded Marina the opportunity to rekindle her friendship with Sir Anton Dolin. Their careers remained intermingled throughout their lives. It was in London that she met and was partnered by one of England's most talented young male dancers, John Gilpin. Along with dancing with him, as well as with Dolin, with Festival Ballet, these two men joined the Svetlova Dance Ensemble as guest artists and went on tour with Marina's troupe, most memorably to India.

John Gilpin was universally acclaimed as one of the leading male ballet dancers of the twentieth century. From the inception of London's Festival, John Gilpin was one of its leading stars of the Festival Ballet company. He later embarked on a career as an actor. Anton Dolin, who had become one of my teachers and who became a good friend of mine, went so far as to call Gilpin one of England's great dancers and a great human being. Gilpin wrote about his admiration for Marina when he described his professional association with her in his book, *A Dance with Life*. For a while, Sir Anton Dolin and Dame Alicia Markova were the directors of Festival Ballet, and Gilpin wrote that Dolin and Markova invited all the great ballet stars to the company as guest artists, which afforded him the opportunity to partner Margot Fonteyn, Tamara Toumonova, Alexandra Danilova, Tatiana Riabouchinska, Carla Fracci, Mia Slavenska, Nathalie Krassovska, Yvette Chauvire, Galina Samsova, Marina Svetlova, and of course Alicia Markova.

> In 1953, during our holiday month in September, Anton Dolin and I were asked to dance in a short tour of India, arranged by Marian Svetlova, our guest ballerina at Festival Ballet ...[9]

Marina made a guest appearance at London's Palladium during the 1959–60 season. On that occasion, Marina danced choreography that was created especially for her by Peter Darrell.

> Wherever she has performed, Marina Svetlova has created a sensation. Her youth, beauty and grace, combined with great talent and intelligence have won her wide acclaim.[10]

In her book, *With Ballet in My Soul,* Impresario Eva Maze describes being on tour in India with Marina, Dolin, and Gilpin. She describes the phenomenal reception they received from the Indian audiences in Bombay:

> Prima Ballerina Marina Svetlova and the young, handsome John Gilpin received huge accolades from both the critics and the audiences.[11]

Maze goes on to report that Marina's ensemble started in Bombay and continued on to New Delhi, where they were treated like royalty. The Svetlova Dance Ensemble seemed to be functioning as a reprise of the reaction generated decades earlier by the Anna Pavlova company. That tour of the Svetlova Dance Ensemble continued on to Calcutta.

Pilot on Pointe

Dance Magazine, May 26, 1953

Somewhere along the line, the *premiere danseuse* became an aviation enthusiast.[12]

The fact that Marina showed an interest in piloting an airplane is not that surprising because her father was an accomplished Russian aviator who flew missions for the Russian aristocracy during the First World War. He emigrated to Paris, where he maintained his own flying school. It was he who taught Marina how to fly an airplane. She was a licensed pilot since the age of sixteen, with more than five hundred solo hours to her credit. When she was leaving North America to perform with the de Basil Original Ballet Russe, she provided her own mode of transportation. When she flew to South America, she piloted her own plane. She also transported the Svetlova Dance Ensemble to Israel, where she was the first American company to perform in that country. Marina, with her company, did twenty concerts in Israel, followed by eight in Greece. She also flew her troupe on to Rome, where Dimitri Romanoff featured her in his *Ballerina and the Bandit* and *Eine Kleine Nacht Musik.*

> When Miss Svetlova is in a hurry to get to an engagement, she merely rents a plane and simply flies there.[13]

Over the Bounding Main

> Marina Svetlova, on this side of the ocean for a flying visit between appearances with the Festival Ballet in London, appeared with the Toronto Symphony Orchestra in August for the third time, to start her 10th Columbia Artist tour this January.[14]

Leading publications such as *Esquire* magazine wrote clever statements about Marina's escapades in the air. The following quip refers to her performances at New York's Metropolitan Opera:

> Her favorite place down here on earth is in the "Dance of the Hours" from *La Gioconda; lots of ballet devotees watching her* have observed that from any angle—as you can see—the hours pass all too quickly.[15]

CHAPTER 8

Col. W. de Basil's Original Ballet Russe

COL. W. de BASIL

Courtesy of Ron Seymour

I do not think the ballet will survive. There is all the machinery, but no driving force. The man who built the machine [Diaghilev] is dead ... Without the puppet master!... the members of the ballet are only lifeless toys. The puppets are sad little things just now.[1]

When the Ballets Russes made its debut in Paris in 1909, the event took the world by storm and literally changed the significant role this ballet company had played in the arts. Actually, the world was forced to realize the influence this ballet company had exerted on human life in general. Some scholars consider the arrival of the Ballets Russes to have been the most significant development in the arts of the twentieth century. Serge Diaghilev was the driving force behind the success of the Ballets Russes and had become an international celebrity.

> When Serge Diaghilev died there was a general impression that with him had died the ballet. Its collaborators, dancers, choreographers and others were dispersed – a flock without a shepherd … all attempts to gather up the threads and start anew failed until Col. W. de Basil made the problem his own and find the right solution.[2]

Col. W. de Basil inadvertently inherited the task of perpetuating the miracle of the excellence bestowed upon the arts by the Ballets Russes of Serge Diaghilev. Not an artist by vocation but a shrewd businessman, de Basil stumbled upon a formula with which he managed to fill the void left by the demise of the Ballets Russes. Diaghilev had become an icon in the world of the arts and was certainly a hard act to follow. Attempt at finding word to address the profound anguish felt by lovers of the arts the world over has been observed in a number of heartfelt words expressed by astute scholars and journalists. The effort to incorporate the words "Ballet Russe" into the name of an organization posed an immense obstacle for the success—or even survival—of any ballet company.

The Russian Ballet Revised

The Monte Carlo Ballet Russe at the Time of Its Arrival in the United States

> After the death of Diaghilev and the subsequent disintegration of his famous ballet … W. de Basil, is now the heir of the famous Diaghilev tradition. W. de Basil is a talented, self-made man … His energy, strong will, and love of ballet have helped him to overcome insurmountable difficulties.[3]

Valarin Svetlov was considered to be the dean of Russian ballet critics and had enjoyed a long career that witnessed the successes of both the Diaghilev Ballets Russes and the subsequent de Basil ballet companies. Svetlov was married to one of the foremost classical ballerinas of the Diaghilev Ballets Russes era, the prima ballerina Vera Trefilova. She enjoyed an exceptional reception, and in 1921, Diaghilev coaxed her out of retirement to portray the role of Princess Aurora in his revival of *The Sleeping Princess.* She was considered to represent the essence of classical ballet. The great English ballet lover, author and journalist Edward Denby expressed the excitement he experienced when he was presented with the opportunity to meet two stellar personalities of the ballet world, Trefilova and Svetloff, whose lives bridged the progression from one ballet era to the next. (In Paris, Marina became one of Treilova's star pupils, and Marina informed me that the last name of her stage name, Marina Svetlova, was a derivative of the last name of Valerian Svetloff.)

> For me, the great treat arranged by Korovin was my meeting with Vera Trefilova, and the *doyen* of ballet critics, Valerian Svetloff. I had worshipped Trefilova for four years … and knew her every little movement by heart.[4]

For whatever reason, from the very beginning, de Basil's prize company was begrudgingly offered a reception riddled with nodes of suspicion and a perception of presumed inferiority. Perhaps it was simply the lack of an immediate box office star lineup that helped initial his efforts to stall. The Ballets Russes fans had become accustomed to seeing established, famed superstars such as Pavlova that were in competition with de Basil, including Les Ballet 1933. Additionally, the tentative start and the turtlelike climb up the ladder of success displayed by the de Basil Original Ballet Russe was undoubtedly owing to de Basil's faith in the warm reception he anticipated that would be awarded the child stars which whom he was fanatically promoted. During the following years, the enthusiasm toward, or even the acceptance of, the new de Basil company was definitely a teeter-totter proposition.

> It had become necessary not only to build at a time of world financial crisis, but, in addition, to overcome on the one hand the hostility of the imagined heirs and their partisans.[5]

The inauguration of de Basil efforts to establish a new ballet company began shortly after the disappearance of the Ballets Russes. De Basil joined forces with Rene Blum, a successful businessman and lover of ballet, and together they formed the Blum/de Basil *Les Ballets Russes de Monte Carlo*. From the very beginning, Blum's soft-spoken, sophisticated personality was overpowered by de Basil's overbearing will and disposition, so even this first Ballet Russe incarnation was considered to have been De Basil's company.

> Ballet must be run by a dictator, but a benevolent despot who is well informed and well advised. Such a man is Colonel de Basil.[6]

Regardless of the animosity directed toward de Basil and the skepticism of the public in general, as well as the critics, some dance scholars chose to give de Basil credit for what they perceived to have been the value of his persistent efforts to make a success of his Ballet Russe.

> Yet it was de Basil who was mainly responsible for the worldwide impact made by the Ballets Russes in the 1930's, de Basil who publicized its new image and steered it into new worlds, and who somehow kept a company in existence …[7]

Marina Svetlova with Alexei Dolinoff

Courtesy of Ron Seymour

Col. W. de Basil planned to build something new. Although he reserved a certain amount of reverence for the company he loved, the Diaghilev Ballets Russes, he chose to found a new company in which youth would rule the day. He selected and created his own bright stars. What daring it took to expect a theatre eager for names and records to accept those thirteen-year-old dancers. He found youth everywhere, awaiting the proper inspiration and direction. He was prepared to face a public with a handful of youngsters in whom he believed. Those youngsters made names for themselves.

> De Basil had 'found a formula by which experience and youth can amalgamate to
> form an exceptional artistic ensemble. He has not only discovered and backed young
> talent but has also evoked something new in the finished artist.'[8]

Although initially the general public was only interested in the entertainment value of ballet, the connoisseur recognized what can only be called the Basil touch—flair, courage, and a touch of adventure that stopped one from taking his offerings for granted. Should he fail in his task and the thread of tradition be interrupted, what was known as Russian ballet would be in danger of extinction.

[The Monte Carlo Ballet] delighted the Diaghilev audiences who feared that with him, his ballet was dead.[9]

That must not be. It was unthinkable that this traveling museum of masterpieces should be destroyed beyond repair. Those who loved the ballet felt confident that just as de Basil was the man to rescue it from neglect, he was also the man to keep it alive.

There can be no doubt that this fresh start saved ballet.[10]

Occasionally, nostalgia wins out. Some folk want to see the older stars and cannot help themselves from viewing young stars as children. However, there exist ballet experts who share de Basil's vision of young dancers as having the potential to be taken as seriously as the more established regulars. Several experts on dance shared the opinion that:

Undoubtedly de Basil is a master psychologist.[11]

No one could have foreseen the effect the de Basil Ballet Russe was to exert upon the social mores of the time:

In its heyday, the company was the darling of the international elite, to which it represented the epitome of cosmopolitanism and sophistication.[12]

Although himself not a ballet dancer, de Basil realized from whence cometh success in accomplishing excellence in the world of dance. Only a company supported by a permanent and well-staffed school can create dancers from the youngest years of their training. Other companies must be satisfied with accepting dancers from a wide range of early training and do their best to instill a company with an indigenous sense of style and character. In the 1930s, the Paris schools of Preobrajenska, Egorova, Kschessinska, and Trefilova were a common denominator in the training of the majority of professional dancers. The de Basil Ballet, along with ballet masters Grigoriev and Tchernicheva, ensured that successive groups of heterogeneous dancers became identified with Russian ballet. "Grigoriev's standards and discipline, his confident expectation that to preserve the Diaghilev heritage and the newer works was a task everyone would recognize to be worth their hardest efforts, created the essential unity of purpose. It ensured that, as Jasinsky and Larkina say, 'even in its less than golden days the de Basil company was a great Ballet Russe.'"[13]

For audiences around the globe, the work of de Basil and his Ballet Russe company had a lasting effect. The appreciation for the work of de Basil and his Original Ballet Russe was heartfelt and truly sincere. For audiences and journalists alike, 1933 seems to have been the pivotal year for de Basil.

The year 1933, when Colonel de Basil brought his company to the Alhambra, marks the beginning of a renaissance not only in the art of ballet but in the taste of its London following ... Colonel de Basil's Russian Ballet fills the Royal Opera House for many months each season.[14]

As detailed in her *Footnotes to the Ballet,* Caryl Brahms remembered thoughts of a friend, R. C. Jenkinson, and shared them with her readers. Jenkins recounted that after having been absent from ballet performances for several years, he returned to the theater to see a 1933 performance of the de Basil company. He was reminded about how about he really loved the ballet and had missed being part of the audience for several years. He wrote that he owed de Basil a great gratitude for having brought ballet back into is life.

In his *Theatrical Dancing in America,* Winthrop Palmer remembers that in 1933, during a performance presented by the de Basil Ballet Russe on December 22, the audience was baffled by a new kind of ballet presented by these Russian dancers. The audacious splendor that Paris audiences had found in the prewar performances of the Diaghilev company was missing. The audience was lamenting the absence of the luscious stage décor by Leon Bakst and the music from their favorite composers, such as Mousorgsky, Rimsky-Korsakov, and Borodin. What the audience was treated to on this prestigious opening night of the de Basil troupe was *Concurence,* choreography by George Balanchine, the George Balanchine Trust, a symphonic ballet by Massine called (Tchaikovsky's) *Fifth Symphony,* and his *Le Beau Danube.* In addition, the de Basil programs seemed to be heavy on charm and slight on imagination. However, most of the audience was at least entertained.

A publicity flyer for the Monte Carlo Ballet Russe of de Basil printed that the company was being presented by Sol Hurok. The brochure labeled the de Basil company as being:

The Sensation of New York, London and Paris, the Monte Carlo Ballet Russe, w. de Basil Director General:

'the most glamorous spectacle in the theatre today …'

In that 1933 flyer, the following reviews were listed under a section called "N. Y. Critics Raved." In the *New York Times,* about the de Basil company, John Martin wrote, "Here is a masterpiece."

In *The N. Y. World Telegram,* Sandborn described the de Basil Ballet Russe in the *NY World Telegram* as being:

Entrancing apparition …
beguiling vision …
perfection itself.

A critic named Gilbert Seldes wrote that the de Basil company was the "Greatest thrill in 10 years." In the *New York Sun,* Henderson described the company as being:

Captivating … infectious …
[inspiring] prolonged applause and cheers.

The *NY Evening Post* described de Basil's company as being "magnificent" and filled with "Evanescent charm, … gay, and riot of color."

The *New Yorker* reported that the Monte Carlo Ballet Russe was "a masterpiece of pace and ingenuity, color and rhythm."

A critic named Bohm described the de Basil Original Ballet Russes in the *NY Herald Tribune* as being "Fascinating … compelling … entrancing … sparkled with vitality."

Critic Robert Garland reported that the company "has youth and beauty, drama and comedy … Highest art …"

Marina Svetlova in *Les Sylphides.*
Photo: S. Shier, Melbourne, Australia, 1940 souvenir program book of the de Basil Original Ballet Russe

However, much—if not most—of the press was overwhelmingly in support of the de Basil Company. Lincoln Kirstein, the wealthy patron of the ballet world, was not as effusive about the talents of Col. W. de Basil or the merits of his company. He made an analogy between the reception by the public of the de Basil company to that being offered to the *Silly Symphonies.* Kirstein's attitude toward de Basil was always somewhat hostile. He was also offended by the fact that Americans thought that ballet meant "Russian." Kirstein seemed more willing to support two Russian companies when they could use their wealth and influence supporting and building an American ballet culture. He was further outraged that America should support two Russian companies.

As was the case with Diaghilev's Ballets Russes, de Basil's Original Ballet Russe made an important contribution to the world of music. Regardless of the fact that George Balanchine was considered by most scholars to represent the ultimate conduit for the introduction of quality music into the ballet world through the Diaghilev Ballets Russes, all journalists were not of like mind. Some of them felt that the musical collaboration that was represented in the de Basil was superior even to that of Balanchine's les Ballets 1933. In addition to Stravinsky, de Basil's Ballet Russe championed the music of Brahms, Berlioz, Tchaikovsky, Beethoven, Handel Scarlatti, and Rimsky-Korsakov. These composers possessed the distinction of their music having been familiar and accepted for years. But de Basil was not content to rely on music composers and designers from the past. He was determined to create a new repertoire and roster of dancers with the eye to the future. He entertained plans for presenting what was new in music and painting, and he formed an advisory committee to keep him informed of what was the best, even most progressive, in various countries around the world.

By 1935, the company had matured and had acquired a personality of its own. It had become a highly sensitive instrument that necessitated not only the maintaining of a crop of highly accomplished dancers but also a stable of skilled and creative choreographers. One ingredient inserted into the recipe for the accomplishment of this feat was part of the genius of de Basil. He had taken in talented dancers from divergent nationalities, and de Basil saw to it that each of them participated in the orthodox ballet training while at the same time demonstrating that which was the best and most characteristic in them.

And everywhere the company has gained enthusiasts, has re-awakened an interest in ballet and has stimulated local and national efforts. In America [ballet caused] nothing but apathy even hostility in many cities, where it was associated with a regiment of synthetic blondes in flimsy dress pirouetting ... between the feature film and the news reel.[15]

This 1935 souvenir booklet includes an entire page entitled "History of Col. W. de Basil's Ballets Russes." Of note here is that the name attached to the company underwent a slight alteration. Now de Basil had assumed the plural form of Ballet Russe, which imitates more directly Diaghilev's spelling ("Ballets Russes"). Printed in the 1935 souvenir booklet is a feature entitled "History of Col. W. de basil's Ballets Russes." The writer of this piece is Edwin Evans—collaborator with the late Serge Diaghilev—and music critic in London. The billing of this author also hints at a more direct offspring of the famous Diaghilev company.

After two successive years ... the English public had so much appreciated his efforts that in the third year an association of 'Friends of the Ballet' has been formed, including thousands of members, from high society. ... down to the working class. No one can imagine a season in London nowadays without Col. W. de Basil's ballets.[16]

The success of the de Basil company may have begun in London, but the company soon became an international treasure. Col. W. de Basil's company was becoming an international company with triumphant success in many European countries. It eventually embarked upon successful tours in the United States.

Its young forces have thereby become thoroughly seasoned artists, and the quality of their performances has earned them international admiration ... Colonel W. de Basil may well look with pride upon the outcome of his labors, which have resulted in the creation of a new link in the history of the ballet.[17]

About a performance of Nijinska's *Les Noces,* on April 20, 1936, John Martin wrote in the *New York Times:*

> The de Basil Ballet Russe should be given a rising vote of thanks by the entire dance community, for here is assuredly one of the great works of our time.[18]

Martin's enthusiasm was mirrored elsewhere:

> And so the great tradition goes on. Long may it prosper.[19]

In an amazing short time, he had laid the foundations, had chosen as his collaborators the strongest and most creative elements of the old organizations, and had mixed them with the new. The actual repertoire had to include the very best in choreography. The ballet has in its repertoire today the largest and most diverse repertoire in the entire history of ballet. During the 1935–36 season, the company packed the vast Metropolitan Opera House during two visits.

In the 1936–37 souvenir program of the Original Ballet Russe, Haskell went on to say that he felt that de Basil had reawakened an interest in ballet and stimulated local and national efforts.

The tally of important artists who made their names with the de Basil Ballet is impressive and the immediate influence of the company in the thirties can hardly be overestimated.[20]

By the time de Basil's Ballet Russe started its fifth American tour in October 1937, ballet had become a small but integral part of American cultural life. Since 1933, the company had toured the United States and Canada for six months every year, thousands of miles every tour, planting the seeds of interest and awareness that continued to grow long after we had move on. In the company's 1937–38 souvenir program, Arnold Haskell wrote:

> Russian Ballet today is truly an International force.[21]

Some experts proclaim that the importance of any ballet company rests in three things: its contribution to choreographic development, the dancers it nurtures and displays, and its value to the audience.

The revivals of ballets from the repertoire of the de Basil Ballet Russe were as carefully rehearsed and as freshly executed as its novelties. "Last year's *Noces* and this year's *Faun* are things to be very grateful for.[22]

On July 29, Igor Schwezoff's *La Lutte Eternelle,* to Schumann's *Etudes Symphoniques,* was presented in Sydney, led by Skibine, Verchinina, Toumonova, Svetlova and Osato.[23]

At the Royal Opera Covent Garden the company completed a record season, three months of full houses. And all the time the repertoire was being increased; "*Scheherazade,*" "*Thamar,*" "*Good Humored ladies,*" and other early works, novelties such as "*Jardin Public*" and d'Erlnger's sparkling "*Cent Baisers*" which brought Madame Nijinska to the company as choreographer.[24]

During the course of many seasons, the personnel of the company had experienced many changes, but there were still several dancers in the company who were with it when it first came to the United States in 1933. Some of these dancers were also becoming recognized as promising choreographers. It seemed as though the creation of new and original ballets was beginning to rival the appearances of its many star dancers.

The choreographer of the company and its first dancer is David Lichine. His personal performances and the performances of his ballets, including *Prodigal Son, Protee, Francesca da Rimini* and *Graduation Ball* were meeting with their accustomed success. There is a rising audience demand for good dance attractions …[25]

> Colonel de Basil has a brilliant troupe. He has first-rate premiers, excellent soloists, and a corps de ballet that has been working together for eight years …[26]

One of the trade publications of the day highlighted Marina's stature in the roster of the de Basil Original Ballet Russe, and it mentioned her in conjunction with the reports of the successes of some of the prominent ballerinas of the day:

There were new names, or names becoming prominent for the first time. Among the listed ballerinas was Marina Svetlova …[27]

Dance Magazine was highly complimentary of Marina Svetlova when it included mention of her in the following quote:

Tamara Grigorieva, Olga Morosova, Anna Volkova, Marina Svetlova, Tatiana Leskova, and Genevieve Moulin lead the feminine contingent.[28]

In his book *The Ballets Russes,* Vincent Garcia-Marquez described the dance world's appreciation of Marina Svetlova as a rising balletic star when he wrote:

The anticipation was especially great because of the reappearance of Baranova, Toumanova and Riabouchinska, as well as the younger dancers Denisova, Svetlova, Moulin, Leskova, Skibine, and Tupine. A whole new generation who had never performed in the States.[29]

After de Basil temporarily split his company into two distinct troupes, many critics felt that the Australian company was the largest and strongest of them all. Although Svetlova toured with the Original Ballet Russe throughout the United States, Mexico, Cuba, and Canada, she was primarily a member of the Australian contingence. In 1941, she was awarded a Citation from the Council of Performing Arts in Sydney. Svetlova danced leading roles in *Les Sylphides, Princess Aurora, Swan Lake, Paganini, l'Apres Midi d'un Faune.* The significance of her appearances in such a variety of roles was reflected by journalists who pointed out that "The Original Ballet Russe is justifiably proud of its repertory which is undoubtedly the largest and the finest of any ballet company."[30]

One critic in Melbourne, Australia, described *Paganini* as a ballet in one act and three scenes created around the legend of the great genius of the violin, Nicolo Paganini. The violinist believed that his talent was a gift from God but became overwhelmed by visions of evil spirits such as envy, scandal, and gossip. Paganini falls victim to his premonitions of doom and finds that his talents for performing and composing are failing him. Toward the end of the ballet, the divine genius reappears, dispels the evil spirits, and ushers Paganini's soul into the heavens. Obviously, the role of the divine genius is the motivation for the entire libretto, and it is the role for which Marina became admired.

> Svetlova, a young dancer in the Pavlova tradition danced the *Divine Genius,* imbued with such an unerring musical sense, she preserved a rhythm in the toes that was enchanting and the like which was never seen before.[31]

Photo: Valente, NY, international favorite of four continents, Australia 1940

The esteemed ballet critic Walter Terry warmed up to the ballet *Paganini* after having attended a number of performances. He became convinced that *Paganini* was a work of genius. He found the ballet to be "brilliant," "profound," and "adult" in its thoughtful study of a great artist.

Col. De Basil Due Here

Having a large repertory, including eleven new ballets which have not yet been seen in America, there is no doubt that the American audience is anxious to see this company again … As soon as Col. De Basil was appointed general director, all disputes which jeopardized the company were washed up.[32]

When it became clear that de Basil was bringing his Original Ballet Russe to the United States, the anticipation went wild. If it is true at all that absence makes the heart grow fonder, it is especially true in reference to Col. De Basil and his company. [33]

Many any newspapers and periodicals, including *Dance Magazine*, wrote pieces that reflected the anticipation of the return of de Basil and his Original Ballet Russe, which was felt across the nation:

> It is not an exaggeration to say that the 1940–41 will be the biggest
> and most exciting season in American ballet history.[34]

The thrill motivated by realization that the Original Ballet Russe, under the general direction of Colonel W. de Basil, would come to America for the season 1940–41 was not universally considered to be prudent. Those who were hostile to the idea argued that it would be foolhardy for Sol Hurok, who was also the manager of the Ballet Russe de Monte Carlo, to bring another major ballet company to the country to provide further competition. "De Basil's detractors criticized the company itself on the grounds that its roster contained too many young and untried dancers."[35]

The great ballet audience from Maine to California and from Texas to Canada has never for a moment forgotten the artistic satisfaction and pleasure the company had been giving them for five seasons, and eagerly awaits its return.[36]

Colonel de Basil's Tenth Season

His Company, Reorganized and Reinforced, Carries out a Transcontinental Tour of the US and Canada

After a series of disasters and mishaps that would have overcome an ordinary person, in 1941, the indefatigable Col. W. de Basil brought his Original Ballet Russe on a tour of the United States and Canada. At the conclusion of the Montreal season, the *Montreal Standard* estimated the Original Ballet Russe performances to have been the most successful stage event in Canadian history. It was also reported that the gross financial success of d Basil's company obliterated all Montreal records for any theatre production. The significance of this success was considered to have been even more remarkable because the Original Ballet Russe was obliged to begin its Canadian tour in Toronto, on the coattails of the Ballet Russe de Monte Carlo.

Col. De Basil's current sojourn in the United States is nothing short of a triumphant return. His company, now as before, is still the Number One ballet company—unbeaten and united, as they say in football.[37]

All the sunny lands south of the border embraced Colonel de Basil as the cultural ambassador of Latin America. This was because everywhere he went, Col. De Basil trained a corps de ballet, founded schools, and worked with the artists of each country to create national folk ballets. In addition, the Original Ballet Russe continued, under his direction, to present the best in ballet from the great choreographers and designers in ballet. The 1941 tour of the Original Ballet Russe that started out in Mexico extended throughout South and Central America for four years, lasting a total of sixteen months of performance there. He encouraged the cooperation and artistic efforts of leading painters, designers, composers, and musicians in the Latin American countries and added to the repertory new ballets combining the folklore of Indians and Spanish history with the technique of ballet. Marina described to me the horror and disappointment of the dancers in Havana, Cuba. She said they had no money and no sense of security. The dancers were coming into the studio extremely fatigued, and many had not eaten properly. Marina described how some of the dancers fainted at the barre. The question of repertoire and relevance thereof is a never-ending conundrum. Ultimate, it seems as though the resolution to this dilemma rests with the proposed choreographic identity of the company and whether or not it wishes to either represent a timely trend or display reverence for an honored heritage. It seems that de Basil was dedicated to accomplishing both, and he provided a well-oiled organization that supported the work of choreographers of all styles.

This talent of de Basil's was demonstrated most vividly in his support for his star "babies." The baby ballerinas of the first company had grown into young ladies in their early twenties. They were considered to be among the finest ballet dancers of their generation. Two of them, Tatiana Riabouchinska and Tamara Toumanova, were with the company in Australia, and the third one, Irina Baranova, was in Hollywood appearing in a motion picture but was expected to rejoin the company after having completed her Hollywood commitments.

From many corners, dancers, fans, and critics were acknowledging the sweeping impact the work of de Basil had on the ballet world.

And everywhere the company has gained enthusiast, has re-awakened an interest in ballet and has stimulated local and national efforts.[38]

Generally speaking, dance historians do not remember de Basil with as much reverence as they do Diaghilev—and perhaps rightfully so. Diaghilev came first in the lineage of the Ballets Russes-es, but de Basil seems to have been the keeper of the flame.

I always had a very great respect for him as my director and now I have a very great admiration for him and for what he did for the world of art.[39]

The colonel believed not only in the continuing development of his own company but also the art in general. He did much to safeguard and shape the future. In the ballerinas' schools in Paris and elsewhere, he had many small wards whose education he supervised. They were debutantes of 1940 and so on. De Basil said that if two out of ten turned out to be premieres danseuses, he would feel rewarded.

Many critics believed that the artists, not the repertoire, represent the company's long-term influence. The de Basil dancers are widely scattered. Alexandra Danilova has been teaching for years at the School of American Ballet in New York City; Tatiana Riabouchinska has a studio in Hollywood; Marina Svetlova teaches in Bloomington …[40]

The tally of important artists who made their names with the de Basil Ballet is impressive and the immediate influence of the company in the 'thirties can hardly be overestimated.[41]

January 1952 saw the ending of an adventure when the last curtain come down on Col. W. de Basil's Original Ballet Russe.

Colonel W. de Basil may well look with pride upon the outcome of his labors, which have resulted in the creation of a new link in the history of the ballet.[42]

Sono Osato was a beloved member of the Original Ballet Russe. She shared her respect for the company and her love for Col. W. de Basil when she wrote in her book, *Distant Dances.* She described a deeply emotional experience she had when visiting the tomb of Col W. de Basil, thirty-five years after his death, when she stood at his grave in Ste. Genieve des Boie, the Russian cemetery near Paris. A few yards away from de Basil's grave, the double-headed eagle of the Romanov lineage decorated the grave of the beloved ballerina Kchessinska. There was a small wooden bench placed near the grave, inviting her fans to experience a moment of peace as they visited Kchessinska's place of rest amidst a neat bed of pansies, surrounded by a plot of manicured grass. By way of contrast, on the de Basil headstone, the Cyrillic lettering was severely worn away.

At the base lay a basket of artificial flowers. Someone had dropped an empty, plastic bottle by his tomb … Whatever physical monument marks de Basil's grave cannot dignify him as much as my memory of him does. The enormous work he did and the fierce tenacity of spirit that drove him will live as long as ballet and its history survives.[43]

CHAPTER 9

La Lutte Éternelle

This ballet proved to be a high point in the early career of Marina Svetlova with the Original Ballet Russe. She was selected by the choreographer to create a solo role in this ballet, one of the more prominent parts for which she received excellent notices.

It was observed by fans that M. Svetlova gave a crystalline performance as Truth in Schwezoff's new ballet.

The *Sydney Morning Herald* felt that *Eternal Struggle* spoke from the heart. No matter how it drafted conflicts of people across the stage, there was always warmth, human feeling within the eye-fulfilling design. Although the ballet did not remain in the repertoire for long, it was a great honor that Balanchine had selected her for whom to create a role in his new ballet.

There are some interesting individual dances in *The Eternal Struggle*. Tamara Toumonova, Sono Osato, Marina Svetlova and Nina Verchinini have occasion to display their prowess …[1]

Yura Skibine, Tamara Toumanova, Sono Osato, and Marina Svetlova in *Lutte Eternelle*. Creator: Kuehn, Nanette, photographer label: H91 49/44 File: br 000258. Courtesy of State Library of Victory.

Marina and I shared a connection with ballet history through Igor Schwezoff. They worked together in de Basil's Original Ballet Russe, where he chose her to be in the first cast of his *Lutte Eternelle.* Years later, Schwezoff invited me to be a piano accompanist for classes he was teaching in New York City. His classes were very successful, and coincidentally, several dancers from the Metropolitan Opera Ballet were regularly in attendance.

Original Ballet Russe, Col A. de Basil, General Director, Los Angeles

Eternal Struggle was composed by Igor Schwezoff to Schuman's *Etudes* and orchestrated beautifully by Antal Dorati, with scenery and costumes by Kathleen and Florence Martin. It was based on the theme of a humanity's struggle against the wretchedness and the helplessness of humankind. Humankind is misled by illusion and held up by obsessions, but through visions of beauty and truth acquires willpower and thus becomes the victor.

> Skibine as the Man, Verichinina as the Woman with Toumonova, Osato, Svetlova and Runanine in the other leading roles clearly project the idea on which this ballet is based … Schwezoff is an interesting choreographer and it will be well to watch for future works from him.[2]

It is enlightening to read about a choreographer's intentions in his ballet. One can only wonder if the statements reflect the objective of the choreography or the creator's interpretation of the artistic commodity. Schwezoff announced about his new ballet that the theme was man's progress toward an ideal beyond worldly things and was symphonic in character. He planned that *Lutte Eternelle* would combine two styles, pure classicism, which would be represented by allegoric figures such as illusion, truth, beauty, and obsessions, and humans headed by The Man would be based on free movement and expressive dancing.

Taking part in the ballet are Grigorieva, Toumonova, Verchinina, Osato, Petroff, Yasinsky, as well as young newcomers to the Company, such as Leskova, Stepanova, Svetlova, Skibine, Ivangine. "I am trying to introduce in my ballet as much dancing as the theme permits so not want to sacrifice dancing for pantomime and am trying to tell the story through sheer dancing.[3]

One can notice that Marina was selected to portray a solo role alongside a few of the most important young stars in the Original Ballet Russe, including Tamara Toumonova, one of the original three baby ballerinas who had already achieved an enviable position among the major dancers of the day.

There were three other new productions in Australia. Igor Schwezov's *La Lutte Eternelle (29 July 1940) was* a re-working of a ballet called *Elckerlyc,* set to Schumann's *Etudes Symphoniques* that he had staged in Amsterdam in 1936. Its cast included Toumanova as Illusion, Osato as Beauty, Svetlova as Truth, as well as Tupinee as Will.[4]

One dance analyst described not only the significance of this Schwezoff ballet in the repertoire of the de Basil company but also emphasized the importance of the new leading roles being offered to Marina. "Another novelty was *The Eternal Struggle,* staged by Schwezoff, an intelligent dancer in the company itself. It is something of a tour de force in keeping allegorical figures properly busy to the music [Schumann's *Etudes Symphoniques*] ..."[5]

The significance of Marina's appearance in the first clast of this ballet is enhance by the manner in which the success of this ballet was being foretold. Walter Terry praised Schwezoff's choreography for *La Lute Eternelle* by observing that he viewed the ballet as "foretelling the possibilities of further effective fusions of the brilliance of ballet with the potency of the modern dance."[6]

Igor Schwezoff.
Photo: *Ballet Russe de Monte Carlo* souvenir program, 1941.

It is very interesting to observe the development of the young dancers, and the way in which they grasp the individual styles of different choreographers.[7]

This statement is particularly applicable when it comes to an analysis of Marina's career with the Original Ballet Russe. She adapted readily to a variety of immensely contrasting styles, from the angular, austerity represented by Balanchine's *Balustrade* to the comedic entertainment qualities as represented in Lichine's *Graduation Ball.*

The Original Ballet Russe Ballet is justifiably proud of its repertoire which is undoubtedly the largest and the finest of any ballet company.[8]

Marina had quickly gained attention as an accomplished classical dancer. However, Schwezoff's ballet gave her the opportunity to hone her skills in more dramatic roles.

The extent to which Marina's presence in the de Basil company can be witnessed in the number of times ballets in which she danced leading roles were programmed.

Eight of the thirty works in the touring company (*Cendrillon, Quest* (premiered in Australia as Etude), *Eternal Struggle, Graduation Ball, Paganini, Pavane, Prodigal Son,* and *Protee* were new.

This ballet was one of Marina's major triumphs with the Original Ballet Russe. Some found her portrayal of truth to be the highlight of the production. It also gave Marina a chance to show a more sympathetic part of her balletic personality in this nonconventional ballet.

The loveliest movement in the ballet comes when m. Svetlova dominates the stage as Truth. Her role is cast in pure classical ballet style and she acquits herself nobly. [9]

Denis Stoll seemed to have some regard for the first version of this ballet, which had been staged in Amsterdam in 1936. He described it as a choreographic symphony which a musician can watch without feeling alternate pangs of fury and sorrow.

Truth danced by Marina Svetlova was an incident of purist loveliness.[10]

Igor Schwezoff was quite an admired performer and became a distinguished and much-loved teacher. Marina and I shared the experience of having worked closely with Schwezoff. I too got to work with Schwezoff when he invited me to be a piano accompanist for classes he was teaching at the Youskevitch School in New York City.

There were plenty of ballet companies, especially in combining classical and modern dance, which possessed imposing lists of choreographic novelties and launched choreographers that entirely lacked the invigorating vitality of the de Basil repertoire.

Many dance enthusiasts felt that "Col. W. de Basil had become an almost legendary figure in the contemporary ballet."

CHAPTER 10

Graduation Ball

Graduation Ball was a popular success from its premiere on March 1, 1940. It instantaneously became the bread and butter of the de Basil Original Ballet Russe. It was dubbed a true charmer and continued as a signature piece in the repertoire of the de Basil company. This ballet held tremendous significance in the development of the Marina Svetlova saga.

Graduation Ball is a ballet in one act. Along with having Lichine as its choreographer, the ballet was set to music by Johann Strauss, which was compiled and orchestrated by Antal Dorati. The scenery and costumes were designed by Alexandre Benois, and they were assembled by Nadejda Benis. The ladies' costumes were executed by O Laros and Antoinette, and the male costumes by A. H. Lester.

The original cast included Marina Svetlova as one of the Junior Girls and as the primary female soloist in the Mathematics and Natural History scene. Tatiana Riabouchinska was a Junior Girl as well as the Mistress of Ceremony. Alexandra Denisova and Tatiana Leskova were also Junior Girls, and Leskova the soloist in Impromptu Dance. Denisova was a soloist in Dance-step Competition. I mention these ladies because they were dancers who interacted more frequently with Marina in other various ballets, such as Balanchine's *Balustrade,* and at one point or another, Svetlova, Leskova, and Denisova each danced the role of the Divine Genius in Lichine's *Protee.* Some of the gentlemen in the cast were David Lichine as Riabouchinska's partner in Perpetuum Mobile, Paul Petroff (one of Marina's partners) as the Scotsman, and Igor Schwezoff as the Old General. It should be remembered that Schwezoff cast Marina to portray a featured role in his ballet *La Lutte Eternelle*, which had its premiere a few months later, on July 29, 1940.

The story begins when a group of cadets from a local military academy arrive to meet a group of young girls at a neighboring Viennese girls' school. The plan is for the boys to escort the girls to a graduation ball. The students self-consciously attempt to pair up for an imminent social dance. Some entertainment ensues, including a solo variation for a drummer boy, followed by a romantic pas de deux, followed by a girl's variation. This is followed by an energetic, vigorous acrobatic competition between two girls. After that episode, the audience is presented with a mock class of Mathematics and Natural History, created by Marina Svetlova, Helene Lineva, and Maria Azrova. In this scene, Svetlova portrayed the main role of the pupil sitting at a desk who was approached by the other two other dancers dressed as balding professors.

The Original Ballet Russe opened its Paris season at the Palais Chaillot on October 7, 1947 … The greatest successes of the season were "*The Prodigal Son*" and "*Graduation Ball*.[1]

After the premiere, part of the review reported in the *Sydney Morning Herald* newspaper described the evening's festivities:

These romping creatures had been imagined with uncommon penetration into juvenile psychology Their pranks had an innocent, darting animation, which enkindled the ballet from the very beginning … It praised the whole cast individually and added, 'it was an evening of splendid dancing in small parts.[2]

Although *Graduation Ball* was and is a great popular success, many scholars were nonplused because the score was not at all original. It consisted of a compilation of various unsophisticated works by Johann Strauss. The collection of dance music included a few ballroom compositions designed to be easily accessible to every stratum of society.

Lichine's *Graduation Ball* is in its type just an operetta to Strauss music, the stock item every company offers … The very first waltz strikes you right away as a little human scene.[3]

Eisel Title: Marina Svetlova as the school girl (center left), Helene Lineva and Maria Azrova as the two teachers (center right and standing front right with butterfly net), and artists of the company, in *Graduation Ball*, the Original Ballet Russe, Australian tour, His Majesty's Theatre, Melbourne, 1940.
Author: Hall, Hugh P. PIC/11102/351 LOC ALBUM 1111/9 courtesy of the National Library of Australia.

An interesting, anecdotal association with this ballet for Svetlova was the fact that once again she was performing alongside many of the leading dancers of the company, including Tatiana Riabouchinska, who danced the role of the Romantic Girl. Marina created the role of the Student

Girl. Marina not only danced alongside the choreographer of this ballet, but she also performed with Igor Schwezoff, who had selected Marina to create a role for him in his *La Lutte Eternelle.*

The opening performance in Melbourne on March 14 [1941] received over thirty calls.[4]

Although there were certain reservations about the music, the other aspects of the production of *Graduation Ball* contributed to making the ballet a tremendous success. In spite of the success of this ballet, there remained some skepticism about the qualifications of Lichine as choreographer.

Lichine, however was not yet established as a choreographic reputation …[5]

David Lichine, who had been a highly respected dancer, had not yet proven himself to be of like stature as choreographer.

In the opinion of some balletomanes, Lichine was beginning to find his sea legs as a choreographer. In his book *Writings,* Denby began to get on board:

Lichine's piece without visible effort to be special, turns out to be a pleasant surprise.[6]

Quickly enough, Lichine's reputation as a choreographer was becoming more widely acknowledged:

If there was any doubt, after '*Graduation Ball*', that Lichine is the choreographic find of the season, here, it was resolved … That theatrical sense which was always a strong element in Lichine's personal performance continued to assert itself …[7]

Arnold Haskell expressed his hopes that Lichine would bring more gravitas to the reputation of the de Basil Original Ballet Russe when he made the following assertion:

The future hope of a very fine company seems undoubtedly to lie with David Lichiine.[8]

Other experts supported Haskell's observation and were inclined to view Lichine's prospects through a longer-reaching telescope: "Lichine as a choreographer of great potential, destined for future prominence."[9]

Marina was obviously a major player with de Basil's Original Ballet Russe, especially in Australia. As a soloist in *Graduation Ball,* she received great visibility. She greatly contributed to the growth of Lichine as a choreographer.

The Australian tour has brought out the fact that beyond a doubt that the future is his … By this time Lichine was coming into his own as a choreographer.[10]

About David Lichine, the esteemed American critic John Martin wrote in the *New York Times*:

His *Graduation Ball* is a work of undeniable talent, fresh in spirit, full of spontaneous invention and totally without swank or pretense. One can think of no other ballet so truly youthful in design and performance.[11]

Not only were his choreographic skills being praised, but he was gaining respect for his versatility for creating ballets of contrasting styles. The *New York Times* remarked that from his earlier ballet *Fils prodigue* to *Graduation Ball* represented commendable choreographic progress:

Lichine had not previously worked in the light comedy vein ... but he found his own style with spectacular success ...

Many fans were in agreement that this ballet was:

Fresh in spirit, full of spontaneous invention and totally without swank or pretense.[12]

Denby, too, liked graduation ball:

Lichine's numbers, instead of being made up out of smug references to what is supposed to be funny, are the actions of real dance characters with all the exuberance of dancing.[13]

Marina Svetlova as the school girl (center left), Helene Lineva and Maria Azrova as the two teachers (standing front right with butterfly net), and the artists of the company, in *Graduation Ball,* the Original Ballet Russe, Australian Tour, his Majesty's Theatre, Melbourne, 1940. Author: Hall, Hugh P. PIC/11102/351 LOC ALBUM 1111/9.

One of the few contemporary works ... [which] may unblushingly called a masterpiece. Irving Kolodin.[14]

After appearances as the Student Girl, Marina enjoyed success with her performances as the Pigtail Girl, one of the leading roles in the ballet.

Helene Lineva and Maria Azrova as the two teachers (standing front left), Marina Svetlova as the school girl (center right), and the artists of the company, in *Graduation Ball*, the Original Ballet Russe, Australian Tour, His Majesty's Theatre, 1940. Author: Hall, Hugh P. PIC/11102/ 356 LOC ALBUM 1111/9.

About Svetlova's performances in this ballet, it was noted that:

She imbued the part with airy grace, playful nonchalance, and a delightful spirit of coquetry.[15]

Although Marina Svetlova had enjoyed success in the role of the Student Girl and had danced as one of the cadets,

Svetlova's power as a mime came to the forte in the role of a pig-tail school girl. She was bouncing with vitality, amusing and unsophisticated and made a small dance convey much.[16]

Critics in Australia could not find enough words to describe their approval of innocent charming effect with which this ballet enthralled the audiences. "The triumph of the time was *Graduation Ball*, which right from its premiere on 1 March, 1940 was a declared charmer.[17]

This ballet seemed to be a born winner: "When it was shown in Melbourne ... it was acclaimed as a sheer delight."[18]

John Martin wrote in the *New York Times* about his concern for the effect that less than first-class dancing could have on choreographers:

With the state of ballet ... the case of younger choreographers is a perplexing one ... All the more honor then to David Lichine, who in the comparatively brief space of seven years has pulled himself up from the tentative beginnings ... to a position where his accomplishments as a choreographer demand not only acknowledgement but respect ...[19]

In spite of all of the wonderful ballets being turned out by other choreographers for the Original Ballet Russe, such as Balanchine, Fokine, and Massine, most experts agreed that *Graduation Ball* was always the biggest draw. During one moment of financial hardship for the Original Ballet Russe, de Basil is reported to have exclaimed, "Thank God for *Graduation Ball!*"[20]

CHAPTER II

Balustrade

It would seem that this ballet was the horse of a different color—heard tell of.

At its premiere, *Balustrade* was confronted by a recalcitrant audience, not shy about demonstrating their disapproval. The new ballet seemed to them to be little more than a repugnant representation of a sort of primitive exoticism. This rude reception undoubtedly contributed to the extremely short shelf life of this ballet. I have viewed the short amount of video that still survives of excerpts from *Balustrade.* Along with my own impressions of the ballet based on this taped footage, I am sharing some astute commentaries on performances of this ballet as expressed by critics and journalists of that time. I am also including some relevant, maybe even surprising, observations about the preparations for the premiere of *Balustrade* as recounted by perhaps the most valuable source, the dancers themselves.

If some of Balanchine's work can be described as nervous, then this one is a nervous breakdown.[1]

The curious fate of Balanchine's ballet is reminiscent of that of the Anthony Tudor's ballet, *Dim Lustre.* Tudor's ballet, for whatever reason, momentarily became his "lost ballet." *Balustrade* was met with great controversy, as was demonstrated by the vehement proclamations of the critics who reported vastly divergent accounts of the merits and inadequacies of this ballet. The effect that the premiere of *Balustrade* had also on the audience was profound, although not necessarily in the preferred manner. However, some ballet historians grew to believe the ballet was a seminal creation in the chronology, if not in the annuls of the Balanchine ballets. Certain authorities viewed the ballet as having been an extraordinary accomplishment in the Stravinsky/Balanchine collaborative enterprise. I am totally fascinated by this ballet and the immediate impact it exerted on the ballet lovers and the artistic community of that day. The published reactions to the premiere of *Balustrade*—both positive and negative—are seriously intriguing.

Balustrade has achieved the posthumous reputation of resounding failure, apart from the haunting designs. It is hard to see just why this is so, except that some leading critics of the time damned it—often a burden a burden too great for a stimulating and original work to survive.[2]

The skepticism surrounding the value and importance of this work is particularly troubling because everything about the creation of this ballet—composer, choreographer, designer, and dancers—seems as though it represented the proverbial recipe for success. Simply approaching the work from an intellectual or analytic point of departure, this ballet should easily have survived, let alone awarded at least a modicum of the significance it would seem to have deserved. Firstly, the choreographer was the sine quo non, George Balanchine, already recognized as a successful choreographer for his creations for Diaghilev's Ballets Russes (e.g., *Apollon Musagete,* 1928, choreography by George Balanchine, the George Balanchine Trust, and *Le Fils Prodigue,* choreographer George Balanchine, the George Balanchine Trust), as well as the Ballet Russe de Monte Carlo. The costume and set designer was Paul Tcherlitchev, a somewhat controversial, surrealist painter of the day who had already scored some success with *las Ballets 1933* for an earlier ballet, *Errante* (choreographer George Balanchine, the George Balanchine Trust), with a score by Franz Schubert. By the time he was designing sets and costumes for Balanchine's *Balustrade* to be presented by the de Basil Original Ballet Russe, Tcherlitchev had already received some acclaim for having been the designer with Ballet Russe de Monte Carlo for Massine's *Noblissima Visione* (1938), music by Paul Hindemith.

The creator of the score for *Balustrade* was none other than Igor Stravinsky, whose collaboration with Balanchine had already become recognized as something exceptional. Truth be told, Balanchine revisited the new Stravinsky score to which the ballet was choreographed on two later occasions, one of these being *Stravinsky Concerto*, and the other, *Stravinsky Violin Concerto* (1972). One might assume that the popularity of these subsequent treatments of the Stravinsky score contributed to the cavalier attitude displayed toward the very existence of *Balustrade.* For whatever reason, and there are many proffered, the fate of this ballet seems to have been sealed immediately following its premier, which took place on January 22, 1941, at the Fifty-First Street Theatre, New York.

Tchelitchov's poetic scenery suggested a fantasie garden and the costumes, fabulous garden creatures … "The décor consisted of a low, white balustrade in perspective with … two pale, macabre, skeletal trees … lit in red against a black background.[3]

> Initially, audiences and critics alike seemed to have become preoccupied with reports of the possible visual impact of the ballet performance: the dancers, the sets, the costumes. In the case of *Balustrade*, perhaps owing to the stature of the composer, there appears to have been given slightly more than usual diffidence to the score and its partnership with the other players in the creation of this ballet. Balanchine is quoted in the *New York Times* as having said that the ballet "has no story but is a contrast of moods in movement and color. It is not an illustration but a reflection of Stravinsky's music."[4]

One might conjecture that such vivid descriptions of a new ballet such as *Balustrade* should have instigated an animal-like curiosity. Balanchine's statement is not only an obeisance to the power generated by Stravinsky's new score, but it supports the concept that there exists an organic, symbiotic relationship between the composer and the choreographer. In the words of Tamara Toumovova, the star ballerina of the production:

Stravinsky was absolutely enchanted … He went into complete ecstasy …[5]

To add fuel to the fire surrounding the alleged failure of the premiere of *Balustrade*, the show had the composer as its conductor. For some cognoscenti, *Balustrade* was seen as a guide post by which the success of other ballets of the time were being gauged.

Tudor's *Pillar of Fire* is the one really good ballet that has been launched in New York since the de Basil company's *Balustrade*.[6]

Casting

In addition, to the talents of the choreographer and the stage designer, *Balustrade* boasted a dream cast, headed by the balletic heartthrob of the day, Tamara Toumonova. It seems to have been Toumonova's presence in New York at that time that was Balanchine's inspiration for the creation of *Balustrade*.

Curiouser and curiouser!

Tamara Toumonova (1919–1996), "the black pearl of ballet," was, along with Baronova and Riabouchinska, one of the three famous baby ballerinas discovered by Balanchine in Paris in the early thirties. Rumor has it that both Baronova and Riabouchinska arrived at separate times during the creation process of the ballet, but each left, claiming that the music was unsuitable or perhaps even too difficult to count. At any rate, the choreographic experience did not turn out to be the personal dream that seemed to have been Balanchine's from the initial planning of this ballet. This could have been disappointing for him on both the artistic and personal levels. It is fascinating to learn about what succeeds and what doesn't in the realization of the original plans for a ballet. "Balanchine's choreography contained further examples of his amazing ingenuity."[8]

The conundrum intensifies. If experts are proclaiming the importance of the creation of this ballet, why has it been forgotten and shelved away as though it were of no artistic value?

Scholars felt that *Balustrade* was a milestone in Balanchine's development. It inaugurated the forties, a prolific decade during which he established definite stylistic preferences and choreographic syntax. This ballet possessed no story and its main concern was for movement as a physical expression of the music.:

It is of interest to note that two previous ballets, *Le Baise de la fee* (Choreography by George Balanchine©The George Balanchine Trust,) and *Jeux de Cartes*, (Choreography by George Balanchine©The Balanachine Trust,) both created in 1937, had libretti, as did most of his works produced since his arrival in the United States (with the notable exception of *Serenade*, (Choreography by George Balanchine©The Balanchine Trust.) [7]

Although *Serenade* (choreography by George Balanchine, the George Balanchine Trust) seems to be directly classic in its style, it makes many of its points by gestures and arrangements that have a sort of pictorial symbolism. It was perceived by some viewers that *Balustrade*, in the first and last parts of it, in which the movement was simple and open, made its effect directly by its dance rhythm and was definitely in the present direction, although it was the wonderfully sensual acrobatics that delighted one part of the audience and shocked another. "Shocking, Balanchine has not been since then, perhaps because shockingness, especially in America, injects a non-dance excitement that interrupts and diminishes the straight dance emotion." [8]

There can be little doubt that Stravinsky was pleased to see his seldomly performed violin concerto take on balletic life. However, Balanchine's abstract choreography won little praise from the critics, who were deeply divided over the Balanchine-Tcherlitchov-Stravinsky *Balustrade.*

Irving Kolodin thought that Balanchine has exceeded himself in the designing of intricate weavings of hands and legs and stunty groupings. But if he has done any more than this, it has escaped the notice of this onlooker. To be sure, one is hardly so naïve as to expect meaning or significance from a ballet, especially one that uses Stravinsky's acidulous and banal violin concerto as a point of departure. [9]

One thing is obvious, *Balustrade* was far ahead of its time. [10]

Denby, reviewing the ballet wrote that he noticed two elements or "motives": the upstretch on the downbeat; and one knee slipping across the other perhaps in a gesture of conventional shame. The first element Balanchine enlarges into the liveliest and lightest of ensemble dances the second element - one of gesture—he elaborate into a long acrobatic trio in which all sorts of "slippings across" are tried—of legs, of bodies, of arms; and this trio ends by a separation, the girl looking reproachful, the boys hanging their heads in shame. "How strangely such a concrete moment tops the abstract acrobatics before it; a discontinuity in one's way of seeing that is bridged by the clearness of placing and the sureness of timing … The most controversial movement was the pas de trois, which Balanchine devised fantastic designs of sensual suggestiveness … This unusual choreographic design inspired boos, cheers, applause and laughter from the audience. [11]

The lobby in favor, however, makes a case that reads differently. Lillian Moore, an accomplished professional dancer of that time, allowed that "some of the patterns employed are startling enough to jar the nerve of the accustomed to more conventional design." [14] She thought that Balanchine had enlarged the scope of the traditional technique with effects of a decidedly acrobatic nature, without ever losing track of the classicism that formed the true foundation of the work.

The much revered and respected composer Virgil Thomson joined Edwin Denby in praising the work, writing in the *New York Herald Tribune* that he felt that it was because of the lack of an ostentatious display of intricate technical passage work and self-conscious lyrical passages that the ballet proved to be an example of continuous choreography. He seemed to feel that this ballet gave Balanchine the opportunity to do what he did best. He built long solos over tightly knit ensemble work. "They seem to have in come out of the music and to walk in closed communion beside it, the closeness of this communion providing an Independence so characteristic of ©Balanchine, that relieved the dancers from any pedestrian obligation to keep step with the measure." [12]

Balanchine's shift from modernism may be due to the fact that he had worked for the last eleven years only in America, generally for American dancers. Certain analysts felt that American dancers, through their incomplete dance training, were obliged to discover their own dance impetus to catapult them to finding the skills that would enable them to carry on in performance. Balanchine's new style may also have been due to a spontaneous change in his point of view, to a new interest in classical coherence, limpidity, and grace that contemporary poetry and music were also beginning to show. In any event, his new style was not an oblique neoclassicism; it was a direct new classicism. It was the new choreographic style of the forties, which was emotional, unlike the proceeding style we knew from *Les Sylphides,* the *Faun, Tricorne, Noces,* and *Apollo* (choreographer George Balanchine, the George Balanchine Trust)—each one a masterpiece, as everyone knows. Balanchine was already recognized by the discerning as a classicist, and classicist he was in comparison to the modern choreographers.

> But even in *Cotillon (*Choreography by George Balanchine© The George Balanchine Trust,*)* which in its open flow gives a clear indication of his present manner, is in its theme a stylized representation of a nonballet form of dancing ... I have the feeling that *Ballustrade* in the first and last part of it, in which the movement was simple and open and made its effect directly by its dance rhythm, was more definitely in the present direction.[13]

John Martin stated about the premiere that "the event need not detain us. Nobody involved in it can have been very serious about it, so there seems to be little reason for anyone else to be." [14]

Some critics agreed that the blatant novelty of composition coupled with the work's odd juxtaposition with programs that contained ballets, such as *Le Marriage d'Aurore* or *Petrouchska*, and the influential bad reviews accounted for its almost immediate disappearance. "It took some time before the music and the dancing became one to this auditori-sectator, however, but the unification was complete when it occurred ..."[15]

Fans found it hard to believe that regardless of all of the eccentricities within the production, parts of the ballet were wonderfully attractive as a spectacle. Some fans became comfortable with the mixture of sheer burlesque, aloof dignity, a hint at eroticism, and the sheer insolence of the spectacle in general. Edwin Denby saw in his new "undissonant," "undeformed," "one-at-a-time" way of dancing a kind of parallel relationship to Miss Graham's new modern-school manner in *Letter to the World* [16].

For the first time in more than three years, George Balanchine has created a new ballet for one of the major companies ... Nevertheless, we doubt very much if *Balustrade* will survive as long as *Cotillon* (Choreography by George Balanchine© The George Balanchine Trust), which was created in 1932, and will probably outlive its choreographer's most recent effort.[17]

Cognoscenti struggled to find appropriate terminology with which to describe Balanchine's new ballet. All seemed to agree that *Balustrade* portended a significant shift in choreographic status quo and that with a unique choreographic vocabulary, Balanchine was forging the way into a new age of ballet creation.

As *Cotillon (*Choreography by George Balanchine © The George Balanchine Trust) had been in the thirties, "*Balustrade* was a milestone in Balanchine's development. It inaugurated the forties, a prolific decade during which he was to establish definite stylistic preferences and choreographic syntax ..."[21]

Dance scholars offered some fascinating insight into this excursion into uncharted waters. "His present style is not an oblique neo-classicism, it is a new direction of classicism."[22]

Some analysts were particularly astute:

I think that this direct enjoyment of dancing as an activity is the central aspect of ballet style that Balanchine has rediscovered.[23]

Audiences and critics alike felt that "*Balustrade* was a stimulating excursion into surrealism. It provoked considerable critical comment, some of it good, some of it most unfavorable. The premiere of *Balustrade* raised near riots in the audience, perhaps the likes of which had not been witnessed since the premiere of Stravinsky's *Le Sacre du Printemps* in 1913. If for no other reason, *Balustrade* should have earned some place in the annuls of Ballet History: audience uproar at premiere of new Balanchine/Stravinsky ballet, *Balustrade.*

Balanchine's *Balustrade*, with a Stravinsky score and a Tchelitchev décor, seemed to be a ballet in the Diaghilev tradition, "a collaboration of first-class artists where one can expect to feel movement, look, and listen with the same degree of sensibility. In such collaborations you can see the poetic quality of dancing better, because all the different aspects of the spectacle have been made by people who believe in its poetry (or if you prefer, as serious) as any other art."[24]

Edwin Denby reported that: *Balustrade* is complex. However, its novelty is that it is not complex in the manner we are accustomed to. The individual dances have almost no angular breaking of the dance impulse or direction. "The impulse is allowed to flow out so to speak, through the arms and legs, which delineate the dance figure lightly, as it were in passing—as they do in our slow dancing. This is all something else than the 'European' style of the thirties."[25]

Although the shelf life of this ballet was relatively short, Marina's participation in the presentation of this ballet did not go unnoticed:

The first two movements, a *Toccata* and an *Aria*, offered extended opportunity to two young ladies of exceptional merit, Tatiana Leskova and Marina Svetlova. These two dancers, well matched in height and in physique, and both such fine technicians that it is difficult to select one or the other for praise.[26]

Toumonova is reported to have said that during one rehearsal of *Balustrade*, Stravinsky remarked to Balanchine, "George, I think that this is the epitome of what I thought."[27]

Another journalist observed the extraordinary effect the third movement had on the audience:

The third movement, an *Aria,* danced by Toumonova, Petroff and Jasinsky,
proved to be an Adagio of a strangeness never equaled![28]

The overall effect was reported to have been something "modern." Judging from the excerpts of the performance of this ballet that I have viewed, the movement was not like any other choreography of George Balanchine that I have ever seen. Yes, the women were on pointe, but their movement was unlike anything heretofore associated with classical pointe work. It resembled something that we in the late twentieth century would have labeled "contemporary ballet." The women sometimes confronted the audience with suggestive thrusts of the hips, usually from side to side. Among the four dancers, there was a considerable amount of lunging and sliding under one another's torsos. Dancers would occasionally find themselves in formations characterized by the interlocking of each legs. Often the dancers were simply rolling over one another, back to back. The men occasionally veered over the balustrade in a quixotic way, as if to be looking for something, reacting to some premonition, or simply positioning themselves for a potential confrontation. Toumonova appeared sometimes with one man in pas de deux movement, alternating with passages of group interaction with two other females. One member of the cast, Sono Osato, felt that her perception of the ballet as a whole was somewhat limited and remarked: "I was cast as a snake, and I spent rehearsals crawling around on the floor."[29]

Toumonova was born as her family was fleeing Bolshevik Russia, though the actual year of her birth is open to question. Her amazing dark beauty, her powerful technique (the famous fouettes), the aura of glamour—all these made her a tremendous international star. Through the years, Balanchine created a wide variety of ballets around her, including *Cotillon, Concurrance* (choreography by George Balanchine, the George Balanchine Trust), *Balustrade*, and the adagio movement of *le Palais de Cristal (Symphony in C)* (choreography by George Balanchine, the George Balanchine Trust). She starred with Massine and Lifar and in 1939 appeared on Broadway with Ethel Merman and Jimmy Durante in *Stars in Your Eyes.* She appeared in many companies, touring incessantly and ending up in California, where she appeared in a number of movies, including *Days of Glory, Tonight We Sing* (she played Pavlova), and Hitchcock's *Torn Curtain.*

Toumonova considered Balanchine to be another-worldly being. She reminisced that he took great care of her. She had come back from Australia with the Colonel de Basil Original Ballet Russe, and Balanchine created *Balustrade* for her. She felt that it was a gift. While she was dancing at the Fifty-First Street Theater, Balanchine and Stravinsky and Tchelitchev religiously attended her performances. During the third week of the season, these three artists came to her and said that they had decided to give her a gift, a diamond necklace. She replied by saying that she thought it to be a fantastic idea. Then they said the diamond necklace would be a ballet created to the violin concerto of Stravinsky, and Tchelitchew would do the costumes and scenery. She believed that the prospect of having such a ballet created for her was almost overwhelming. She thought that this was more than a diamond necklace. It was beyond anything she could ever have dreamed of. They began to rehearse the ballet. Balanchine brought the recording of the Dushkin performance and played it for her. She found the score to be a bit intimidating, but Balanchine told her not to be alarmed by the sound, insisting that it was a very special sound, very clear, very pure, and attempted to convince her that she would understand it more when she started rehearsing it. It was very sharp, very long, and there were movements that shocked her mother. Georgi Melitonovich would turn to her and tell her that she had an alarmed look in her eye. The choreography was different from any other he had done for her, and quite daring. She was no longer the little girl in *Fastes.* She felt that by that time, she was able to produce what he wanted, and it was pure at the same time. There was absolutely no expression, which was extraordinary for her because usually there was a dramatic or sad or coquettish expression.

The time came to have costume fittings, and then she understood what Balanchine meant about the diamond necklace. Her costume was full of diamonds, rubies, and emeralds. On her head was a half moon, a sparkling crescent, and even her shoes were jeweled. Whatever movements were required, she had to figure out what she was doing, and at certain points on opening night, two or three people in the audience shouted, "Ah!" or, "Oh!" because it was a shock. What she liked about *Balustrade* was that it had a tremendous amount of long movement. Stravinsky's music had a sharpness, but it also had a continuity. Balanchine picked it up beautifully. Toumonova had tremendous adagio technique, and through hard work, she had high extensions. Balanchine did not use her technical footwork. She felt that he wanted to see her more or less like a strange remote being, a statue, not quite alive. Her contract ended, and she left the company. She joined the Denham company, and she felt that they had no one else suitable for her role. Toumonova said that *Balustrade* has been written about as though it were not a success, but that was not accurate. Although for her it was not a success in the manner of *Black Swan,* it was an artistic success, which for her was more important than anything else. An example of the complicated situations that arose among the rival companies and their choreographers was that she "could not take the ballet to Denham because Balanchine wouldn't allow it. And Denham wouldn't want it because it had been done for de Basil."[30]

There exist conflicting reports about the casting of the ballet and even the exact number of movements it included. Interestingly, the original cast of *Balustrade* is recorded differently by Garcia from Sorely. Sorely reports: *Tocatta*, Leskova, Jasinsky, with eight supporting girls. In the second movement (*Aria*), Svetlova and Petroff were joined by Sonia Orlova and Irina Zarova (Yvonne Mounsey), and the trio of Toumanova, Jasinsky, and Petrov came in the third movement (also called *Aria*). She makes no mention of the fourth movement, *Capriccio*.

In His book *Ballets Russes,* Garcia-Marquez records:

Original Cast; *Toccata*, Tatiana Leskova, Roman Jasnsky and corps de ballet.; *Aria I*, Galina Razoumova, Paul Petroff, Sonia Orlova, Irina Zorova, and corps de ballet; *Aria II*, Tamara Toumanova, Roman Jasinksky, Paul Petroff,; *Capriccio,* Entire Cast.

Dancers at the premiere: 1st movement, *toccata*: Tatiana Leskova, Roman Jasinsky, 8 women; 2nd movement *Aria: I,* Marina Svetlova, Paul Petroff, Sonia Orlova, Irina Zarova, 8 women; 3rd movement, *Aria II*: Tamara Toumanova, Jasinsky, Petroff; 4th movement: *Capriccio*: Toumanova, Leskova, Svetlova, Jasinsky, Petroff, 12 women.[31]

Nevertheless, the entire cast of this ballet is rather impressive. Balanchine selected Marina Svetlova to be in the first cast. He set a solo for her in the second movement (*Aria*). She also appeared with Toumanova in the fourth movement, called *Capriccio*. This event demonstrated the way in which Svetlova was being groomed to don the garb of baby ballerina and how she had quickly found herself thrust into the top echelon of ballet dancers of the day.

When it comes to evaluating the strengths and weaknesses of a ballet, is it not advisable to listen to the attitudes of the dancers who helped create the ballet? The dancers would at least have an insider's viewpoint. In the New York Library for the Performing Arts, there exists a tape of an interview between Tatiana Leskova and Kathy Matheson. It is generally agreed that Leskova was in the original cast of *Balustrade*, and here is a paraphrase of this interview, which illustrates the impact of the announcement that Balanchine was coming to the de Basil Ballet Russe. Furthermore, he was going to create a new ballet for them:

Leskova said that even before Balanchine came to the de Basil company, the dancers worshipped him because they had heard so much about him. They were thrilled that he was going to create a new ballet for them. She said that she had a lovely costume done by Tchelitchev. Madame Karinska did the costumes. A lovely base costume, all painted. It was white painted over with blue veins on it.

Lovely. It was very modern. At the premiere, half of the audience whistled, and half clapped. It was a scandal. I loved the ballet. I was furious. Leskova was not certain that it was Marina Svetlova who danced the premiere, although her name was in the program.

Leskova remembered that for about three weeks, Mr. Stravinsky came to rehearsals. She found that Balanchine's choreography was very difficult. "You think it's not possible to do … Some what Mr. Balanchine puts out, it's a miracle. He says you do it to the right. Now you land there underneath the leg. One of those steps he used in *Agon* Choreography by George Balanchine© The George Balanchine Trust … If he would have asked me to do anything on top of my head, it just would be easy …"

Leskova remembers that when Balanchine came to a rehearsal, he always arrived with a little pencil and the music. He and Stravinsky were very friendly.

When she was reminded that the reviews were not all positive, she called it a scandal. Some of the reviews were very favorable. Some were not. She recalled that some critics did not like it, and it didn't last that long, which didn't make any sense at all. She contended that the ballet disappeared because we did not give it any more. The company went on tour to Canada. She felt that the costumes were very special. Toumomova's was full of diamonds and other sparkling embellishments. She thought that maybe it looked a little cheap in a way. "My costume was beautiful. Her costume was all in black with stones all over, here in front. The boys were with stones here: head and waist? She allowed that maybe for the time It looked cheap but I don't think so … While *Cotillon* contained implicit sexual overtones, in *Balustrade* they found more open expression."[32]

Balustrade is remembered chiefly for an erotic trio, and for the fantastic designs by Paul Tchelitchev. These included a setting of a low white balustrade that accounted for the title, and a stunning black jewel-encrusted costume for Toumanova, with a fringed georgette skirt drawn between the legs, black silk tights embroidered with sequins and brilliants and long black gloves with pendant crystal drops at the finger tips.[33]

Toumanova's black leotard was backless, and the edge of the scoop in the back that came down to her waist was set of by a ring of diamond-like jewels. Her costume was set off by those of surrounding women who wore costumes that were long and flowing, silk-like, floor-length gowns with flowing veils and pseudo wings on their shoulders. The effect of these costumes was startling by way of contrast with that Toumanova and was somewhat confusing as to raison d'etre or dramatic intent. "The choreography has its triplicate roots in the American jazzdance, post Wigmanesque hauteur and out and out ballet."[34]

Balustrade Is danced to Stravinsky's Violin Concerto, music that seems to me easy to go along with from the rhythmic side as it is full of references to our usual slow dancing, the kind you see anywhere from a burlesque to a Hollywood production number.[35]

There were some artists who felt that the elaborate and decorative nature of the costumes and the setting embodied "the tradition that painters and musicians should not give up their character when they work for dancers; the tradition that a dance evening is a natural pleasure for a civilized person."[36]

One critic who attended the premiere of *Balustrade* opined that since 1940, it seemed that Balanchine's choreographic style had discovered ways to place the dancer's momentum in motion.

"The spring of the steps and the thrust of the gesture clarify and characterize the dancer's changing impetus ... His present style is not an oblique neo-classicism, it is a direct new classicism."[37]

This work is intriguing and fascinating, not only because I have a penchant for becoming absorbed with the obscure but because, in many ways, *Balustrade* holds tremendous significance for the world of dance.

That having been said, this ballet has suffered from a life languishing in total obscurity.

Balustrade was considered to have been ... a collaboration of first class artists where one can expect to feel movement, look, and listen with the same degree of sensibility. In such collaborations you can see the poetic quality of dancing better, because all the different aspects of the spectacle have been made by people who believe in its poetry.[38]

~This sounds like a recipe for success.~

Toumanova is reported to have declared:

Cotillon and *Balustrade* exploited my personality at two different epochs of my life, not only psychologically, but physically as well ... *Balustrade* was imbued with a femininity that was alien to me in 1932.

Toumonova believed that *Balustrade* was like an ocean, a crescendo of waves composed by dancers in motion but always with a strong sense of symmetry.

She perhaps, more than any other dancer I can speak of, is the perfect exponent of Balanchine's choreographic inventions.[39]

Roman Jasinsky, Marina Svetlova, Paul Petroff, Tatiana Leskova.
Photo: Cosmo-Sileo.
Courtesy of Jerome Robbins Dance Division, the New York Public Library.

One item that seems to be agreed upon is that the sets and costumes were memorable. Some found the costuming to be "original," and some found it to be "outrageous." It seems rather unanimously agreed, however, that they were "memorable," if not inspired. Toumonova wore a black, backless leotard on which diamond/jewels outlined the edge.

The effect of the costuming was off-putting. Svetlova had what appears to be antlers on her head with a long, draping wraparound that sported a colorful, abstract design across the bodice, complete with fringe along the edges.

The female lead for "Aria" was dressed in a chiffon dress in shades of pink and grey … The women in Aria II wore a black sleeveless dress, with a georgette skirt fringed down the center, and long black gloves. The bodice of the dress, the gloves, and the toe shoes were ornamented with rhinestone; a small crescent moon crowned on her head. Her two companions had turtle-necked black leotards and tights and visorless caps. The caps, the turtle-necked collars, the belts, and slippers were also adorned with rhinestones. In the fourth movement, the dancers from aria II again wore the black outfits … that became lost against the black background, so that the audience could only discern heads with rhinestone-studded headpieces and black toe shoes and elbow-length gloves also ornamented with light-reflecting gems.

> This unusual choreographic design inspired boos, cheers,
> applause and laughter from the audience.[40]

One of the ultimate fascinations I find in *Balustrade* is the uncanny interplay and interrelationship among the scenery, the costumes, and the choreography. One is inextricable from the other. Granted, one can look back to Nijinsky's *Faun,* for example, and observe a similar interplay among the various aspect of the whole, but in *Balustrade*, the interaction seems to have dictated the demise of the ballet.

I must add that in *Balustrade* the costumes are elegant but annoying … the materials are such that after the first minute or so they look like a wilted bunch of rags cutting the line of the body at the knee, obscuring the differentiation of steps, and messing up the dance. And the Trio costumes look too publicly sexy; they take away from this erotic dance its mysterious juvenile modesty. Still, it was right of the management to take a first-rate painter for a work of this kind; an artist's mistake is infuriating, but not vulgar.[41]

The music and dance critic for *Saturday Evening Post,* Irving Kolodin, went on to comment on costumes "that look vaguely what a bat might wear if dressed by Hattie Carnegie, but allowed that the movement contained many sequences that were original in their viewpoint and full of crispy distinctive patterns."[42]

However, all did not agree. Lillian Moore wrote in *The Dancing Times:*

Balustrade presented by the de Basil Ballet Russe … proved to be a stimulating excursion into surrealism. As is usually the case with Balanchine's more daring ventures, it provoked considerable critical and commentary, some of it good and some of it most unfavorable …

Toumonova, Pettrof, and Jasinsky performed a trio in which the female dancers' legs hooked in various positions around her partner's waist; the dancers wore black outfits that became lost against the black background, so that the audience could discern only heads with rhinestone-studded headpieces and black toe shoes and elbow-length gloves, also ornamented with light-reflecting gems. "The female role in *Balustrade* was expanded from the one in *Cotillon*, resulting in the transformation of the enigmatic adolescent into an enigmatic woman."[43]

In *Balustrade*, some dance journalists felt that the finale departed considerably from the closing process in Balanchine's early works.

It was a grandiose formation of dancers collectively performing with great impetus a continuous sequence of movements that were fascinating in their powerful and breath-taking effect. in Balustrade While *Cotillon,* (Choreography by George Balanchine ©The George Balanchine Trust), contained implicit sexual overtones, in *Balustrade* they found more open expression.[44]

Many of the peculiarities seen in the construction of the choreography for *Balustrade* were in embryo form in *Cotillon*, and in 1941, he developed them further. First, there was very intricate pointe work, as if the toes were weaving the most complex designs.

Some of these steps and other choreographic motifs recurred throughout the ballet. There was also a more accentuated concern for line. Not only the line of the individual movement of each dancer, but the overall geometric constructions of the groups.[45]

Along with widespread reservations about the merits of the choreography and the value of the elusive raison d'etre of the ballet in general, the sets were minimal, and the effect of the scenery was questionable; but then there was the topic of the of the impact of the costuming. Following are some observations from the experts. One begins with a statement by one critic who attended the premiere of *Balustrade* about the lack of unanimity over the assessment of the values of the visual: "Beautifully costumed and boasting a scenic design of unarming simplicity."[46]

I have the impression that *Balustrade* in the first and last parts of it [Svetlova] in which the movement was simple and open made its effect directly in the present direction [modernism], although it was the wonderful sensual acrobatics of the middle section that delighted one part of the audience and shocked another.[47]

Audiences and critics alike were genuinely baffled by what they were watching.

It was a continuous process of assembling and fragmenting, dominated by a strong sense of organizational structure but achieved with such speed and precision that the spectator was taken by surprise with each new formation. And yet, there was also an elaborate construction that provided a feeling of slow motion that enhanced the work's duality.[48]

The composer was not dismayed by the recalcitrance of the audiences to his new creation:

Stravinsky himself considered *Balustrade* to be 'one of the most satisfying visualization of any of my theatre works … a dance dialogue in perfect co-ordination with the dialogues of the music.[49]

The mystery surrounding the apocalypse of Balanchine's *Balustrade* is intensified by the fact that several significant books on dance, written by highly respected authors such as Arnold Haskell and Lincoln Kirstein, completely ignore its existence. To add insult to injury, the volume entitled *Reading Dance* by Robert Gottlieb goes so far as to include a section entitled "Balanchine Lost Ballets" in which the existence of *Balustrade* goes totally without mention.

> Tudor's *Pillar of Fire* is the one really good ballet that has been launched
> in New York since the de Basil company's *Balustrade*.[50]

One critic who attended the premiere of *Balustrade* wrote:

Balustrade is one of the important new works in the repertory. Often may it be repeated.[51]

Regrettably:

It was repeated exactly twice.[52]

CHAPTER 12

Battle of the Ballets Russes-es

The War of the Ballet was the battle cry. I don't know if this was concocted as publicity stunt or if it emanated from a frightened competitor.[1]

Most dance enthusiasts would agree that rivalry between coexisting ballet companies is nothing rare in the dance world. However, in the post-Diaghilev era, which began in 1929 with the disbandment of the Ballets Russes, the intensity of the struggle surrounding the transfer of power among the subsequent companies resulted in an intense quest for preeminence. To compound the confusion, many of these companies attempted to ensure their own success by incorporating the words "Ballet Russe" into the title of their respective companies.

Ten years ago, lovers of ballet were mourning over the disappearance of the art, expressing dubious hope that perhaps in another twenty or thirty years there would come another Diaghilev.[2]

For this reason, ballet aficionados of the 1930s were ripe for the emergence of a suitable ballet company to fill the void experienced by the disappearance of the exalted Diaghilev Ballets Russes. A state of anxious anticipation was prevalent among fans who were desperate for the arrival of a quality ballet company—hopefully replete with a requisite number of star dancers—to remedy the situation. As multiple ballet companies emerged, more or less simultaneously, and presented themselves as contenders for the crown, it was certainly predictable that bitter disputes would ensue. Welcome to the ballet debacle of the 1930s and the 1940s.

With Diaghilev dead, the Ballet Russe dynasty was a disputed kingdom. Laying claim to it in a dramatic gesture worthy of the most flamboyant theatre ...[3]

The frequent and often unpleasant arguments among the directors of the various ballet companies, Serge Denham, Rene Blum, Leonide Massine, and Col. W. de Basil—all pretenders to the Diaghilev thrown—began while Marina was absorbed in her studies with the illustrious Parisian ballet teachers of that time. Most of her teachers were former ballerinas from the Russian Imperial Ballet, and each of their schools was being canvassed for young recruits for the budding Ballet Russe companies. George Balanchine, a former dancer and choreographer for Serge Diaghilev, along with Col. W. de Basil, a former officer of the Russian Army, were perhaps the most visible scouts.

Historians disagree in their interpretations of the mélange among ballet companies that emerged in the wake of the death of Diaghilev. The confusion is not abetted by the manner in which the would-be successors shuffled around in various roles they might play in the subsequent incarnations of the Ballets Russes.

In 1932, after two years of experimenting and groping, Rene Blum formed his first company, the Ballet Russe de Monte Carlo. The basis of this company was already established when Mr. de Basil offered to combine his efforts with those of Blum. The company was named Rene Blum and de Basil.

Shortly after the inception of the Blum/de Basil Ballets Russes de Monte Carlo, the ballet cognoscenti considered the company essentially to be the de Basil company. For the next several years, the directorship of the various companies was the source of tremendous confusion as to who was leading which company at any given time. Also, the frequent changing of names of the organizations added insult to injury.

When de Basil began at Monte Carlo, his stars were so young that he had to pretend that the real stars would appear later in the season! He knew these girls of seventeen and eighteen were the only 'stars' he had … but he also knew that the public would want no others, once they had been given an opportunity to prove their skill.[4]

The Ballet Russe de Monte Carlo, under the sole directorship of de Basil, made a spectacular London debut at the Alhambra Theater in 1933. The arrival of this ballet company was generally considered to have been a huge success. However, all attendees at the opening performance were not in concordance as to the merits of the proposed successor to the Diaghilev Ballets Russes. Some fans were disappointed with the whole affair because they missed their favorite stars of the Ballets Russes, such as their adored Karsavina and their beloved Nijinsky.

In 1933, Robert Garland reported in the *NY World-Telegram* that the de Basil Ballet Russe de Monte Carlo company was:

The Highest Art to Reach Our Shores.[5]

The roster of dancers in the Monte Carlo Ballet was comprised mostly of dancers from the Diaghilev company. At its inception, the direction was shared between Rene Blum, long interested in the direction of the theatre of Monte Carlo, and Colonel de Basil, an alleged ex-Cossack concert manager. Added to the collection of the experienced dancers was the introduction of the much heralded new baby stars, Tamara Toumanova, Tatiana Riabouchinska, and Irina Baronova, whom Balanchine had discovered in the legendary dancing schools in Paris. Along with Balanchine, they joined the Blum-de Basil Ballet Russe.

The first taste of ballet left us more eager than ever to welcome the next rivals … In its origin, *Les Ballets 1933* was a fragment of the Monte Carlo Ballet, the result of one of those quarrels unfortunately possible at any moment in the dancing world.[6]

Blum and de Basil argued incessantly, and their ballet company split into two faction companies. When de Basil officially parted ways with Blum in 1934, he formed the Ballets Russes du Col. W. de Basil. This company ultimately adopted the name of Original Ballet Russe. At that time, there existed also the Massine-Blum Ballet Russe de Monte Carlo, which turned into the Denham Ballet Russe de Monte Carlo. George Balanchine functioned briefly as maître de ballet for the Massine company but fortunately created outstanding ballets for each of the combative companies. Throughout the decade, the clashes that arose between the de Basil companies and those of Massine, Blum, Denham were inevitable. By 1935, the group was then known as the "Col. W. De Basil's Ballets Russes de Monte-Carlo." There follows a rather large portrait of de Basil, under scripted with the statement, "Colonel de Basil, Founder and General Director." In this company, we still have Rene Blum listed as artistic director and Leonide Massine as maître de ballet and artistic collaborator (also one of the leading male dancers). Blum willed his Ballet Russe de Monte Carlo to Denham, which shortly thereafter became known as Massine's Ballet Russe de Monte Carlo.

The Winter of 1937–38 was a time of turmoil in the Russian ballet world. There was widespread feeling that to run two major Russian ballet companies in competition, splitting the repertoire and leading dancers, might spell disaster all round.[7]

From 1938 onwards, few people have really been clear about the Ballet Russe identities and countless ambiguous or incorrect entries in the encyclopedias worldwide have made it all worse. [8]

Denham Ballet Russe

Due to the last unpleasantness in the world of Russian ballet, descent from the Imperial days has been like the Greek Orthodox Church itself, split … There are the Montagues of the house of Colonel de Basil, and the Capulets of the house of the Mr. Serge Denhan … There were a lot of Montagues who wouldn't mind being Capulets, and some Capulets who weren't so damn sure, themselves. [1938][9]

With few exceptions, the company included most of the principal dancers and personnel introduced in 1933. In New York there was one important addition to the roster when Balanchine was invited to rehearse *Cotillon*. [1940] Tatiana Riabouchinska … has endeared herself during several seasons with the thousands of balletomanes throughout the country who are having an opportunity to see her again this season in her most popular roles.

Among the newcomers is the American ballerina, Nana Gollner, who came to Col. De Basil from Ballet Theatre and had previously danced with the Rene Blum company in Europe.[10]

Some of the ballet public felt that the seemingly never-ending hostility among the rival ballet companies was in danger of having a negative effect on the art world in general. However, ballet dancers and ballet companies were generating more interest among the social elite, and the obvious lack of cordiality among the ballet companies, their directors, and their patrons was not widely welcomed.

Throughout the first months of 1938 the press in both London and New York devoted considerable attention to the fate of the two rival companies. The Battle of the Ballets became an artistic and social war that involved some of the most prominent art personalities of the time.[11]

Many ballet scholars concurred that the tension being propagated by persistent dueling in the ballet world was certainly unseemly. It was producing a malaise that many fans feared would be impossible to overcome.

London balletomanes were caught up in the great ballet 'war' of 1938, between Massine and the Colonel de Basil … De Basil's company was at Covent Garden while Massine's was dancing around the corner in Drury Lane.[12]

As a result of the bitter animosity that prevailed among the different companies throughout the 1930s, the selection of a champion was inevitable. Some fans and critics came to the conclusion that by 1938:

The Original Ballet Russe was superior to any other ballet company of the time.[13]

From the moment de Basil discovered a seventeen-year-old Marina Svetlova in one of those ballet studios in Paris in 1938, she was on her way to becoming a leader for the next crop of de Basil baby ballerinas. Upon her entrance into de Basil's company, a network of committed dancers and choreographers emerged within the company, which aided Marina in developing professional alliances with some of the most important members of the several ballet companies active at that time.

After having changed its name many times, late in 1939, the succession of the de Basil ballet companies assumed the name Original Ballet Russe, which it kept until the closing of the company in 1948. Marina remained with this company for three seasons. The change of the name of the de Basil company did not diminish the compulsion to compare the two versions of the Ballet Russe, although the judgmental impulse may have become more tempered.

The Original Ballet Russe is not just another version of the Monte Carlo; it has a quality of its own, and a particularly pleasant atmosphere. It hasn't of course as much prestige, but it seems to have more dance to it, more buoyancy.[14]

The rivalry between the Ballet Russe companies took a toll on the ballet fans and the critics who explicitly expressed their displeasure.

The confrontation of the two Russian companies was resented by many of their admirers. [1939][15]

London was captivated by the appearance of two major ballet companies during the same season. One could attend performances presented by the Massine-Blum Ballet Russe de Monte Carlo company at Drury Lane, followed by shows presented by the de Basil troupe. The London audiences were treated to premieres of several ballets offered by each company. One year, the Massine-Blum company presented three new Massine ballets: *Gaiete Parisienne, Seventh Symphony,* and *Noblissima Visione.* The de Basil company offered *Cendrillon,* choreographed by Michel Fokine, and *Protee,* choreographed by David Lichine. The highlights of the season seemed to be the Fokine ballets found in the repertoires of each ballet company. The pervasive presence of his ballets prompted the renowned ballet critic Arnold Haskell to call Fokine the father of modern Russian ballet, and he felt that even in his least inspired works, he offered an invaluable lesson to all dancers.

In the opinion of some Australian ballet critics, when the Original Ballet Russe performed in Australia in 1939, audiences were elated. Apparently the audiences had tired of seeing the rival Ballet Russe company, which had been appearing in Australia for several seasons. They found the Ballet Russe de Monte Carlo to consist of dancers who seemed to be uninterested in the quality of their performance. The audiences felt that the Massine Ballet Russe company brought tired dancers accompanied by dirty and ragged costumes. Fans were flocking to see the young, fresh, and vibrant dancers of the Original Ballet Russe. The audiences saw the company as being fresh and brimming with excitement. They found the costumes of the Original Ballet Russe to be clean, crisp, and beautiful. The dancers appeared to be rested, and they seemed capable of executing the most difficult enchainment with ease and grace. The dancers left the audience with the impression that their energy was unlimited. The artistic deterioration of Denham's Ballet Russe de Monte Carlo prompted Hurok's to join forces again with de Basil.

It seems that fortune had shown upon the Original Ballet Russe during the 1940–41 season because the de Basil company followed on the heels of the Massine Ballet Russe de Monte Carlo company in their performances at the Met. Apparently the Massine company had just presented one of its poorest seasons.

All fans were not receptive to the animosity that infiltrated the battling Ballet Russe companies. Considering the fact that several dancers left one company to join the other, it is not difficult to understand the dilemma in which the ballet fans found themselves.

V. Grigorieff, Tamara Grigorieff, Vera Nemchinova, Marina Svetlova, Serge Grigorieff (i.e., Obukoffo, Bellvue Hill, South Wales, 1940). Author: Repin, Ivan Dmitrievich (1940), National Library of Australia, Bib ID 4468 701.

V. Grigoriev was a dancer and son of Serge Grigoriev. Tamara Grigorieva was a ballerina in the Original Ballet Russe. Nemchinova was one of the reigning ballerinas of the Ballets Russes, and she was a ballerina with the Rene Blum Ballet Russe de Monte Carlo, guest artist with the Original Ballet Russe, and guest artist with the Ballet Theatre, and she floated effortlessly from company to company. Marina described to me how much positive impact Nemchinova had on her and how Nemchinova had helped her along as she progressed through the ranks of the Original Ballet Russe. Lubov Tchernicheva was a dancer and *regisseur* of the Diaghilev Ballets Russes, and she became regisseur general of the de Basil Original Ballet Russe. Serge Grigoriev was a dancer with Diaghilev.

The auspices are perhaps unusually fortunate for the success of the Original Ballet Russe, not only because it has been absent for a long time but also because it comes on the heels of what is undoubtedly the least distinguished season Massine's company has given [1940].[16]

Some dance experts felt that the difference between the Original Ballet Russe and the Monte Carlo Ballet Russe was only the way in which they were run. Both companies were filled with highly accomplished dancers.

These organizations are nearly on a par of front-rank virtuosity.[17]

Other experts felt that, as is the case in the corporate world, free enterprise encourages a better product. And it should be remembered that the ballet war extended beyond the shores of the Thames.

Col. De Basil is a real person of the theatre, and he has contributed much to the theatre and to ballet in particular throughout the world. That is why it is a source of satisfaction to everyone that his company is again active and successful in the theatres of this country.[18]

Colonel de Basil's Ballet Victorious
As Ballet Number One of the World

In 1939, when *Dance Magazine* announced in its Dance Attractions last February that the Original Ballet Russe, under the general direction of Colonel W. de Basil, would come to America for the season 1940–41, to most ballet fans, the news sounded fantastic. There were some who were always inclined to find something to complain about and they argued that it would be foolhardy for Sol Hurok, already manager of the Ballet Russe de Monte Carlo, to bring another major ballet company to the country to provide further competition. Those fans who were de Basil's detractors criticized the company itself on the grounds that its roster contained too many young and untried dancers.

Colonel de Basil and his Original Ballet Russe did safely arrive in the United States … for what will doubtless become the longest run of any ballet company in a single theatre … The personnel of the Original Ballet Russe, especially in its feminine part, is high above anything that has been seen in hereabouts in a long while.[19]

The compulsion to compare and criticize the rival Russian companies was not limited to their expertise on stage. The companies were even held up, one against the other, based on box office success. The following observation was made in *Dance Magazine* in 1941:

The valiant Colonel's organization is practically all it was promised or threatened to be … the cast includes a flock of young soloists whose names will shine brightly on the ballet horizon for years to come, among them Alexandra Denisova, Genevieve Moulin, Marina Svetlova, Tatiana Leskova, Anna Volkova. [20]

Every so often, somebody still asks whether or not the ballet is a genuinely popular form of dance, whether or not American audiences are 'ready' for it, whether or not it is an alien thing with only a snob appeal. As for the popularity of ballet as theatrical amusement, one has only to point to the transcontinental tours of the de Basil troupe.[20]

Although most individuals—myself included—would point to the Diaghilev Ballets Russes as the most significant development in the world of the arts in the twentieth century, one must acknowledge that after the disappearance of that company, ferocious contention among ballet fans persisted. Opposing factions were adamant about proclaiming the superiority of their favorite company.

No other company in history has achieved the international prominence of de Basil's Ballets Russes de Monte Carlo.[21]

Obviously, many fans and critics alike felt that it was the de Basil Original Ballet Russe that had snatched the gold ring. However, the impressions of the ongoing Ballet Russe skirmishes were not unanimously in de Basil's favor. Here is a perfect example of the battle of the ballets:

Most spectacular is that the major ballet company of the world—the Ballet Russe de Monte Carlo, headed by Leonid Massine …[23]

The Massine Ballet Russe de Monte Carlo at one point during the 1930s became associated with a successful businessman named Sergei I. Denham. Thereafter, the Massine Ballet Russe de Monte Carlo was sometimes referred to as the Denham company.

Audiences now wanted to be able to make comparisons with Denham's company … From the opening performance, it became clear that de Basil's company was the leading company … although the Monte Carlo surpassed it in classical danseurs nobles, he praised the de Basil's new group for having 'more body and unity as a company.'[24]

While Denham was assuming the directorship of the Ballet Russe de Monte Carlo, Massine was in the process of forming his own small touring ensemble called Ballet Russe Highlights (as if we needed another ballet company with the mention of "Ballet Russe" in its name).

Therefore, comparison between a de Basil Ballet Russe company and a Denham Ballet Russe and a Massine Highlight of the Ballet Russe became part of the game when Denham became a noticeable player. Denham is reported to have written in a letter to *Dance Magazine* saying that, in his opinion, there was no issue of one company being better than the other. He believed that both had a diversified repertory and a fine group of artists, and if you liked ballet, you would enjoy them both.

Ballet Russe versus Ballet Theatre

As if things were not bad enough, the war between the opposing versions of the Ballet Russe became even more complex with the advent of the American Ballet, which had been the dream child of Richard Pleasant since 1939. Directly prior to the formation of the Ballet Theatre, Mikhail Mordkin had a ballet company, with Lucia Chase (future founder and director of American Ballet

Theatre) as his prima ballerina. An associate of Mordkin was Richard Pleasant, who envisioned a large company of superior quality so that it would be capable of competing with the best companies in the world.

The enthusiasm for the emergence of American Ballet Theatre as a worthy competitor of the Russian companies was genuine and widespread. The illustrious impresario, Sol Hurok wrote a telling letter that "would testify eloquently to two facets of the current state of ballet in America; number one, that America is now host to more than one ballet company.[25]

Bombardment of Ballet in New York

Ballet Theatre opened also on April 9th at the Metropolitan Opera House, played to a full house and has been doing so well ever since that it had added two more weeks to the season. So much for the ballet war and those who shouted about unfair competition.[26]

Richard Pleasant's dream had become a success. Curiously enough, Pleasant also had a connection with the de Basil Original Ballet Russe during Marina's tenure with that ballet company. "Mr. Pleasant's troupe gave the foremost ensemble performances of whatever work was undertaken by any large company within our memory."[27]

CHAPTER 13

The Great Migration

Westward Ho! The Dance!

The spirit which stirred Columbus is abroad again, and now every dancer is ready to confess that his dearest dream is to come to America … The receptiveness of the American audience, together with the aesthetic understanding of the American artists … are the signs which point to American supremacy in the dance.[1]

The above article holds particular significance because the author of these words was the husband of Vera Trefilova, Marina's prized teacher. Added to the association of the writer with Marina's teacher and the connection between the author and the prima ballerina, Marina told me that the inspiration for the creation of her stage name was provided by the last name of this author, Valerian Svetloff.

From the point of view of one dance scholar, before the massive arrival of European dancers, the plight of ballet in America was pretty dismal:

During the Nineteenth Century, America was nothing if not a balletic wasteland.[2]

Marina's efforts with her own group, the Svetlova Dance Ensemble, were intended to reverse this statement. Her career represented a wholesome mission to contribute to the relocation process of the center of the dance world from the East to the West (from Europe to America). With many stops along the way, Marina's dance career zigzagged across the globe, from Europe to America. She began in Paris and eventually made her way to New York. She left Paris and immediately joined the de Basil Original Ballet Russe. With this company, she performed extensively throughout Australia. After a few years in Australia, Cuba, and South America, she landed in the United States. Within a few years of her arrival in New York, she incorporated into her dance obligations in New York an excursion westward across America with her own dance ensemble to bring classical dance to a new audience. After traveling as far west as Hawaii, she eventually settled in Dallas, Texas. A few years later, Marina added Manchester and Dorset, Vermont, to her itinerary. As a coda, she moved to Bloomington, Indiana, where she became a professor at Indiana University.

Ballet Takes Sanctuary—In America

The Art of Ballet travelled first from Italy to France; from there to Russia and Scandinavia; from there to England. Now, it would appear, it has found its stronghold and its security here in this vast country, the United States of America.[3]

Not all experts were of like mind, however. Some felt that the influx of foreigners did not necessarily represent a positive event in the history of American ballet. Owing to the fact that America is an extremely young nation, it should have been a forgone conclusion that when Europeans arrived in America, bringing with them centuries of tradition in ballet, American Ballet would start out naturally as European. Any ballet company arriving in America, calling it their home, was actually an American ballet company. Whether they called themselves "Ballet Russe" or "Monte Carlo Ballet" or Original Ballet Russe," there was not yet a ballet company called "Ballet Americana," so if a company made America their home, then they were American Ballet, unless they wanted to be identified as a long-term guest company. Until America had enough time to establish a homegrown team, there was no opposition party. Even les Ballets 1933 was populated mostly by Europeans. It did originally have Maria Tallchief, who was perhaps the originator of a truly American ballet presence.

There is little doubt that New York, not Russia or France is currently the center of ballet activity.[4]

Just as European dancers had their sights set on destination West, America was ripe and ready for the arrival of the foreign dancers.

Now as never before is America—and more specifically the western hemisphere—the cultural haven of the world…The Ballet Russe de Monte Carlo was the first to attach itself to America…Next season this country will also harbor the de Basil company.[5]

Marina was a member of the de Basil Original Ballet Russe. With this company, she was immediately part of the great migration.

There may have been no Diaghilev to guide and supervise it, but de Basil's company extended the frontiers of ballet, particularly in America!…[6]

Some ballet scholars were concerned that the influence of the European presence in ballet was prohibitive of America's ability and desire to create a uniquely American product.

Every so often somebody still asks whether or not the ballet is a genuinely popular form of dance, whether or not American audiences are 'ready' for it, whether or not it is an alien thing with only a snob appeal. As for the popularity of ballet as theatrical amusement, one has only to point to the transcontinental tours of the de Basil troupe.[7]

However, everyone did not share in the enthusiasm about the influx of especially Russian ballet companies.

But ballet itself is in a bad way because Americans have been led to believe that *Russianballet* is one single word ... it is my purpose to investigate that here, Russian ballet has meant world-ballet from 1910 up to about the year 1935.[8]

From time to time, the question surfaced as to whether or not ballet was truly a popular dance idiom and if American audiences were ready to accept it as such. One often wondered if ballet was merely an elitist's amusing pastime. Apparently, many experts credited de Basil and the transcontinental tours of his ballet company with turning ballet into a viable and agreeable theatrical statement for all Americans.

When de Basil was asked whether or not he felt that there was going to be too much ballet in America, he replied:

I do not feel there can be too much ... This country is so eager for art... It is ironic, but probably true, that Europe, which nourished America, will soon need the invigoration of the culture which only America may still enjoy.[9]

Many experts agreed that in America:

There is a rising audience demand for good dance attractions.[10]

A Heritage for Ballet in America

America, the land where the soot of tradition has not yet settled into its valleys, the land where it is impossible to change the river's course to wash away the sedimentary grime of civilization, should be proud of what its loom produces.[11]

These articles reveled in the eagerness for the promotion of dance in America and supported the significance of Marina Svetlova's endeavors not only to bring dance to the hinterlands but also to develop a nationwide, knowledgeable audience for dance.

Ballet in America is still young, still in a state where it requires careful nurturing, loving fostering.[12]

Marina Svetlova's ambition to bring ballet westward across America was kindled while she was a member of the de Basil Original Ballet Russe.

Another season of ballet has begun—this is the fifth annual visit of Colonel de Basil's Russian Ballet to America ... and in those five years and the two years before the Ballet has covered much ground, both artistic and in miles. The present company has toured America from coast to coast in succession.[13]

Appreciation for the untiring efforts of de Basil to foster a love for ballet, not only around the world but especially in America, did not go unnoticed. Praises for his work and the accomplishments of his company were not limited to publicity publications circulated by his own organization but were recognized by the international press:

Five years in succession Col. De Basil has been showing our country the most there was in ballet, the greatest ballet compositions, the finest ballet dancers … he has been developing a great ballet audience, a fine and sincere appreciation for the ballet. The most outstanding ballet company in the world, it has taught American audiences to expect of ballet the best it can produce.[14]

Colonel de Basil was totally dedicated to promoting excellence in ballet as a viable performance art form. The crowning accomplishment was the success of his Original Ballet Russe, which was the emerald in the crown of the various companies had directed. He was on a mission:

I believe that the American public loves the ballet and my company will bring it to them.

Although there is much argument and disagreement about the value and the validity of the influence of foreign dance on American dance, dancers themselves often articulate their own perception and feelings about the situation. The talented dancer Sono Osato, who became a member of the de Basil Original Ballet Russe, felt honored to have had the opportunity to grow up watching the Russian dancers. She loved their gallantry, their humor, and their passion, and she cherished the pleasure that one got by bringing pleasure to others:

The unspoken love the Russians shared for their art gave them the strength to endure any hardship. The depth of their souls and the breadth of their emotions filled their dancing with magic and their daily lives with philosophical acceptance. Without their dedication, America would never had known the ballet.[15]

Dance World
by Paul R. Milton
America Becoming World Dance Headquarters

Until years ago … the dance revolved largely around a London-Paris axis. But now this is changing. America is becoming … the world center of dance. … the Ballet Russe de Monte Carlo, headed by Leonid Massine is financed 90% by American capital. No longer do English pounds dictate the life of the company.[16]

The above journalist went on to point out that the Ballet Russe played longer in the United States than in any other country or on any other continent in the world. He felt that this demonstrated to the dance world that no company of this size could prosper without an extensive American tour.

Although many were initially intrigued, if not excited, about the notion of bringing ballet to the North American continent, it is fascinating to read the various reactions to the concept. Some comments were written by informed enthusiasts, and some represented purely gut reactions. There seemed to be a consensus, however, that ballet in America was something new, and most believed that it was worth giving it a try.

The following is an observation that offered hope to the prospects of success for ballet in America:

It is most inspiriting to note that ballet, long appreciated and warmly supported abroad, has within the last few years become popular, on an ever-increasing scale, here in America … The American public loves ballet and has taken it into its heart.[17]

One playbill for the de Basil Ballet Ruse de Monte Carlo boasted of a rite of passage, proclaiming:

To America with Ballet
The Triumph of a Generation

S. Hurok Presents
The Monte Carlo Ballet Russe …

Another consideration concerning the effort to find an American ballet is from where do the dancers come—how to find American dancers? Although many wonderful dancers were trained abroad, particularly in Paris after the immigration of those universally recognized, Russian genius teachers, some felt that American dancers should be taught by American teachers:

His plans, he [de Basil] said, have always included the foundation of a great ballet school which will give Americans something to look up to.[18]

Before heading out to the western United States, Marina Svetlova solidified her presence in New York City. In the early 1940s, as a guest artist, she danced with the Ballet Theatre. She performed in a variety of roles, including *Aurora's Wedding, Graduation Ball, les Sylphides, Spectre de la Rose, Bluebeard*, and *Pas de Quatre.* In 1943, she became the prima ballerina of the Metropolitan.
Skeptics maintained that:

Ballet is not indigenous to the North American continent.[19]

Although she realized that her mission would be an uphill battle, Marina Svetlova vowed to spread the knowledge and love of ballet across America. She was creating her own narrative. Her western sojourn led her to spend several seasons in Texas.

American ballet is now just a babe whose swaddling clothes are well made and well kept. … his dreams are about people he does not know … Let our hero roam among the Alleghenies, descend into their valleys, visit the miner, the steel workers, their children … Let him strength his arms in Texas.[20]

Many scholars agreed that spreading an appreciation for ballet across the country had always been an uphill battle:

We all know the hard history of ballet in America.[21]

De Basil was not only a shrewd businessman, but he had an understanding about the necessary groundwork that needed to be laid and perpetuated for the creation of a superior product. He calculated where to look for the necessary ingredients needed for the establishing of a sound foundation of a ballet company, those being talented and well-trained dancers, and he had an uncanny instinct for what would sell. Unlike several of his contemporaries and predecessors, including Serge Diaghilev, the de Basil Original Ballet Russe finished its existence in the black.

Ballet and Hurok have been linked by threads as shear as and indestructible as nylon. For it was Hurok who brought Ballet to America.[22]

Hurok's success with the promotion of ballet in the West was not a one-way road but rather a joint effort:

Hurok brought America to Ballet.[23]

Most people who are familiar with the name Sol Hurok know that not only did he represent dancers such as Anna Pavlova and Isadora Duncan, but his name is associated with the presentation of major instrumentalists, such violinists as Mischa Elman and Eugen Ysaye. He also represented leading singers the likes of Luisa Tetrazzini and Marion Anderson, the first black singer to appear at the Metropolitan Opera. He brought the composers Alexander Glazounov and Richard Strauss to America.

One thing, however, appears certain to me. … major attractions have come from Europe, [and] are seriously beginning to explore the American grounds … There is a big job to be done in America with American artist, especially dancers. They deserve all the attention and encouragement they can get.[24]

Dance historians point to the fact that the greatest ballet theatres are those found in Petrograd and Moscow, the Grand Opera of Paris, the Danish Royal Theatre in Copenhagen, and La Scala in Milan. Each of these theatres has its own school, its own traditions, its own repertoire, its own artistic individuality and glorious history …

The love and adaptability for the dance in Americans, their exceptional sense of rhythm, the vitality and energy of a healthy nation, the talent of the individual dancers, all this leads to the conclusion that the ballet, in order to continue its development, needs a new soil, such a place is the soil of America.[25]

Ballet in America was in a critical state, attempting to identify its identity and then to convince the American audience that said identity had a validity both in America and in the world.

It is most inspiriting to note that ballet, long appreciated and warmly supported abroad, has within the last few years become popular, on an ever-increasing scale, here in America … The American public loves ballet and has taken it into its heart.[26]

This opinion certainly leads credence to the assertion that Ballet will or has already found its footing in America. However, it was understood that achieving success with selling ballet to America was a joint venture: both the ballet and its audience need developing.[27]

If someone fifteen years ago had predicted that ballet would become the fastest growing segment of American show business, and that the geographic center of ballet activity would switch from Paris to New York within a decade, he would have been looked upon as an optimistic madman.[28]

It seemed that the year-by-year increase in ballet's popularity began in 1933 when S. Hurok brought Col. W. de Basil's Monte Carlo Ballet to America. By that time, the major companies were on this side of the Atlantic. Good dancers were to be found everywhere. The Americanization of ballet was under way. The Ballet Russe de Monte Carlo had accumulated its entire corps de ballet in America, as well as many of its top soloists. Among the seventeen or so nations represented, Americans were the preponderant group. The Ballet Theatre was so dramatically homegrown that it billed itself as "the first American-born of the big-time ballet companies." Americans did not limit the scope of their presence in the dance world to merely being dancers in ballet companies. The Ballet Russe de Monte Carlo launched Agnes de Mille by introducing her *Rodeo*. Ruth Page created for the company *Frankie and Johnny* and *The Bells*, and Todd Bolenger set his *Comedia Ballettica*. Choreographers for the Original Ballet Russe included John Taras, twenty-six-year-old New Yorker became known for his ballets *Camille* and *Constatia*.

No one can deny that during the last few seasons American dancers have been seen with satisfying frequency.[29]

Here is how the esteemed dance historian Lincoln Kirstein sums up the consideration of how it was possible for American dance to evolve from foreign roots:

Russian Ballet in America: 1919–1936

Most of the Original Diaghilev troupe came to the Americas in 1916 … But far more than the Russian visit, the Americans have benefitted from the Russians' stay. Michael Fokine, Jove of the Age remained in New York, has taught with his unique pedagogical mastery many of the best of the present generation of American-born dancers …[30]

Many ballet authorities believe that American ballet had developed a standard of technique internationally valid. "People are aware that our ballet is not an imitation of the pre-war Ballet Russe manner but … it compares favorably in enough respects with the post-war ballet style abroad to make one hope it will continue a development so soundly started."[31]

The Arrival of Ballet Theatre

With the genesis of the Ballet Theatre, an enormous collaboration was instilled among at least a dozen choreographers. The company boasted a huge complement of dancers and an impressive roster of designers and costumers. This became apparent during an initial three-and-a-half-week season in Manhattan's Center Theatre in Radio City. The financial support of the enterprise was American, and—most important of all—the atmosphere of the Ballet Theatre was completely indigenous. Founded on the principle that it aimed to present all phases of ballet and to preserve in its repertoire examples of the work of the various important eras of ballet history, the Ballet Theatre generated an amazing response among the public, and they came in droves for three weeks. New people had been brought into the dance public. By touching a sympathetic nerve among the uninitiated folk, "ballet took another step on its road to becoming an art close to the people, not one reserved exclusively for ermine-caped box holders and cousins of the Czar."[32]

Audiences were starting to have an almost proprietary interest in our American ballet companies. They felt they had some real connection with American-born and bred dancers. "Audiences cannot look at the American ballet companies at the present, expecting to find them replicas of the Russians … The creation of a really American ballet depends in a great part on our audiences who must have fresh eyes and open minds."[33]

One should be reminded that all is not beautiful at the ballet. A more clinical analysis of the beast is worth keeping in mind:

The promotion of ballet in America may be a nervous excitement full of frustration and love for some of us, but for others it's big business pure and simple.[34]

Many ballet buffs are more optimistic:

An American ballet movement may well have a preponderant influence on the future of the arts, not only here, but elsewhere in the world.[35]

Svetlova's performances with Ballet Theatre were recognized as being of the highest caliber, and she also received extensive glowing appreciation for those performances from audience and critics alike.

Ballet at Lewisohn: Les Sylphides and *Patrouchka:* 'In *Les Sylphides,* the first number on the program, Miss Markova, as well as Miss Hightower and Miss Svetlova, began extremely well.'[36]

In this instance, Marina Svetlova was a featured soloist alongside two of the reigning prima donnas of the time. Markova was one of the world's most esteemed ballerinas in the romantic style, and Rosella Hightower, a Native American Indian, had achieved fame as another of the world's star ballerinas of that time. In some ways, they functioned as a catalyst in bringing Svetlova from the Original Ballet Russe to the Metropolitan Opera.

Barn Dance, done by Catherine Littlefield for the Littlefield Ballet is a robust success of ballet with a true American style … Eugene Loring's *Yankee Clipper* is another example of a truly American ballet … the dance of friendship alone marks it as an American work.[37]

Ballet—The American Position

Statistically speaking, by 1940, ballet had become naturalized. It was no longer viewed as being foreign. It had become homegrown because "almost everyone on stage was born and trained in America, and it was for their kind of dance gift and their American look that the new productions were being created. Their collective innocent American flavor in action was a novelty in big-time ballet but it appeared natural and enjoyable to the audience in attendance."[38]

Americans generally love good dancing if they are allowed to see it.[39]

Enthusiasm for the success of ballet in America was rivaled only by its self-confidence:

The quality of the distinguished amateur becoming a finished professional is also a very theatrical asset, and the Americans can't be beat at it.[40]

New York had witnessed many memorable nights of ballet in its past but never any organized achievement to match the extraordinary success being achieved at that time by Ballet Theatre in the Center Theater. Marina danced as a guest artist during the 1941–42 season. Individual dancing had reached high levels in many fields. Under one management or another, the miraculous Russians had delighted thousands of fans. Here at last was a solidly American organization that brought together a wealth of talents from many countries and put their creations, old and new, on the stage with a freshness and an intelligence that honestly earned the enthusiastic support accorded its performances. Their success represented an unmistakable coming of age on the part of the American ballet. Music had become an essential part of the pattern of American life.

The ballet was simply one of its myriad forms —marvelous when it is done well … The music lovers of the city have every right to be proud of this new organization and its significance for the future.[41]

Collaboration is the keyword used to describe the effort. The Ballet Theatre had mastered this phenomenon.

In all this has been a very active summer for ballet, and a very successful one. If there are still skeptics who doubt the growing popularity of ballet in America, let them delve into the results of the past season and into prospects of the oncoming one. They'll change their minds.[42]

The critics, the scholars, and the audiences of that time agreed that:

Ballet, according to three million Americans, is here to stay.[43]

CHAPTER 14

Jacob's Pillow

Jacob's Pillow is among the thoroughbreds of dance institutions because it holds the record for being the oldest internationally acclaimed summer dance festival in the United States. The Jacob's Pillow mission is to support dance creation, presentation, education, and preservation and to engage and deepen public appreciation and support for dance.

The purpose of the Jacob's Pillow Dance Festival, Inc. is to provide students with the finest possible dance education, to provide many dancers with the opportunity to reach the public.[1]

It was Shawn himself who invited Marina Svetlova to perform at the Pillow.

The Pillow's 1942 ten week-festival championed comprehensiveness. Its veteran and emerging performers represented the world of dance [including] Svetlova.[2]

My own experiences at Jacob's Pillow were twofold. My first visit involved performing the duties of a ballet class pianist. There was no mistaking that the place was extraordinary. It felt like walking through living ballet history. It was an honor to be allowed to enter its hallowed halls.

Jacob's Pillow, July 24, 1944. "Faith's dearest child is miracle"—so wrote a great poet. The miracle had been born, due to the faith of a few devoted friends whose contributions enabled us to carry out through this past year, and open again this summer. They believed that the work we are doing here is valuable.[3]

Along with his wife, Ruth St. Denis, the founding of America's homegrown dance institution was established. The Pillow, as it affectionately came to be called, was not only a training ground for young dancers and debutant dance groups but a prominent performance venue located in Becket, Massachusetts. This much loved and respected institution has remained a revered dance spot since its inception in 1940. The Pillow is a National Historic Landmark.

Ted Shawn wrote a book entitled *How Beautiful Upon the Mountain*. It is a history of Jacob's Pillow. The list of the performing guest artists for the first season of performances names many already well-known and established artists, including Nathalie Krassovska, Thalia Mara, and la Meri. Marina Svetlova was listed as prima ballerina. She made appearances in such capacity for several subsequent seasons. In addition, she was the only ballerina to receive a full-page photo, taken by John Lindquist.

John Linquist Collection, 1910–1985 MS, the (482) Harvard Theatre
Collection, Houghton Library, Harvard University.

Ambassador of Dance

Undoubtedly, Ted Shawn's six-month visit to Australia during 1947 will go down in the annuls of American dance history as an event of unparalleled success. The Australian critics were as enthusiastic as the huge number of dance fans in attendance. Some of the dance journalists wrote that Ted Shawn, the American dancer, was the most striking personality to have enlivened Melbourne for many a day. Ted Shawn astonished, delighted, and overwhelmed the audience. He was an artist of world stature. Throughout his tour of the principal cities of Australia, Shawn also gave classes in each city. Since those in attendance at these classes included ballet, modern dancers, teachers, and physical education instructors, Shawn was able to absorb as well as influence every phase of dance culture in each city. More importantly, according to Shawn, these classes served to break down the sense of competitive barriers between these different types of dancers and helped to establish an understanding and unity that was heretofore unknown. He termed this dance ceremony as well worth his trip halfway around the world.

"I have seen some of the greatest dancers in the world and now I have seen them equaled. This has been one of the most marvelous experiences of my life …" [4]

Many dance students have shared memories of their experiences at the Pillow. One of the recurring themes was that of hard work, both as student and as staff. Time spent by dancers at the Pillow was truly a way of life. One student described how a letter had arrived from Papa Shawn inviting her to be a scholarship student at the Pillow the coming summer (1943). She felt that returning to the Pillow was more exciting than going home for Christmas. Students came a week early in June to get things ready for the 1943 season. In the evening, they assembled in the stone cottage for the first meal together. Chatter was rather animated until Papa Shawn rose and raised his arms over them in a blessing. "With a warm smile, he welcomed us all and announced the events for the coming summer. Joe Pilates was already here. Natasha Krassovska and Grant Mouradoff of the *Ballet Russe de Monte Carlo* would be teaching Classical Ballet … Marina Svetlova were coming later." [5]

In 1942, Svetlova danced in the opening season of Jacob's Pillow, where she became a frequent guest performer. She appeared that first season in performances under the direction of Bronislava Nijinska. Jacob's Pillow was and is a much-loved performance venue for dance, and it was an enormous honor to have played such a vital role in its inception. Obviously, Ted Shawn held Marina in high esteem and was not shy about acknowledging her as a major artist in the dance world.

One dance student explained that on the very first day at Jacob's Pillow, one's scope of dance exploded exponentially from personal joy to the deep appreciation for each new dance form. And the day was not over yet. After supper, hanging out in the old barn entrance, getting to know a few people, students learned that Madame (Branislava Nijinska) was rehearsing in the studio. As the students quietly sneaked into the small observer's bench above the mirror, they "watched Madame Nijinska … demonstrate the *porte de bras* for a very pretty ballerina, Marina Svetlova … Then Papa Shawn shoo-ed us out, so we went to the theater where Asadata Defora was rehearsing with his Sierra Leone drummers." [6]

As part of the 1944 Jacob's Pillow lineup of guest faculty, there appeared an announcement of anticipated stellar instruction: guests artists in the theatre on August 19 would include notable teachers and dancers, such as Marina Svetlova.

... Today, as always, Ted Shawn's vision for dance is so great that it reaches far beyond the borders of his own land.[7]

La Meri, a much-respected dancer and teacher of ethnological dance forms, described the institution as the dancer's dream come true. Here, young people from every part of the country could spend nine happy weeks every summer learning dance and its allied crafts. She remembered that when one drove up to Jacob's Pillow during the day, the air seemed to be filled with the sounds of pianos, drums, castanets, finger cymbals, hammering, even the hum of sewing machines. She pointed out that these sounds were the very spirit of Jacob's Pillow. They represented the rehearsing, the performing, and the learning that went on constantly. She insisted that it was not all work because there was also some magic involved. This mystery manifested itself in the form of friendly contact with visiting artists who appeared at the Pillow's weekend concerts. Mr. Shawn's second project was promoting the Jacob's Pillow Dance Festival Company, which at times left its home to tour the country. "She believed firmly that this company is what the Pillow stands for—the many forms that are taken by the art of dance and she reminisced that, like many other dancers, 'I am grateful that one day, twenty-two years ago, when Ted Shawn rested his head on a great stone slab beside a tumbledown farmhouse and dreamed the dream of Jacob's Pillow.'"[8]

How Beautiful Upon the Mountain
Summer of 1942—First Season in The New Theatre

MARINA SVETLOVA: When Mme. Bronislava Nijinska produced her two ballets on the Jacob's Pillow Dance Festival, 1942, Nina Youskevitch and Marina Svetlova were the two prima Ballerinas. Marina Svetlova returns to dance at Jacob's Pillow again this summer (1943) after completing her California season with Ballet Theatre.[9]

CONTEMPORY EUROPEAN BALLET. Madame Bronislava Nijinska presented her ballets: *Etudes* to music of J. S. Bach, *E Minor Concerto* to music of Chopin. Stars: Marina Svetlova, Nina Youskevitch, Nikita Talin ....[10]

Many individuals active in the Arts proclaim that the art of the dance has many unique qualities, chief among which is that it is the only art in which we, ourselves, is the stuff.[11]

Shawn recalled that the last performance Walter Terry witnessed and reviewed before being inducted into the army, was the opening performance at Jacob's Pillow on July 9th, 1942. He said to the crowd that just a few days ago, he had received a letter from him, dated "Somewhere in the in the Middle East, June 24, 1943" ...[12]

Walter Terry believed strongly that the arts must be kept flourishing at all costs, and the clean spirit of creation must continue regardless of the worldwide destruction being caused by the war. He believed that there were thousands, perhaps millions, who agreed with him and that when the war was over, they would want to go back not only to their homes and people but to theatres, music, and dance. They would act as cathartics for a war-laden past and as a guide to a future that must be creative. He said all this quite honestly and unmelodramatically, because although he had not yet been subjected to the physical horrors of war, he thought that the battle was justified and that the world would flourish for all humankind, not just for a nation alone. Shawn shared some of a letter he had received from Terry shortly before he left for active duty. Terry wrote that he believed with all his heart and soul that the artist can and must play a role in the reconstruction. If he does nothing but bring great art to the consciousness of humanity, then he will have accomplished a miracle for the entire world, "for surely no one can behold a great work of art and not absorb some of its harmony, its sense of structure, its logic and its vision, and surely it follows that, if these qualities are observed by man, the peoples of this world would at last be worthy of the Great Creator whom they profess to worship. So, Shawn, keep up the battle at home, and bring the great art of human movement to everyone you can reach."[13]

… the last two weeks of the season Marina Svetlova will also teach and dance, as our prima ballerina.[14]

The Pillow's 1942 ten week-festival championed comprehensiveness. Its veteran and emerging performers represented the world of dance … Marina Svetlova.[15]

I had subsequent visits to the Pillow as an audience member. There was a small amphitheater-like stage where I saw the Nutmeg dancers. In the main hall, I had seen some professional guest dancers from France.

Jacob's Pillow has had a long with French dance artists. Notable engagements include a 1942 performance by Marina Svetlova, a young French-American ballerina born in Paris, the first of many Pillow appearances.[16]

Shawn's vision for dance was so great that it reached far beyond the boundaries of his own land. This vision had already taken him to Europe, Asia, Africa and Australia.

Where it will take him next remains to be seen; it may lead him to south America, back to Australia or to his own Jacob's Pillow. One thing is certain, however, and that is that American dancers and citizens can salute with pride their ambassador of dance—Ted Shawn.

A benefit for the Jacob's Pillow Dance Festival will be held in the Hunter College Assembly Hall (December 29,1948.) Among those participating will be Marina Svetlova …[17]

In 1942, a new student at Jacob's Pillow named Barbara Hastie wrote an essay describing her early experiences at this haven for the arts. Highlights of her musings included mention of both Ted Shawn and Marina Svetlova.

I found out that here at this school Ted Shawn strove to keep the art of dance going no matter what the outside world said, or what was the cost. My program for the day consisted of: Body conditioning, Joseph Pilates; Advanced Ballet, Grant Mouradoff, Nathalie Krassovska and Marina Svetlova.[18]

Dance—A Vital Technique for the Theatre

In the Dance Shawn, the dean and curator-pioneer, takes a new step in the interest of American dance...

For the first time in dance history a completely American company, prairie-born, cornfed and homespun... offers a cycle of self-contained, interrelated dance dramas, in which divertissement is given no place or play except for a brief period at the end of the cycle.[19]

CHAPTER 15

Opera Ballet

According to the Opera House tradition, the ballerina counted above all, the work itself was subservient to her.[1]

Photo: Bruno of Hollywood, courtesy of the Metropolitan Opera

The origins of ballet in operas can be traced back to the *opera-comique* of the eighteenth century. At that time, opera lovers remained satisfied that the ballet portion of an opera was to be an agreeable display of pretty girls in attractive costumes. Dance in opera, although mandatory in Paris, was considered to have fulfilled its function in an opera when it provided an evening's pleasant, unobtrusive divertissement. In Paris, a short ballet scene was expected to appear in the second act, and a more extensive presence in the third act of every opera that hoped for success and longed for repeated performances. The French preoccupation with the inclusion of a ballet in opera even caused certain Italian opera composers such as Giuseppe Verdi to feel obliged to rewrite their operas to include the de rigor ballet scene. Fortunately, some of these opera ballet scores became acknowledged as music possessing more gravitas than existing merely as vehicles to accompany incidental ballet scenes in most operas. Some of the music composed with the sole intention of enhancing opera performances became the basis for the creation of ballets that could stand on their own, independent of the opera for which they were originally composed.

When opera houses engaged choreographers, the management often expected something extraordinary to be produced. Were the dancers less than distinguished, somehow the choreographer was obliged to turn the proverbial cow's ear into a silk purse. Not only did the choreographer need to address the level of accomplishment displayed by his dancers, but he had to address the limitations presented by the house in which he was required to function. This not only included the size of the stage but also the lighting capabilities and the sightline presented by the dimensions of the auditorium and the proscenium.

What Is Wrong with Opera Ballet?

When opera managers go overboard for really good dancing, they are in for extravagances, misunderstandings, recriminations, and triumphant premieres … So one can accept our present 'well-meaning but not very able' Metropolitan ballet … as a modest substitute for a glorious inconvenience.[2]

One of the drawbacks facing ballet in the opera was that the public had found their singing stars who had become box office. Diaghilev may have had his Nijinsky, but the opera had its Caruso—and its Louisa Tetrazzini, its Lili Pons, its Mary Garden. Also, one could more easily present an opera without dancers because along with ballet came specific stage requirements. Families could not be treated to having ballet with the opera brought into their homes. It was a flimsy argument to repudiate the value of ballet in opera. In many operas, ballet was not the add-on, as some would have it. Obviously, some opera audiences attended the opera primarily for the singing, but given time and distinguished balletic participation, audiences could be seduced into adding ballet to the list of anticipated delights experienced during a night in the theatre.

Opera has become enmeshed in a rather sticky web of tradition … an unfortunate limitation for contemporary composers, designers, singers, and most assuredly for its dancers. Its dancers, in fact, seem to be—traditionally—at the bottom of everybody's lists, from the General Manager's to the buff's in the back row of the family circle.[3]

Some authorities on opera performance were slightly more precise when opining what they believed opera should accomplish when attempting to achieve the optimum goal:

My belief is that one must give the public what it wants, to survive in the theatre. The public loves dancing, but it also wants audible enjoyment. There must be song and speech coupled with the dance for a full evening's entertainment.[4]

There is no doubting the commitment of the dancers in the Metropolitan Opera Ballet Company. Their efforts challenged the meaning of the word "dedication." The length of the season of the Metropolitan Opera Ballet rivals that of any other ballet company.

Behind the Scenes of Ballet

Many dance experts agreed that the Metropolitan Opera of New York City should have a permanent ballet, not simply a group of dancers to perform incidental dances in the operas. The ballet company should have a definite season of its own, of reasonable duration, combined with a well-equipped stage, an orchestra, and its own school to supply the ballet company with its own product.

As things stand, [1939] the artistic aspect does not come into consideration until the financial one has been satisfactorily cleared up. I repeat, the keystone of the ballet structure at the Metropolitan is the *desire* of the management to have a ballet company worthy of the Metropolitan name.[5]

Immediately prior to Marina becoming prima ballerina at the Metropolitan Opera, the following symposium took place in New York City.

Opera Guild

On one occasion, the Metropolitan Opera Guild's Round Table addressed the longstanding disappointment with the status of ballet in New York's opera season. The Met director, Edward Johnson, felt that the ballet, like a spectacular bride, brought beauty and grace to the opera. He also observed that ballet had a positive impact on creating the "atmosphere, mood and color" of the production.

Anton Dolin opined that the ballet at the Met should be of the same caliber as the singing there. He felt that the opera audience should see dance stars and hear opera stars. He stated that one evening a week for ballet would pack the Met as the Ballet Theatre had packed it in the spring. He insisted that the Met should have a first-class ballet. His insistence was received with loud applause. A male soloist dancer at the Met, Alexis Dolinoff, asserted that if the ballet dancers at the Met were given more opportunity, they could produce more inspired performances. He mentioned that were any rehearsals to be cut out, they were always those of the ballet. The dancers had to assume many responsibilities that no one else wanted. The dancers were employed in dramatic scenes owing to the fact that they moved more expressively to music. Dolinoff observed that ticket revenue was usually greater for the operas that had ballets. He also pointed out that the Paris Opera was billed as *of music, of dance, and of opera.* The esteemed choreographer Agnes de Mille pointed out that the Met had been one of the forces of an American national theatre. She suggested that the Met should function for dance as it had for the art of singing. She went on to point out that America had produced perhaps the three most famous artists of the twentieth century, Duncan, St. Denis, and Graham. She lamented that America had championed the world of the arts in concert, theatre, and ballet, but no American dancer or American choreographer had ever been invited to appear at the Met.

In Europe, young dancers and choreographers had the opportunity to grow up, learn, and develop in opera ballets, but not in America! … All the American dancers ask is that the Met open the door to the dance.[6]

With the goal of improving the ballet contingent at the Metropolitan Opera, the general director of the Met, Edward Johnson, disbanded the opera contingent at the Metropolitan Opera in 1935 and engaged the newly formed American Ballet, directed by George Balanchine. However, their approach to opera ballet was so unique that the dependable subscribers of the Metropolitan "Horse Shoe" were unnerved in a way that they had never been by the former, rather placid routine presented by the Metropolitan Opera Ballet company.

Balanchine was choreographer at the Met in New York from 1935 to 1938. Prior to that time and afterward, he also staged opera ballets in Monte Carlo, Paris, Denmark, Buenos Aires, and Italy. Balanchine claimed that the most important ingredient for the success of opera ballet was the cooperation of the administration of the opera house with the opera ballet company. Failure of ballet in the operas was because opera companies didn't want ballet to be excessively good. He thought they considered ballet as an art inferior to opera.

On the reduced-rate Sunday-night concert programs, Balanchine presented some of his greatest ballets to date, and he managed to provoke considerable controversy with a new version of a work that was already in the repertoire of the Metropolitan Opera. This opera was Gluck's *Orpheo*.

At the Metropolitan Opera, Balanchine found that his efforts at championing the cause of the opera ballet were not greeted enthusiastically. Ballet in opera was accepted by the management of the Metropolitan Opera management only under protest. He felt that his attempts at offering up choreography of a personal and imaginative character was virtually impossible to achieve within the confines of the opera ballet, at least as was permitted within the confines of the Metropolitan Opera. After three years of frustrated efforts, he chose to withdraw from his position at the Met.

Balanchine was not alone in proclaiming that the low level of accomplishment of the ballet contingent of most operas was often owing to the cavalier attitude assumed by the presiding administration of the opera house. It was much easier to blame the choreographer or the dancers for the undistinguished ballet scenes in an opera than to admit a modicum of responsibility for having deprived the ballet component of the productions of an appropriate and professional level of support and cooperation.

After Balanchine's departure, ballet at the Met generally reverted to old productions … Nevertheless, stellar artists of the period danced there, including Felia Doubrovska, Maria Gambarella and Marina Svetlova.[7]

Operas Marina Appeared in at New York's Metropolitan Opera:

La Gioconda—Almicare Ponchielli

> This work was perhaps the most significant opera for Marina during her decadelong tenure as prima ballerina at the Metropolitan Opera in New York City. Along with many performances of the entire production at the Met, Marina appeared as soloist in the famous act 3 "Dance of the Hours" during a multitude of Metropolitan Opera Gala presentations.

Gypsy Dance, from "Mignon"

Photo: Maurice Seymour, courtesy of *Opera News* archives

Mignon—Amboise Thomas

The Gypsy Dance of Act I was opera balletics of a superior class, thanks to Marina Svetlova, a dainty and technically resourceful ballerina.[8]

Carmen—Georges Bizet

It is a good deal pleasanter to speak of the fourth-act ballet in *Carmen*. Miss Svetlova's toe dance with fan and mantilla and in a brief ballet skirt … was an amusing novelty and didn't look out of place at all. It was also the best dancing I have seen at the Met …[9]

Midsummer's Night Dream—Boris Romanoff

Opera's first important ballet of the 1947–48 season was unveiled at a Christmas matinee, during the colossal snowstorm of the 26th of December, It was a little snowed under, but not by the storm. Principals Marina Svetlova, Edward Caton and Leon Vargas, in the order named, fared well enough in Boris Romanoff's ballet *A Midsummer's Night Dream* …[10]

Photo: Bruno of Hollywood, courtesy of the *Opera News* archives

Prince Igor—Alexandre Borodin

Polovtsian Dances from this opera is perhaps the most obvious choice in this category. These dances are orchestral tours de forces and are frequently performed worldwide, independent of the opera, on orchestral concerts.

An Anniversary for Prince Igor

Thirty years ago this week, December 30, 1915, a large audience gathered at the Metropolitan for the first performance in America of Borodin's Prince Igor ... the opera had a strange history ... the critics found a serious fault with Borodin's libretto ... and a serious fault with the music ... the Herald said 'it is an opera of choruses and ballet, embellished with obbligatos by the principals' ...

But though the chorus was 'the backbone, the background, the mainstay of the opera' the ballet was also an important feature … The usual Metropolitan ballet had been augmented by a group of men, 'said to be real Tartars,' who danced 'with real abandon.'[11]

La Traviata—Giuseppe Verdi

This is one of the operas for which Marina earned extensive acclaim. She was also frequently invited to do the choreography for this opera by opera companies around the country. This opera relies heavily upon the choreographer's acumen for dealing with the choreographic requirements in devising designs for chorus members during crowd scenes, along with movement for the principal singers. The opera also has a very exposed and famous dance for an accomplished and attractive Spanish dancer during act 3 at Flora's high-society party. Marina Svetlova was engaged to create the choreography for a production of *La Traviata* for the Dallas Opera. The production had been originally been planned as a vehicle for Maria Callas. This offered Svetlova the opportunity to collaborate with the internationally admired and respected stage director and designer Franco Zeffirelli. This man had achieved great worldwide recognition through the success of several productions he had created for several of the great opera houses of the world, including Italy's la Scala, the capital of the world of opera. Zeffirelli also directed productions for the much-loved Covent Garden of London and New York's venerated Metropolitan Opera. Zeffirelli received further international success for his production of the film of *Romeo and Juliet* starring Leonard Whiting and Olivia Hussy as the star-crossed young lovers.

Aida—Giuseppe Verdi

    Act 2, scene 2—very famous triumphal scene

Samson et Dalil—Camille Saint-Saens

    Act 3, scene 2—Festive Bacchanale ballet scene

Manon—Jules Massenet

    Perhaps third most popular French opera (next to *Carmen* and *Faust)*. Act 3, scene 1, extensive dance scene representing the ballet from the Paris Opera.

Le Coq d'Or—Nikolai Andreevich Rimsky-Korsakoff

    Ballet dancers mime the off-stage singers. Act 2, slave girls do slow, sensual suggestive dance. Ballet Theatre Ratmansky ballet production in 2018.

The Bartered Bride—Bedrich Smetana

    Act 1, scene 5, Polka (a dance that Marina often performed at galas)
    Act 2, scene 1, Furiant
    Act 3, scene 2, Dance of the Comedians

Lakme—Leo Delibes

    Famous veil dance

Louise—Charpentier
Dances for street crowds and trips to the local dressmaker

Marina Svetlova in *Louise*.
Photo: Bruno of Hollywood, courtesy of *Opera News* archives.

There were ballet experts who sympathized with the plight of the ballet dancer in operas of the eighteenth and nineteenth centuries:

Opera Ballet, too long treated as a step-child in the dance world … the general public has become increasingly conscious of ballet in opera and such noted choreographers as Anthony Tudor, at the Metropolitan Opera House, and Charles Weidman, at the New York City Opera Company, are in large measure responsible for this upswing in interest …[12]

What Some Choreographers Have Done to Improve Ballet in Opera

Though ballets in opera must conform to the opera period, and innovation and experiment are therefore limited, the Metropolitan has signed a new choreographer, Boris Romanoff to put new life into its ballet.[13]

Zachary Solov, a choreographer for the Metropolitan Opera Ballet (1951–1960), has added something to the argument. This highly respected choreographer was quoted as having said:

I believe the choreography of the ballet should be the lifeblood of an opera.[14]

After leaving the Metropolitan Opera as its prima ballerina, Marina began to make her contribution to the improvement of the state of ballet in opera. Occasionally, she danced in her own productions:

Andrea Chenier—Umberto Giordano

In act 1 of this opera, the choreographic responsibilities included creating some stately court dances, which included the guests dancing a Gavotte. Act 2 required the setting of movement for street dances.

Fort Worth's *Andrea Chenier* Scores …

The first act was highlighted by some charming dancing, whose choreography was supplied by Marina Svetlova.[15]

Die Fledermaus—Johann Strauss

This is an opera/operetta that is filled with dance sequences. In act 2, although in the original version of this opera, along with there is what seems to be an endless number of wonderful waltzes, Strauss also wrote a number of national dances in act 2, which have customarily been replaced by an interpolated waltz and Polka *(Unter Donner und Blitz)*.

[*Die Flerdermaus*] supplied serious relief for the comedy … Guest dancer Malenko Banovitch is absolutely dazzling … parred with Marina Svetlova (who has choreographed the ballet) the evening absolutely stopped still … they and the corps make it difficult to bring one's self back to the opera.[16]

Tannhauser—Richard Wagner

This opera contains a famous "Bachannal," which is a favorite ballet scene for many operagoers. As the name might suggest, the dance usually depicts a level of debauchery that holds the prize for such scenes in all opera. This music, along with the overture to the opera, is frequently programmed by symphony orchestras.

The success of the work on this occasion was due to the very well-prepared production of Carlo Maestrini, with extremely evocative sets and costumes by Lorenzo Ghilia and Peter Hall, wonderfully lit by Robert L. Benson, and with exciting choreography by Marina Svetlova.[17]

As had been demonstrated by Coll. W. de Basil in his determination to establish his Original Ballet Russe Company as a superior institution, the attempt at achieving excellence in a ballet company usually required a grassroots effort. The Metropolitan was determined to make a success of its resident ballet company. To assist in achieving that goal, in 1945 the Metropolitan Opera procured the talents, both as teacher and as ballet master, of the distinguished ballet genius Edward Caton.

Opera ballet in America, as demonstrated by the Metropolitan, is improving. Men like Caton are working actively toward a broader responsibilities of opera ballets, toward greater recognition of their importance In performances. One quality characterizes all those connected with opera ballet; a deep-rooted love for the magnificence which is opera in all its traditional splendor.[18]

Ballet Auditions

Edward Caton will concentrate on his work with the Metropolitan Opera ballet and the new professional class which has been organized for him by the opera management … he will stress discipline—not the enforced control of an objective power, but the inner discipline of mind and heart over body which to him is the essence of a successful ballet.[19]

Dancers as well as opera house directors were determined to make a go of it. Although it may have seemed that all odds were against the company, as is the case with most major ballet companies around the world, the establishment of a superior Metropolitan Opera Ballet School was truly an inspiration. It wasn't long before the news of the formation of the outstanding ballet school of the Metropolitan Opera became widely circulated. Aspiring young ballet dancers lined up for the opportunity to audition for admittance to the highly respected new ballet school.

Dozens of women in black tights and jerseys, dozens of boys with their shirt-tails tied about slender waists have gone through the classic drill … Mr. Caton declares himself as deeply impressed by the talent of his prospective students.[20]

All of the operas in which Marina appeared at the Metropolitan Opera contained extensive ballet scenes. In addition, she was frequently invited to dance on the special opera galas presented by the Metropolitan Opera. I have given special mention to these occasions because they contained solo performances by Marina. I have also included the names of particular singers, owing to their international fame or because these singers became faculty members of the School of Music at Indiana University, Bloomington.

This list of Marina's performances with the Metropolitan Opera illustrates the immense obligation one undertakes as a dancer in the Metropolitan Opera Ballet Company. The gala events are listed individually, including the names of singers who also appeared on the given concert. Repertory opera performances are separated from the gala listings and are listed horizontally.

Metropolitan Opera Debut
American Academy of Music, Philadelphia, Pennsylvania
Sir Thomas Beecham, Conductor

Carmen
November 23, 1943

Photo: Maurice Seymour, courtesy of *Opera News* archives

Debut at Metropolitan Opera House, New York, New York,
Carmen
November 29, 1943

Marina Svetlova almost stopped the show.[21]

Along with having danced in hundreds of complete ballets at the Metropolitan between 1944 and 1949 (see index), Svetlova danced in several Metropolitan Opera Galas. This allowed her to appear alongside many of the greatest opera singers of her day. Some of these singers became Svetlova's colleagues at Indiana University.

Gala
December 5, 1943
Astrid Varney, Leonard Warren, Stella Roman; Marina: "Dance of the Hours"

Gala
December 19, 1943
James Melton, "Il mi Tesoro"; Marina: solo dance from *Carmen*

Gala
December 26, 1943
Marina: "Dance of the Hours," *Carmen* dances, *Bartered Bride,* "Polka"

Gala
January 9, 1944
Faust, act 1, Nicola Moscona; Marina: *Bartered Bride,* "Polka"

Gala
January 16, 1944
Frank Valentin Alfio from *Cavaleria*; Marina: *Aida,* act 2 dances, Polovtsian dances

Gala

January 23, 1944

Boris Godounov, Kurt Baum Inn Scene; Polovtsian dances

Gala

January 30, 1944

Aida ballet dances

Gala

February 6, 1944

Laurence Tibbett, "Vissione fugitive," *Herodiade*

Gala

February 13, 1944

Nadine Connor Pagliacci excerpts, Harshaw *Voce di donna*; Marina: "Polovtsian" and *Carmen* dances

Gala

February 20, 1944

Mignon, act 2, Patrice Munsel, Irra Petina; Marina: "Dance of the Hours"

Gala

March 26, 1944

Licia Albanese, soprano; Marina: *Aida* dances

Gala

December 3, 1944

Licia Albanese, "un bel di," "Sempre Libera"; Marina: *Aida* dances

Gala

December 10, 1944

Margaret Harshaw, *Trovatore; Aida,* act 2, scene 1; Marina: *Lakme* dances

Gala

January 7, 1945

Regina Resnik, *Aida,* act 3; Jan Peerce, *la Juive-Rachel;* Marina: *Lakme, Carmen* dances

Gala

January 14, 1945

Jennie Tourel; Marina: dances from *Mignon*

Marina Svetlova in *Mignon*.

Photo: Maurice Seymour, courtesy of *Metropolitan Opera News*.

Gala

January 21, 1945

Lipton, *Favorite, Faust*; Marina: dances from *Carmen*

Gala

January 28, 1945

Enzio Pinza; Marina, "Dance of the Hours," *Carmen* dances

Gala

February 11, 1945

Richard Tucker, "cielo e mare" from *la Gioconda*; Marina, "Dance of the Hours," *Lakme* dances

Gala

March 4, 1945

Walter Cassel, *Faust*, "avant de quitter"; Marina, dances from *Lakme*

Gala

March 18, 1945

Walter Cassel, *Valentin Faust*; Marina: "Dance of the Hours"

Gala

December 9, 1945

Harshaw, *voce di donna Gioconda*; Marina: "Dance of the Hours"

Gala

December 16, 1945

Leonard Warren, *largo al;* Martha Lipton, Madalena, *Rigoletto*;
Marina: "Dance of the Hours," *Lakme* "Hindu dances"

Gala

January 6, 1946

Charles Kullman, Magaret Harshaw, Eleanor Steber, Bjoerling; Marina: "Dance of the Hours"

Gala

January 13, 1946

Charles Kullman, *il mi Tesoro*; Harshaw, *mio Fernando*; Marina: *Lakme, Bayader* veil dance

Gala

January 20, 1946

Marina: dances from *Lakme, Bayader* veil dance

Gala

January 27, 1946

Leonard Warren, *largo al*; *Martha* Lipton Madalena, *Rigoletto*;
Marina: "Dance of the Hours," *Lakme* "Hindu dances:

Marina Svetlova in *Lakme.*
Photo: Bruno of Hollywood, courtesy of *Opera News* archives.

Gala

March 3, 1946

Dorothy Kirsten, soprano; Marina: *Lakme* dances, veil dance, *Bayadera*, Romanof choreography

Gala

January 11, 1949

Regina Resnik, Charles Kullman, Martha Lipton, Margaret Harshaw, Nicola Moscona, *Aida,* act 2; Marina: solo dances

The Metropolitan Opera Gala performances presented opportunities for Marina to be featured as a solo dancer. However, the great number of full opera performances, some of which also featured Marina in solo roles, was extensive and bore testimony to the grueling rehearsal and performance schedule demanded of the dancers in the Metropolitan Opera Ballet Company.

Marina Svetlova's last Metropolitan performance:

Aida

May 13, 1950

Marina Svetlova offered the best dancing I have seen at the Met.[22]

Former Metropolitan dancers may be found working in Broadway musicals, television variety shows, the New York City Ballet, and European groups. Many have achieved distinction, Bruce Marks and Sally Wilson among them.

The ballet's roster is always crowded with talent. They tend to be worldly and articulate, less self-conscience than dancers who have confined their minds and bodies to the purely classical mold. They are poised, intelligent 'theater people' in the best sense.[23]

It was reported by *Dance Magazine* that among the celebrated dancers and choreographers who have worked with the Metropolitan Opera Ballet Company, one finds the names of George Balanchine, Anna Pavlova, Adolph Bolm, Rosina Galli, Luigi Albaretini, Ruth Page, Boris Romanoff, Felia Doubrovska, Ruthanna Boris, Maria Gambarelli, Anatol Vilzak, and Marina Svetlova … "all famous in their day."[24]

An article in the *Sun Times* supported the above statement made by *Dance Magazine* when this newspaper made the following assertion about Marina Svetlova:

The Prima Ballerina's indefatigable spirit soars beyond the confines of the Metropolitan Opera House.[25]

NYC Opera

When Marina left the Metropolitan Opera Ballet Company, she joined the ballet contingent at the New York City Opera Company. Her arrival at the New York City Opera was heralded by a front page photo of the *Musical Courier.*

132

One of the busiest ballerinas, Miss Svetlova joined the New York City Opera immediately after the conclusion of her annual nationwide concert tour … she has toured the United States and Canada for seven consecutive seasons.[26]

From 1951 to 1952, Svetlova was prima ballerina at the New York City Opera Company.

Marina Svetlova will be in the company's new production of Massenet's *Manon*. Miss Svetlova, it will be remembered was prima ballerina of the Met Opera for several seasons and every season since 1944, she has toured the country with her own concert group.[27]

Obviously, Marina was a highly successful ballerina with both the Metropolitan Opera and the New York City Opera companies. She was given the distinction of being granted the title of prima ballerina with both of these organizations.

One of the chief assets of the current production of Massenet's *Manon* at the New York City Center is the dancing of Marina Svetlova in the Cour de la Reine scene … Her gifts are already well known to opera goers in New York through her work with the Metropolitan Opera.[28]

Marina's performances have certainly been seen as exceptional. One journalist was exuberant in his description of the power of her performances:

Her performances stopped the operas, something few dancers have done.[29]

CHAPTER 16

Choreography

Already famous while still in her 20's, Svetlova is a choreographer as well as a performer, constantly adding new ballets to add to her extensive repertoire.[1]

When I asked what aspect of her multifaceted career proved to be the most challenging, without hesitation, she stated that creating compelling choreography for operas that had already been choreographed many times by other choreographers was surely the most daunting. Many dancers cannot or do not choreograph. Some choreographers are not dancers. Some artists, such as Marina Svetlova, excel at both dancing and choreographing.

Above all else, a choreographer should engage the onlooker. He or she should bring the audience into a conversation. This proposal does not need to be a fifty-fifty proposition, but there must exist a dialogue.

Primarily, the function of ballet is to tell a story.[2]

For centuries, ballets were expected to be created around a given narrative. Even as early as Dauberval's *la Fille mal Guardee* (1789), ballets managed to present a literary argument, which is often referred to as the ballet's "libretto." This custom continued throughout the nineteenth century, culminating with the ballets of Marius Petipa. Although the plots may have seemed somewhat superficial, his ballets were constructed around a given theme or possessed an obvious story line. Audiences generally expected a theme or a tale. Even ballets such as Tchaikovsky's *Swan Lake* contain scenes of mostly pantomime sprinkled throughout the show. Especially Russian audiences were disappointed with a ballet that eschewed the inclusion of a certain amount of mime, which they took very seriously.

Romeo and Juliet ... ... Tchaikovsky

Marina Svetlova and Robert Roland.

Photo: Bruno of Hollywood, courtesy of *Metropolitan Opera News.*

Another writer shared a similar notion but with a bit more specificity:

How to tell his story in pantomime in the simplest manner possible, without the need of extraneous literary explanation.[3]

~A choreographer is an author whose words are his dancers
who form his sentences as they tell his story.~

What is choreography? To qualify as choreography, a dance must consist of more than a mere arrangement of steps. Successful choreography is the projection of a specific idea or emotion into dance. Choreography is a search for truth as defined by prescribed movement of the human body.

By the close of the nineteenth century, dances were already being created with the intention of providing the audience with a satisfactory theatrical experience based primarily on the visual impact of the production, rather than on the dramatization of a given libretto. The American performer Loie Fuller (1862–1928) was already producing dance performances that incorporated flowing veils and imaginative lighting into her productions, minimizing the reliance on a narrative to be conveyed through movement.

A ballet may contain a story, but the visual spectacle, not the story, is the essential element.[4]

A choreographer who was a contemporary of Fuller was the American dance icon Isadora Duncan (1878–1927). She was another dancer and choreographer who embraced the notion of a plotless dance composition. Where Fuller had emphasized a dance form that relied heavily upon the effect of unique costuming and lighting, Duncan focused on a choreographic methodology that transferred Fuller's use of flowing scarfs into a type of fluid body movement. Her predilection for a freer, less predictable approach to movement was a reaction against the highly stylized, somewhat rigid choreographic inclinations being observed in the classical ballet mores of the day. It is believed that her revolutionary approach to creating dance movement influenced the neoromantic work of Michel Fokine (1880–1942).

A ballet usually tells a story too and so it uses pantomime: but people don't go for the pantomime, they go for the dancing.[5]

The following observation was made by choreographer Andrea Miller. She pushed the boundaries of innovative choreography with her dance company, Gallim Dance, and was trained especially at the Juilliard School. Her company has performed widely, including at New York City's Soho Joyce and Jewish Community Center. She and her company have been in residence at the Baryshnikov Arts Center.

I feel like every piece I make kills part of me, destroys something—and then it also invigorates something else.[6]

One ballet fan was heard to have expressed his admiration for a given choreographer when he exclaimed, "I think you are a wonderful geographer!"

Although the storytelling ballet or even the predilection for presenting pantomime through dance may today appear to be anachronistic, neither was extinct during the midtwentieth century.

Even the staid Metropolitan Opera, which has weathered as many trends and crazes as it has depressions has not been unaffected by the public fondness for stories in dance form.[7]

One writer observed that the challenge of creating engaging choreography was not the providence only of operatic productions.

In the scarcely remembered days … when the word 'choreography' was a tongue-twisting stranger on Broadway, and anyone who prescribed a ballet sequence for the crucial close of the first act in a musical would have been eased with clucking tenderness into a straightjacket.[8]

A dancer must ideally be capable of everything.[9]

This description of Fokine and his energy while running around the room prompts me to remember a day long ago when I was invited to be a guest pianist to accompany a class taught by E. Virginia Williams, former ballet pedagogue and artistic director of the Boston Ballet. By that time, she was upper middle-aged or older and somewhat rotund. She was exasperated by the inability of a classroom filled with young ballet students to use more energy and to cover more territory in the classroom during one enchainment in the center. She boldly took to motion and demonstrated what she meant. She proceeded to execute the combination with such enviable, energetic commitment and to exhibit such a robust, gobbling-up space it was truly eye-opening.

I am also reminded of the first time I watched Luigi, the illustrious jazz dance pedagogue, demonstrate a combination while I was taking his class. Although his performing days were long past, he demonstrated his vision of the way one of his combinations was to be executed. His movement was smooth as silk. He effortlessly glided across the floor as though it were made of the smoothest, shiniest piece of marble to be found anywhere. After witnessing that excellence in movement, I thought that there was no hope for me.

Generally speaking, a *ballet* is a theatrical representation achieved through terms dancing.[10]

One could advance the discussion about the alleged duty of a ballet to proclaim a narrative by wondering if the material should be derived from a known source, or if a choreographer can convey a totally original plot. From my point of view, were a ballet to depict or design a legend of some sort, the message could be about music rather than words. After a few viewings, I found that Balanchine's *Concerto Barocco,* for example, tells its own story. In a collaboration among the choreographer, the dancers, and the musicians, I see two ballerinas telling the tale of two solo violins as presented in J. S. Bach's *Concerto for Two Violins* in D minor. The first solo ballerina initiates a phrase of the score in unison with the first solo violin. Her movement is then imitated in canon by the second ballerina, likewise in unison with the second solo violin. The two ballerinas then weave patterns around each other while interacting with the corps de ballet girls who imitate the texture of the orchestral strings. In the second movement, the solo male dancer arrives on the scene and in some ways could be seen to represent the basso continuo in the orchestral score because he provides the foundation over which the solo violins (and one of the ballerinas) and the other string instruments flow. The third movement represents the assimilation of the contributing players in the composition. For me, watching this ballet is akin to reading a score, reading a book, or, in other words, watching dancers as they are telling Bach's aural story.

George Balanchine is not only the choreographer's choreographer; he is also the dancer's choreographer.[11]

As the cultural tastes and expectations in the arts evolved throughout the twentieth century, Marina found herself producing progressive, even abstract ballets. Owing to the fact that she usually designed the lighting and created the costumes for the Svetlova Dance Ensemble, her productions occasionally harkened back to the trademark creations of Loie Fuller. In addition, Marina was a dancer and choreographer who had received enormous acclaim through her performances in ballets that had been devised by Michel Fokine. She also was chosen by Balanchine to create a role in one of his ballets. Marina developed her own style of choreography, which represented an amalgamation of the choreographic innovations evident in the three early giants of the dance world, Fuller, Duncan, and Fokine.

The members were well costumed and staged and lighting effects added to the artistry of all the members.[12]

Although Marina's dance compositions were an amalgamation of some of the divergent approaches to choreography as espoused by these three dance personalities, Marina never lost track of her pure, classical training that provided her with a solid, secure foundation that enabled her to form her own choreographic vocabulary.

What Does a Choreographer Do?

In one article for her "Looking at the Dance" column for *Dance Magazine*, the esteemed dance critic Ann Barzel described that during a televised NBC show, she heard one performer sing:

They're doing choreography: it doesn't mean a thing, it's just choreography.[13]

Choreographers Are Special People

Doris Humphrey was a Pioneer of American Modern Dance who inspired many developing choreographers with her words of wisdom and support. She was a featured dancer with the Denishawn Dance company. Doris Humphrey believed that owing to the fact that good choreographers are scarce, one should inquire into the characteristic qualifications required of a successful choreographer. She felt that without some of the traits and attitudes of the creative mind, any dancer would be foolish to take up such a difficult and demanding enterprise as choreography. She advanced that the dancer's medium is the body, which is much more than words, musical notes, or paint.

The uniqueness of each personality, beginning with their own, should always be considered. They should honestly ask themselves, "What do I believe in? What do I want to say?" Humphrey believed that she should figuratively put a stethoscope to her own heart and listen to those mysterious inner voices. In composing for other dancers, she must have a high regard for their individualities. She believed that this mining for gold in personalities is one of the great rewards of the choreographer. She maintained that one of the great interests of a choreographer should be in people—the audience as well as the dancers, and yes, the choreographer:

The function of a choreographer is to express balletic ideas, thought and emotion in a way that first and foremost pleases him.[14]

The following statement was made by the accomplished dancer and teacher Richard Thomas. Was he merely bemoaning what he felt to be his own inadequacy when it came to choreographic skills, or was he actually expressing the reverence he held for inspired choreographers with whom he had worked?

I knew I couldn't choreograph—you have to have a talent to choreograph.[15]

It is not a prerequisite that a choreographer have been an accomplished dancer in order to devise an interesting, if not successful ballet. However, a good choreographer must have a firm command over the dance vocabulary with which he or she is working:

Ballet technique simplifies the problem for the choreographer in a way, say, a piano simplifies the problem of a composer who wants to arrange noises so they will be interesting to listen to.[16]

A gifted choreographer possesses an instinct for the kinetic implications inherent in the movement being constructed. It is helpful when the dance composer possesses an active, if not vivid imagination. They should also have a concept of movement in time and space as well as a vision of color as demonstrated through costumes and scenic design. Perhaps one reason that there seems to be a dearth of good choreographers is the fact that it is difficult to find individuals who possess all of these attributes.

Dance Magazine published an interesting outlook on the plight of a choreographer who was looking for some motivation to start a project:

How to Compose a Dance

You want a reason for a dance … You wear a winter coat. Why? Because it's cold. You hit someone. Why? Because you are angry. You laugh—because something is funny. There is always a reason. The reason for a dance is called CONTENT.[17]

Miss Svetlova has had a long and fine career. She is mainly a dancer, but she stages, choreographs—she has done it all.[18]

Marina's accomplishments as a choreographer for opera were almost as well sung and as far-reaching as was her career as a ballerina. After having spent nearly a decade performing as a leading dancer in opera houses around the world, it was a natural progression for her to become a leading designer of movement for opera ballet.

After her own performance schedule was less stringent, Svetlova became the director of several regional ballet companies and professional opera houses, including Kansas City Performing Arts, Lake George Opera Company, the Caramoor Festival in Westchester, New York, and the Delaware Opera. She created choreography for each of these companies, and the press, both local and international, were highly appreciative of Marina's choreographic endeavors. She was also interested in observing and promoting the work of other choreographers. She was always open to hearing about the ways in which other choreographers approached the challenge of creating original choreography.

-A choreographer is a ventriloquist who speaks through his dancers.-

Marina was presented with a singular challenge when she set about to devise movement for one of her most unique creations. She was engaged to create the choreography for the Purcell masque/opera/ballet *Faery Queen*. Marina received extraordinary international recognition as a choreographer of merit when it was learned that the star of the Purcell production was to be none other than the world's prima ballerina assoluta of the day, Dame Margot Fonteyn. This work deals with an ancient myth, and Marina depicted the story without resorting to pantomime. Of course, the choreography was a departure from the predictable *enchainements* of the traditional classical ballet *methode*, and one might notice in her *Faery Queen* traces of the innovative choreographic vocabulary to which Marina was introduced while creating a role in Balanchine's *Ballustrade*. Marina's movement composed for this Purcell work was both fascinating and well constructed.

Ballet Director for the Dallas civic Opera, Mme. Svetlova is also associated with the Houston, Fort Worth and Seattle city operas. Widely acclaimed for her choreography, Svetlova's most recent work for the Dallas company was her new choreography for Dame Margot Fonteyn.[19]

I saw Marina appear in the role she created for Fonteyn. I found Marina's portrayal of the princess to be expressive and engaging. The work as a whole was fascinating, and it was an enormous crowd-pleaser.

Miss Svetlova has devised some handsome stretches of dance and some wonderful sculpture-like pairings … Miss Svetlova provided Labis with an impressive variation which was danced with surety and provided the virtuoso sparks to be found in *The Faery Queen*.[20]

When Marina's *Faery Queen* went on tour, audiences and critics were highly impressed. *Time* magazine reported that Marina's choreography was in perfect accord with Purcell's music. From the very beginning, they felt that she revealed a combination of superb skill and sublime confidence in her ability to construct the masque in a style that was "charming and exquisitely simple."

There are many operas in the standard repertory that allow for the choreographer to revel in the creation of ballet scenes prescribed to be performed for actual dancers. However, the most complete staging of an opera occurs when an imaginative choreographer can suggest intriguing, yet noninvasive movement to be executed by the solo singers. Examples of this type of opera are Strauss's *Salome* and Massenet's *Thais*. Both of these works have dance scenes that provide the leading soprano their own solo dance scene.

An even greater challenge is presented to an opera ballet choreographer when one's duties entail devising movement for crowd scenes, at the discretion of the stage director. Envisioning interesting stage movement for large numbers of nondancers can be overwhelming. The task of organizing the troupes and efficiently communicating your plan to them can often lead to a state of acute frustration. Marina was particularly adept at dealing with the masses and explaining her concepts in an orderly fashion, avoiding being perceived by the chorus as condescending.

An annotated list of choreography created by Marina Svetlova for companies around the world follows:

Eugene Onegin—Peter Ilyitch Tchaikovsky

This is a choreographer's dream come true. This opera is filled with first-class Tchaikovsky dance compositions.
Act 2, scene 1, Waltz
Act 3, scene 2, Polonaise

I Vespri Siciliani—Giuseppe Verdi

- A choreographer's dream come true -- one of the most extensive ballet scenes in all opera. The engaging ballet scenario is entitled *The Seasons*. As the title would suggest, the scenario consists of separate scenes, starting with winter, followed by spring, summer, and autumn. This dance sequence is the dream come true of every opera ballet choreographer. The music is frequently excerpted from the opera for the purpose of creating independent works to be presented on ballet programs unrelated to the opera.

Macbeth—Giuseppe Verdi

Here is another Verdi opera requiring extensive ballet choreography. Contrary to what one might expect to find in an operatic work depicting Shakespeare's tragic epic, this opera contains a huge ballet scene in act 3, as well as later in that act a scene for chorus and ballet. This is a ballet in Marin's repertoire as choreographer.

Un Ballo in Maschera—Giuseppe Verdi

As the title of this opera would suggest, there exist extensive court dances throughout this opera. I had the honor of dancing on a production of this opera that was expertly choreographed by Kent Stowell, former principal dancer from the New York City Ballet Company, who went on to become an associate director of the Pacific Northwest Ballet Company.

Il Trovatore—Giuseppe Verdi

Extensive ballet scene for the reworking of this ballet for the de rigor of the Parisian ballet audience. Some musicologists have referred to this opera as containing "perfect ballet music." Based on the ballet music from this opera, Verdi has been labeled by some opera buffs "the Tchaikovsky of Italian opera ballet music."

Rigoletto—Giuseppe Verdi

If requested by the director, the choreographer may engage in devising intriguing movement for the hunchback as well as crowd scenes.

Faust—Charles Gounod

This opera is considered the most popular French opera ever written and has been performed worldwide, translated into several different languages. This opera contains what is arguably the most well known of all opera ballet scenes, the extensive *Walpurgis Nacht*, act 4, scene 1. Owing to the fact that this opera has gained avid affection from operagoers around the world—rivaled only by Bizet's *Carmen*—*Faust* has never left the repertoire since its debut in 1859. This work can present to the opera ballet choreographer enormous challenges. It can also represent the realization of a lifelong aspiration of a choreographer to revel in the creation of a cherished operatic ballet sequence.

Romeo and Juliet—Charles Gounod

In this opera, there exists an aria sung by the lead soprano known as "Juliet's Waltz." This poses a challenge for the choreographer, as did Strauss's *Salome,* because the choreographer might be called upon to create dance movement that would need to accommodate the dance skills possessed by the soprano. Also, in all fairness, one might notice that she must negotiate some intricate vocal maneuvers while she dances.

Salome—Richard Strauss

Dance of the Seven Veils presents the opera ballet choreographer with an enormous challenge. The dance is obviously choreographed for the title role soprano. For this reason, the choreography must be sympathetic to the possible (probable?) dance limitations presented by the singer. However, the dance is often performed by a soloist from the opera ballet, where the imagination of the choreographer can be somewhat more expansive.

Don Giovanni—Wolfgang Amadeus Mozart

It is considered Mozart's most extensive ballet music in any of his operas. There is a large party scene at the end of the opera, during which different groups of dances simultaneously execute their respective dances, which are written in contrasting meters. The nobility dance a minuet in triple meter. In a party scene at the end of the opera, he scores three different styles of dancing to be performed simultaneously: nobility, minuet, accompanied by a peasant dance and a contradance. Meanwhile, one of the lead singers, Leporello, is presenting a peasant dance. The choreography for the scene is rather challenging to construct, and managing to have it performed appropriately is another obstacle to be conquered.

The Marriage of Figaro—Wolfgang Amadeus Mozart

Figaro contains a famous fandango, a Spanish lively dance in triple meter, complete with castanets, guitars, singing, and hand clapping, for solo dancers.

Boris Godounov—Modest Moussorgsky

This opera calls upon a choreographer's skill with organizing large crowd scenes and devising engrossing dances, often presented by amateur dancers. There is a formal coronation scene, and in the third act, the opera contains a formal polonaise, act 3, scene 2.

The Elixir of Love—Gaetano Donizetti

Donizetti contains inspired ballet music. In addition, there are opportunities to incorporate some limited choreographed dance steps for the soldiers.

Julius Caesar—George Frederick Handel

This opera has been referred to as "Handel's greatest heroic opera." At any rate, it is his most celebrated opera. It requires a great deal of choreography, and it was one of Marina's triumphs. The opera necessitates a great deal of repositioning and parading of troupes. Occasionally, there is dancing accompanying solo arias, which requires skill on the part of the choreographer in the constructing of dance choreography that will not interfere with the singing. There are scenes with idyllic, lyrical movement for groups of innocent maiden types. By way of contrast, some scenes in this opera demand exotic, sensual movement from the dancers.

Manon Lescaut—Giacomo Puccini

In act 2 of this opera, there is a scene that calls for a dancing master. This character dances a legitimate gavotte with the prima donna. She then sings a gavotte, which again leaves room for some sophisticated choreography for the prima donna.

La Rondine—Giacomo Puccini

Although not frequently performed by comparison with many of Puccini's other operas, *La Rondine* contains some fun Viennese-type waltzes. Act 1 of this opera also calls for choreography for dances with more modern dance music, such as a tango. In act 2, along with more waltzes, there appears a foxtrot. Act 2 contains more waltzes.

Hansel and Gretel—Engelbert Humperdinck

In spite of the fact that there is no official ballet in this opera, the choreographic requisites are demanding in their own way. The work is filled with character and folk dances. The most famous among these is the duet dance, "Brother, Come and Dance with Me."

The Ballad of Baby Doe—Douglas Moore

The plot and staging of this opera revolve around a turn-of-the-century old opera house in Leadville, Colorado. There are play-within-a-play scenes that require dancehall choreography to be performed by dancers on a set stage for the other cast members.

Lucia di Lammermoor—Gaetano Donizetti

Act 2 and act 3 of this opera each contain scenes that depict celebrations in conjunction with an impending wedding ceremony. Most of this dancing portrays revelries surrounding the much-anticipated event. Much of the dancing includes movement for the opera chorus, into which can be inserted lively set dances.

Marina was often invited to create traditional folk dances, as well as classical ballet scenes to be inserted into repertory operas. The travels around the world of the Svetlova Dance Ensemble provided Marina with a choreographic vocabulary with which to represent national dances from countries as far away from the United States as Israel and India.

Marina's accomplishments as a dance composer include many entries that are not exclusive to opera ballet. I had the good fortune to have performed in some of her strictly ballet productions. I had the privilege of dancing in some of them.

Autumn Leaves

Pavlova was particularly fond of this ballet which, except for an occasionally divertissement, was her only achievement as choreography.[21]

This was truly a unique dance experience for me. Marina invited me to dance the role of North Wind in a ballet she was producing. I was hesitant, because I had decided to begin winding down my career in dance and focus more on music. However, I became more and more interested in the project after she explained to me that it was a ballet from the Pavlova repertoire. Eventually I became more excited by the possibility because the role turned out to be wild and wooly, which was not the type of role I had come to be associated with. I am reminded of a time when I asked Kirsten Simone, prima ballerina of the Royal Danish Ballet and world expert on the Bournonville technique, what her favorite was that she had performed during her extensive career. I was expecting her to say *Les Sylphide, Giselle,* or even *Swan Lake.* With an uncanny, mischievous look, she jubilantly replied *Carmen* and described how much she enjoyed the opportunity to be the spitfire gypsy after having been the refined sylph in all the other ballets she had performed. I became excited by the opportunity not only to perform in a ballet with such historical significance but also to realize a role of significant solo technical demands along with beautiful partnering scenes. From the get-go, Svetlova was totally self-confident. She taught the role to me as if she had performed it herself. I was rather amazed at her confidence and expertise. I was slightly doubtful as to the authenticity of the choreography. However, when Dolin arrived and coached me in the role, he was not at all skeptical of Marina's reconstruction. This made me lose my skepticism. Owing to the fact that I was to appear with no tights on, she assured me not to worry, that she would bring me some "Texas dirt" soil, which would offer the same effect. I also had some wonderful pas de deux partnering obligations in this ballet, to beautiful Chopin music. Svetlova was particularly helpful in conveying to me and my ballerina fine touches to make the dances more compelling. There were some difficult lifts, and I relied upon Dolin for advice. He mentioned to me that he knew so much about achieving the lifts because in his years of doing pas de deux episodes with Markova, it had been particularly troublesome because he claimed that she never jumped much when performing a lift because it detracted from her the soft, effortless image of herself she was conveying. I found Marina Svetlova to be very knowledgeable and quite easy to work with.

My belief is that one must give the public what it wants, to survive in the theatre. The public loves dancing, but it also wants audible enjoyment. There must be song and speech coupled with the dance for a full evening's entertainment …[22]

Marina Svetlova with Igor Stravinsky,
Located in the Indiana University Archives

l'Histoire du Soldat

The clear and uncomplicated joy of a maiden rescued by a handsome young man.

This observation appeared in the *New York Times* when the newspaper described the effect of Marina's choreography for *l'Histoire du Soldat.* She also danced the role of the princess.

In 1972, I had the privilege of not only seeing Svetlova and Dolin reprise their roles in this ballet at Indiana University, Bloomington, but on occasion, I played the clarinet part in the chamber ensemble that accompanied the ballet. The run of these performances was quite successful.

This work played an enormous role in the career of Marina Svetlova as both ballerina and choreographer. The work is a multifaceted, sometimes confusing composition that has found an identity in various formats. It is described by Stravinsky as a theatre piece to be read, played, and danced. Originally it was scored for piano and clarinet but has evolved into a few different variations on the original idea. This composition played a major role in the continuity of the Svetlova career.

Along with many appearances around the country as the maiden in this work, she assisted Igor Stravinsky in the restaging of his *l'Histoire du Soldat* for the Seattle Opera Company. Stravinsky invited her to Seattle to help him recreate the staging and the choreography. Stravinsky said to Marina, "After I saw you dance the part, I wouldn't change a single note." In this Washington performance, the cast included the illustrious Cyril Richard as narrator and Rock Hudson as the narrator. Her performances frequently involved appearances of the esteemed dancer Sir Anton Dolin in the role of the devil. Another notable performance that included the choreography and dancing of Marina was the ballet at New York's Caramoor Arts Center in 1968, with Edward Villella portraying the soldier. The production was conducted by Julius Rudel from the New York City Opera. It was with that opera company that Marina had created the role of the maiden. She and Dolin also presented this work at the Vermont Center for the Arts.

Ruth Page, another dancer/choreographer, also had a connection with *l'Histoire.* She performed the role of the maiden in the debut performance of *l'Histoire du Soldat* for the League of American Composers. I mention Ruth page because she and Marina had much in common. Page was also the first dancer at the Metropolitan Opera to be given the appellation premiere danseuse. They both were prolific choreographers of ballet for operas. Ruth Page became the director of the ballet for the Chicago Opera, and both of these women were instrumental in promoting appreciation for opera ballet.

One variable in the success of choreography is the capacity of the audience to digest the ingredients mixed into the dough of the creation of the ballet. One must not be convinced that each viewer will be primed to devour the recipe with the same palate. The spectator brings his or her life experience to the table, and with the digestion of the recipe, each gourmand will probably not leave equally satisfied. However, an audience member should bring to the unveiling of the main course an eagerness to meet the choreographer on common ground. The message from the choreographer to each participant (audience) need not be translated into the individual language of each individual audience member, but the assemblage of steps and movement must speak, if not sing, to the audience member. The audience member should exert an effort toward the digestion of the dish being rendered up by the choreographer. In other words, the choreographer is the chef who selects and mixes the ingredients that cooperate in the serving up of a dish of which he or she is proud. The audience member must be ready for the feast.

Just as it is important to remember that the choreographic statement is a result of evolution, so is it imperative to have a grasp of the historical context in which it is couched. As is the case with accomplished musicians, a good choreographer knows when to reign in their gifts in a given area. As a clarinetist, I remember being coached by a distinguished musician who admonished me for allowing my gift at sustaining long phrases of music to interfere with the necessity to form shorter and more delineated phrases. Likewise, a skilled choreographer will not allow a favorite form of movement to become a hindrance by employing it too frequently, or allowing it to get in the way of other elements that are also important—especially when they themselves may be performing in their own works. Were a choreographer a good turner, for example, one often sees repeated pirouettes throughout his ballet, especially when he is choreographing on himself. I have seen a choreographer who was creating a piece for himself and a young petit ballerina. The work was filled with lifts. This brings up another consideration. Some choreographers rely on stock classroom combinations. Now, perhaps this is appropriate at times in a work such as Lander's *Etudes,* which was created for the purpose of intentionally depicting the content and construction of a usual ballet class.

The plan of a choreography is a great pleasure … it is that clear sharp sense of our own natural way of living that makes a moment of ballet speak to the complete consciousness; that makes choreography look beautiful.[23]

~A choreographer creates in his brain, dances in his mind, and revels in his senses.~

In some ways, a choreographer is reminiscent of a potter. Before actually beginning to shape their creation, they throw an amorphous clump of clay onto a potter's wheel and then imagine how to transform the virgin clump of clay into a stylized shape that realizes their quest for a visual fulfilment. In some ways, for a choreographer, the clay is analogous to the dancers—the material with which the ballet is to be shaped. The potter has the wheel, which is a utensil that doubles as a sturdy surface against which the potter forms a creation while supplying its own movement into the mix. A choreographer has the floor, a constant surface upon which their movement will be formed, and the dancers are their clay with which the ballet is composed.

Its science is difficult to acquire and its practice, rare … As in other arts, there are different levels of creation: choreography may be interpretive or decorative, or more importantly, inventive and creative.[24]

~A choreographer is an orator of movement:
he speaks so that others may see.~

Although the majority of Svetlova's choreography was based in classical ball, she also delved into more modern movement. She respected and admired quality choreography for modern dance. Here are observations made by some stellar choreographers for modern dance.

Mary Wigman, born in Hanover, West Germany, was a pioneer in German modern dance early in the twentieth century. She was also a philosopher. She founded the Mary Wigman Central Institute in Dresden and believed that dance was the most fleeting of all arts. She advocated for experimental choreography. She also felt that choreography was a dichotomy in that it was in the moment but could also perpetuate itself infinitely. She stated that it awakens joy in us, moves us, and makes us tremble. She also felt that it brings happiness and freedom and becomes a part of the human condition when it has found fullness in us. She believed that we should have a dance art worthy of us as human beings. She thought that the dignity of dance lies in the most noble of instruments, the human body. She felt that the dance was larger in scope than the dancer. She saw that it is difficult to understand the connection between the drive to create dance and the consummated creation, and that coming at it from the opposite direction, one cannot easily look behind the creation to the experience that inspired it. She firmly believed that "we are weaving the cloth of time."

All choreography does not need to be prescribed. Choreography can even evolve by chance. Witness the extensive success of the choreographer Merce Cunningham (1919–2009). He found his own process by which to create ballets. He often capitalized on the concept of chance and even randomness in the creation of some of his ballets. His ballet *Collage* (1952) was his first "chance" work. He found that even a spontaneous role of dice could act as a catalyst for the production of a valid, satisfying choreographic statement. He was a member of the Martha Graham Dance Company and eventually—as did Marina—formed his own company, where he had more control over the product and the process. Cunningham once said:

I take myself seriously as an artist, and I want people who doubt that to understand what that means and also to realize that art-making for me is anticipation in the world of ideas.[25]

The following vignette demonstrates how choreography is not limited to ballet and modern dance. This story revolves around an event that is not a stylization meant for the stage. It is taken from a real-life tale, rather than a stylized representation, and shows how colloquial movement can also be turned into a stylized choreographic statement.

New Orleans Marching Bands, a Choreographer's Delight

I quickly parked my car and double-timed back to the scene. I was not the only one … I, too, found myself in the rapidly growing ranks of the parade, no longer walking but, but strutting and suddenly dancing … It is hard to describe the sensation it gave me.[26]

From the mouths of babes: this description of the effect the choreography had on this young man is so well expressed and devoid of any traces of self-consciousness that one cannot but be at once impressed—no, amazed—that he found a friend in his naïveté, which prompted him to brilliantly express his reactions. It was a feast day for those interested in dance folklore or in theatrical staging and choreography. There was an abundance of rare and inventive movement on display.

The dancing was pure natural movement completely untrained and unconscious, but with unmistakable origin in the distant shores of Africa … The atmosphere was enhanced by the hilarious high spirits of the participants. The overwhelming feeling of happiness and pleasure reflected in radiant faces was altogether contagious.[27]

One might conclude that this was the real thing. It is certainly difficult for many professionals to accept the fact that for some artists, the devising of choreography is as simple as all that. Notice how the following statement represents a totally divergent conviction.

Now, creating a ballet is a complex affair, even though, as actually performed, it may appear fluently simple in its sustained flow of colorful sequences. Creating a successful ballet calls for the closest, most sympathetic group action.[28]

~A choreographer is an arbiter of time,
of space, of movement.~

Choreography is the fluid architecture of human mass in space and time.[29]

A choreographer operates as the sun within their own solar system. Their dancers are planets that revolve around them in their own unique orbits. They seem to be engaging in a sort of hide-and-seek where the bright stars seem to take refuse in the shadows of their own alter egos. In other words, through his choreography, the choreographer is the center of the universe.

Every ballet I do is, for me, the solving of a balletic problem … the playwright writes his play and hands it on to a producer who animates it for him and puts in on the stage, a choreographer does all this himself.[30]

The choreographer is the proverbial tie that binds. They hold the ballet together by providing material with which the dancers can remain solitary, separate, yet united.

In some ways, the relationship of the choreographer to their dancers is very much like that between lovers. This a romantic notion, but is it always true? Sometimes, lovers are tender with each other, such as the Ashton treatment of the Camille story in his *Marguerite and Armand.* However, sometimes lovers have spats; John Cranko's *The Taming of the Shrew* is case in point(e) (please excuse the pun).

No choreographer wants to be treated as a person who just adorns and creates for the big names.[31]

~A choreographer is the dancer's postage stamp.~

Differences and similarities have been among other major choreographers. Sometimes the inspiration for a dance comes strictly from the static designs of the images, what some call the poses. Choreographers capture their inspiration from their own karma.

While the choreographic counterpoint of a typical Massine ballet is based upon the foundations of his amused observation, that of a Fokine work springs from a quality of sheer emotion.[32]

Massine choreographed roles specifically for Marina in two of his ballets. The first, *Amphion*, was created in 1924 for one of Ida Rubinstein's first companies, which premiered in Paris in 1924. Massine revisited and reworked the choreography for his ballet *Mademoiselle Angot* for Svetlova at the New York City Ballet Company in 1950.

~A choreographer is an interlocutor of movement.~

The trouble with any choreographic interpretation of a classical symphony. . . .is that the dancing is bound to emphasize the least important aspect of the music. . . .[33]

I remember once being in the audience for a dance performance at Skidmore College. The bill included a ballet choreographed by Deborah Fernandez. I found myself feeling as though I was sharing in the choreographic creation. At a given moment, for example, I sensed that I understood the exact impulse that stimulated a given connection of movements, and I felt as though at that moment I was cooperating in the creation of the choreography. I caught myself saying to myself that Deborah had "got it right."

Creating a dance is not much different from entering a trackless jungle. There are neither highroads nor neat arrows to point the way.[34]

The famed Modern Dance choreographer Daniel Nagrin goes on to opine that:

To make matters worse, experience is a trap, because each new dance is a new jungle. Rules, principals and theories can be just so much excess baggage.[35]

A prominent dance journalist, Caryl Brahms, who was writing during the 1930s, made the following observations. She felt that the play of gravity was not a force in play only in modern dance.

Gravity is the second quality that is to be found in Fokine's work. . . . [36]

These words encouraged in me a reminiscence of a beautiful book of poems written by Joan Kunsch. In her *Playing with Gravity,* Kunsch has created a collection of poems based on her career and experiences as dancer, choreographer, traveler, translator, and thinker. Kunsch expresses sensitive insight into the mystery of creating movement.

Playing with Gravity
by

Joan Kunsch

A Question of Choreography

Who dances into mind
when images appear
with bodies light enough
to be anywhere thought moves them?
Figures wreathe into slow falls
play with gravity …

Choreography! Motion from where?
Who is dancing
When images come to mind?
Others may speak of a Muse. Look there—
An ethereal playground
For countless beings made of light.
All dancing.[37]

When Marina was dancing with American Ballet Theatre in the 1942–43 season, she worked with Anthony Tudor. It was as though his emotionally fraught ballets were a continuation of the sort of ballet that Massine had begun to create. Compared to the choreographic style of both Fokine and Balanchine, two choreographic giants in the early twentieth century, Tudor was interested in promoting a different message.

Capable dance-writers are rare. Choreographers of fresh impulse and genuine creativity are rarer. Today they may be counted upon the fingers of two hands with digits to spare. One suspects they are born, not made.[38]

A good choreographer transforms the natural movements of the human body into stylized physical statements. They then use that vocabulary to design an avenue into the human heart. Then the choreography in tandem with the dedication of the dancers manipulate the preconceived limitations presented by the human condition into a reflection of universal harmony—the dance of life. Although it sounds like a superhuman event, a true choreographer can convey to the dancers and audience their vision, their intentions through the language of dance. One exciting aspect of being an experienced choreographer is that a dance composer may select the language of movement with which they choose to speak, or they may prefer to function as a polyglot and call upon a variety of languages with which to speak. Some choreographers are idea choreographers, in that they are motivated by a thought or a specific drama. Other choreographers prefer to coax their conversations out of the impulses suggested by the music with which they are collaborating.

Dancers must always be at the mercy of choreographers to whom they entrust themselves … They remain the creatures of the choreographer.[39]

~A choreographer is the ultimate puppeteer: he pulls the strings that initiate the movement.~

After all is said and done, a prerequisite for fulfilling the responsibilities of a dance composer is very simple. Arnold Haskell wrote:

The first duty of the choreographer is to create good ballet.[40]

Music and Choreography

Marina had realized extensive success in ballets based on Chopin scores, I believe that her first love was Brahms. That having been said, she was always eager to take up the challenge of creating choreography to more contemporary music. As a choreographer, as was the case with her dancing, Marina was extremely versatile. She was fond of jazz and especially enjoyed collaborations with the renowned jazz artist David Baker at Indiana University. Her musical instincts were enviable, and she enjoyed being challenged by new and unique projects.

Many choreographers and dance pedagogues find a supporting grid work in the music. Another consideration presents itself: Does music support the movement, or is it the reverse? Does the choreography support the music? Or are they of equal importance? If one chooses not to enlist the interface of music, there is no escaping the temporal reality, that Father Time waits for no one. The choreography must breathe as a living force. I couldn't agree more.

Being a musician, my attitude may be a bit biased, but I heartily agree with the following observation:

Music determines dances more than any other single element.[41]

A ballet that is choreographically, musically and scenically first class is a big event in the in the Dance world.[42]

Many a musicologist would undoubtedly proffer a similar sentiment concerning the creation of an exceptional symphony.

~Dancers sing the choreographer's song.~

Choreography may, for instance be delayed by dancing a cadenza, as it was in the old ballets, when the story was conveyed in long passages of mime, and subsequently embroidered, coloratura-like, by the *Ballerina*.[43]

There is Riabouchinska, the coloratura of the ballet.[44]

When I began studying ballet, I was struck by the way in which dancers and choreographers counted music. I soon realized that dancers tend to count by melodic cells. Some count by rhythmic impulse and group them either by beat or by groups of beats, sometimes both. Musicians tend to divide a musical phrase into smaller units, which is to say counting by beats rather than by measures. After that, a good musician camouflages the beats and transforms them into larger groupings or phrases.

I can always invent movement, and sometimes it can be fitted into the right place, but that is not choreography. It is the music that dictates the whole shape of the work.[45]

One writer found a poetic way of stating what he felt to be the obligation of dance composers when he wrote:

It is the *orchestration* of dancing that is the choreographer's function.[46]

After a few years as a dancer and owing to the fact that most dancers knew that I was a pianist (some knew clarinetist, as well), I was often asked to teach Music for Dancers. I find the concept of "music for dancers" to be somewhat insulting. I always find that expression to connote dumbing down to the dancer.

Why Not Dancers for Music?

I loved to dance because ballet was usually a physical expression of beautiful music, beautifully performed. I began to realize that one reason certain dancers habitually dance off the music is because individuals tend to think there is a difference between "music" and "music for dance." I understand the course title Music for Dance; the only justifiable use of this title is to apply it to music that was composed specifically to be used as a basis for choreography. A perfect example of this principle comes from the composer Igor Stravinsky. Of all of the spectacular Balanchine/Stravinsky collaborative ventures, few of the compositions that Balanchine turned into his incomparable choreographic masterpieces, only a handful of the Stravinsky scores were composed as music for dance. One of my favorite Stravinsky scores is *le Sacre du Printemps,* which was composed as a ballet score. Happily, it is such a fabulous composition that it has found its way into the standard repertory of most major symphony orchestras. Then there is another work of genius, Balanchine's *Agon,* choreography by George Balanchine. The score to this ballet was composed not specifically as music for dance but became a terrific ballet in the hands of Balanchine.

That the music of a ballet can be so treated as a separate element is evidence in itself of the comparative immaturity of the art … Most of the outstanding ballets of the past have been outpourings of choreographic ideas into ready-made vessels.[47]

The first obvious indication to many listeners that they are hearing a piece of ballet music is that they notice a plethora of repetitive, heavily accented downbeats. That is not to say that there is no music for dance that is lyrical in nature, but when first approaching such pieces, the music does not proclaim itself to be music for dance. For example, when one approaches a Chopin nocturne, usually the first impression is of listening to a beautiful piano solo. However, when one first hears the coda to the famous *Pas de Deux* from *le Corsaire,* the reaction is frequently one of, "Oh, there's music for dance." Yes, one might argue that these standard ballet gems serve a function and perhaps function as an aural representation of the dancer's power. Unfortunately, the constant thud that permeates many of these scores eventually becomes somewhat unlistenable, such as the "Anvil Chorus" from Verdi's *Il Trovatore.*

Musicality means two things: both the ear to seize and follow rhythm, and the comprehension of the atmosphere and content of the music.[48]

When one wishes to find a way to utilize music in the creation of movement or in the performance thereof, the operative word, or concept, if you will, is *articulation.* Obviously there exists a variety of ways to initiate movement, be it lyrical or abrupt, fast or slow. Although it is common in dance, as it is in music, to equate articulation with the crisp, brisk execution of a given task, slow, legato music or dancing also requires a clear initiation of a particular phrase.

For those of the general audience who have not had too wide an acquaintance with the ballet, it is the music which assumes a more prominent role in the scheme of events.[49]

Bombastic

This is the category that most people refer to as music for dance—especially ballet. Strong beats can be used as punctuation marks, as in exclamation points, but when exclamation marks become incessant, they relinquish their effectiveness. In all fairness, virtually every pas de deux in the classical ballet has an example of the slow, romantic melodic adagio, followed by the female variation, which can be languid and lyrical but is usually terse and crisp. The pas de deux ends with a coda that can be quick and light but is often unbearably bombastic. Drigo's coda to the famous pas de deux from his ballet *Le Corsair* is an example of music from the ballet that is almost unlistenable were it to be performed as a concert piece.

Honest ballet choreography is not based on choice bits or wow moments … it is based on coherent sequences, on a positive rhythm. The sustaining rhythm sets off one phrase after another … and finally gives the sense of a rhythmic beginning and ending, of a dramatic progress which conveys a human sentiment.[50]

Early on in my studies of how to create dance movement, I was instructed by an accomplished dance composer that the best choreography is often achieved by selecting less than great music. These words of advice once came back to me. I witnessed a ballet that had been choreographed to Beethoven's entire Ninth Symphony. The ballet was a total disaster. The music far overshadowed the choreography, the ballet was far too long, and it demonstrated the validity of the statement that all music is not suitable for choreography.

Another scholar observed that ballets often fail when the audience finds that:

Their interest was exhausted due to the over-familiarity of their music.[51]

The most obvious example of this phenomenon is Ravel's *Bolero.* If ever there were a piece of music that is more repetitious, used in many a cartoon, and prevalent in much canned music, I am not familiar with it. Another such piece is the Overture to William Tell: Bugs Bunny to the rescue!

Not everything available is suitable. Even the convinced preference of a certain choreographer for a chosen composer is no guarantee of sensibility. [52]

As we saw with Erick Hawkins, although he preferred to work with live musicians, some choreographers and dancers assert that "pure movement has nothing to do with music." To me, this is an oxymoron. I have been a dancer, a musician, and a dance musician, and I can't conceive of dance having nothing to do with music. I find it impossible to separate the two.

Concepts of time in rhythmic divisions are the base of any truly contemporary dance-style.[53]

Finally, our choreographer better have something to say.[54]

CHAPTER 17

Touring

The Travels of Terpsichore

Every year since 1944 Svetlova had toured with her own group, giving as many as 96 concerts in one year. She appeared with her own group in Israel and Greece in 1953, and her most recent seasons have included concerts in Switzerland, Holland, Greece. Spain, Italy on British television and in Helsinki.[1]

Tour American Style

It is not difficult to realize the lasting effect that Marina, especially through traveling to concerts with her own performing ensemble, had on the world of ballet. One could contend that the impact of her extensive touring activities as a distinguished ballerina made an impact on the other arts as well.

American ballet is of the trouper variety Indeed ... Outside the artistic conglomerations of choreographers, dancers, composers and designers, who form the nuclei of 'the companies,' American ballet has a life in the popular theater of musicals, television, and films. More than in any of these, it thrives most wonderfully on the road.[2]

There is also the phenomenon of a method of performing known as run-outs. This is an event that is also experienced in the world of classical music performances. A run-out is the name given to a performance that is usually no more than a one-day excursion, where the artists leave their home base and present a one-shot concert. These events sometimes occur in the afternoon of an evening concert in the home base of the organization and usually do not involve the necessity of an overnight stay.

Regional manners and mores in the thirties and forties were at the same time weird and wonderful to foreign dancers. Marina was once invited to attend a dinner reception sponsored by a group of local dignitaries.

Marina ... was once pressed to accept a dinner invitation ... on the stage of the local concert hall where she had lately been a performer in the ballet ... she and her five civic dignitary hosts sat down to sup. To Svetlova's astonishment, an audience of six hundred took their seats ... and amiably watched the ballerina consume fried chicken ...[3]

155

Marina Svetlova, who, with her company, is doing 20 concerts in Israel, followed by 8 in Greece, is also doing some fancy flying back and forth from Rome where Dimitri Romanoff is staging *Ballerina and the Bandit* and *Eine Kleine Nacht Musik* with her in the leading roles.[4]

When one considers the distances and the amount of time required to arrive at performance venues all across America and in many other parts of the world, it is easy to understand why Marina said, "I think I travel more than I dance."

Remembering that when in the United States, the Svetlova Dance Ensemble usually drove from coast to coast in a family van, it is easy to imagine that their tours were always an adventure.

On tour at present is another dance concert that cannot help but be popular. The beautiful and gifted Marina Svetlova … has created a happy and colorful program that gives thrills, laughs and a thoroughly enjoyable evening of dance entertainment.[5]

We were looking forward to this important performance at the end of a tiring week and were sorry to find poor working arrangements … Next day the company returned to New York via chartered bus and truck … Heated arguments went on about the relative merits of train versus bus travel.[6]

One journalist made a comment describing another aspect of the effect of the years of tours of the Svetlova Dance Ensemble.

Her travels have provided incidental anecdotes that make the history of modern ballet in America as colorful as that of older times.[7]

As I quoted in an earlier chapter, it was the troupers of the twentieth century who made it their mission to fertilize an awareness of ballet in the lives of all Americans.

During the Nineteenth Century, America was nothing if not a balletic wasteland.[8]

In the twentieth century, the establishment of small touring companies became the vogue. These groups could have been considered in competition with one another, including the Markova Dolin venture, the Franklin Danilova troupe, the Ballet Russe Highlights, and many others. When the authority on American dance, Olga Maynard, offered an assessment of the relative artistic contributions made by several independent touring troupes, she came to this conclusion:

Few have done so well as Marina Svetlova, and how many have survived as long?[9]

Markova-Dolin Company

In spite of the fact that this troupe consisted of two of the biggest names in the international ballet world, their touring troupe was not particularly successful. Luckily, the lack of extensive success of this group led Dolin and Markova to establish one of London's foremost performing ensembles, the Festival Ballet.

Ballet Russe Highlights

The raison d'etre of Leonide Massine's Ballet Russe Highlights was to present to ballet audiences new choreographic compositions created to short pieces of delightful music. Along with the new choreographic sketches, the traditional pas de deux and variations were performed in their entirety. Composers represented in the Leonide *Ballet Russe Highlights* were Chopin, Strauss, Ravel, Rachmaninoff, Rossini, Tchaikovsky, Weber, de Falla, Brahms, Beethoven, Moussorgsky, Rimsky-Korasakoff, Bach, Gliere, Nabokoff, and Offenbach. Major stars appearing in the ballet were Irina Baronova, Andre Eglevsky, Yurek Lazowsky, Kathryn Lee, Anna Istomina, and Massine himself as dancer and choreographer-director. Well-known ballet musical directors often conducted. It would seem that this ensemble should have flourished internationally.

All ballet fans were not impressed with the level of accomplishment of Massine's freelance troupe.

Two exceptions to the rather limp tradition set by the Ballet Russe Highlights Company and the Markova-Dolin are Mia Slavenska Variante and Marina Svetlova's company.[10]

Olga Maynard believed that these intenerate souls were among the most—or were the most reckless—devotees of American ballet. Without them, America would have been destitute of dance arts. Unfortunately, American ballet dancers were obliged to travel about the United States in toleration of substandard conditions. The most expedient answer to the dilemma of how to at least minimize the hardships incurred during their ambulant existence would be for every major city in the country to support a theater in which theatrical artists could perform. Meanwhile, one proffered that America must make do with its troupers who gave to an audience more than their money's worth at the box office. Distinguished touring groups brought dance to the general audience that was of a quality and style far more provocative than simple entertainment. Olga Maynard felt that in spite of the growing popularity of dance in America,

Most of the little touring groups fail for one reason or another. Those that survive do so by a combination of stamina and fortitude ... they are able to draw responses from the audience. This is not something done only by gesture or plot but ... by a magnetic quality conveyed by the dancer ...[11]

Even while being subjected to grueling tours, years on end, some dancers manage to maintain their technique in top condition. What is the inspiration? one might wonder. Some of them say that it is the art that keeps them forging onward. Some of the troupers have a more down-to-earth explanation. They contend that their pathway to survival in the face of nearly insurmountable odds is to develop a skill whereby one might benefit from striking a union between a calculated muscular control and the inevitable nervous reflex. The adrenaline rush has seen many a dancer through a performance.

Trail blazing does have romance. First, one must have the conviction that there is an immortality in sincere effort ... To spend one's life efforts on almost uncharted ground has every aspect of bondage, but to one with imagination and creative ability its very obstacles are an advantage ... because he is a creative artist.[12]

Some philosophers contend that after a lifetime of performances on the stages of the world, moving through Europe and the Americas, not only from city to city and theatre to theatre, the stage is the only place many of them come alive.

A great dancer … has more than once been lost as a trouper, either by a lack in temperament, or from an incapacity or a refusal to adapt to the rigors, mental and physical, of touring. But when the truly great dancers are also troupers, nothing exceeds their thrilling rapport with their enormous theatre audience.[13]

Anton Dolin, my friend and mentor, occasionally went on tour as Marina's partner. The gifted young English dancer John Gilpin was one of Marina's partners in London and went on tour with the Svetlova Dance Ensemble. He reminisced about the way in which Marina acted as her own stage manager and went so far as to arrange the lighting for her numerous tours. On one occasion, after the troupe had arrived in Bombay, Marina attempted to arrange a lighting rehearsal with the local stage crew. They insisted that they did not require a rehearsal. Marina pointed out that they did not even know what the repertoire was that her ensemble was about to perform. They replied that they felt confident that they knew the routine because they had already had a ballerina come to their city to perform, and they knew the drill.

'When was that?' asked Marina. 'In 1920.' Marina could not believe her ears. 'Who was it, she asked, amazed. 'Anna Pavlova' came the reply … eventually Marina persuaded them to give us a lighting rehearsal, using the same equipment that had been used for Pavlova more than thirty years previously.[14]

One journalist described how the touring artists helped to combat the prejudice that the thrill of live ballet performances was reserved for the elite patrons who lived in the major metropolises. Most patrons of the arts believe that:

There is need of creative artists who have vision enough to see that the future of dance is going to depend on inspired leaders throughout the country who can see the value and romance of building from the ground up an appreciation for the art at home.[15]

Here are a few examples of the impact that Marina's performances while on tour had on her audiences. I have selected the following statements to illustrate how attendees from a variety of locations seemed to concur that Marina's performances not only demonstrated her level of excellence while dancing the classics but also the attention she paid to selecting a repertoire that represented a wide range, designed to please a diverse collection of fans.

Fresh from the Hills … Ballet in the Hills

Svetlova promptly appeared to do a beautiful solo dance programmed as Variation from Faust Ballet … I thought she was wonderful … the lovely girl seemed to have materialized from Ozark haze, a creation of willow wands and milkweed fuzz tossed about on a mountain breeze.[16]

Vera Zorina, a leading ballerina with the Ballet Russe de Monte Carlo, also made important appearances in the musical comedy, ballet, and films. She also went on to make her mark in Hollywood. She found touring to be quite burdensome:

I found traveling for one-night stands all over the United States quite exhausting, even though in small towns the same program would be presented each night. There is little chance for class or practice because so much time is spent on the trains.[17]

Zorina said that all one can do realistically is to try not to get too physically exhausted. She went on to assert that a dancer has to have a very strong constitution to stand it, as well as strong nerves.

She frequently dances on arty television programs in America and England, and her partners, in recent seasons, when she appeared at world festivals, included George Zoritch and Anton Dolin. Svetlova [has been] the darling, for fifteen years, of community concert in America.[18]

Many dance enthusiasts hasten to point out that Marina not only made it her mission to bring dance performances to those who had never had a chance to see live ballet, but she also encouraged them to increase the scope of their appreciation for the art form.

She epitomizes The Ballet in style and form ... and is lithe, chic and striking ... Svetlova's audience sees a dancer of quality and distinguished attainments, and it is to the credit of American ballet that its audience has educated itself to discriminating standards.[19]

Ballet Troupe Well Received

The Kingsport, Tennessee, concertgoers had their first taste of ballet as a Community Programs offering on a Saturday night. Judging from the extended applause and numerous encores they gave the Russian ballerina Marina Svetlova and her concert troupe, those in attendance enjoyed it and showed their approval with extroverted exuberance. The brilliant performance of the Svetlova Dance Ensemble marked the debut of the 1945–46 concert season for Community Programs and packed the Dobyns-Bennett auditorium to well over capacity. Some fans felt that it was their youthful exuberance and spirit of high comedy, as much as their artistry, perhaps, that won over Saturday night's premiere audience to the trio of dancers and their accomplishments. Their artistry was there in abundance, as even a novice balletomane soon could see:

The two artists who had been the epitome of grace and artistry moments before were transformed into gawky and ludicrous star pupils of the typical dance school. In the latter Mlle Svetlova bourlesqued in high style the gentle sexiness ... in a medley of familiar 90's tunes.[20]

Another fan described the effect that one of Marina's concerts had on her and the audience in attendance: she felt that the classic grace and dignity of the ballet was most successfully demonstrated in their presentation of the *Grand Pas de Deux Classique*, which was followed by a ballet set to music by Franz Liszt. This ballet was called *Adagio and Coda*. The audience agreed that the piece was performed with exquisite precision by Svetlova and her partner, Alexis Dolinoff, who was also a leading dancer of the Metropolitan Opera Association. Among Marina's solos, the Princess Aurora variation and the Jalieate Dance of the Elfs were enthusiastically received. The duet numbers by Svetlova and her partner, Dolinoff, varied from somber-hued and lyric "Meditation" from *Thais* to the lighthearted and romantic *Viennese Waltz* by Johann Strauss, in which Svetlova was a debutante at her first ball, and Dolinoff appeared as a dashing Prussian officer.

The beautiful and gifted Marina Svetlova with Alexei Dolinoff, Adriana Otero, Spanish Dance and concert pianist Sergei Molavsky has created a happy, colorful program that gives thrills, laughs and a thoroughly enjoyable evening of dance entertainment.[21]

Wherever she performed, Marina enthralled her audiences with the variety of the repertoire she selected for her troupe to present at each event.

She is obliged to run the whole gamut of ballet to satisfy individual tastes in her vast audience, and he has a mobile gift in interpretation, from her evocative "Camille to her fiery *Don Quixote* variation.[22]

Marina Svetlova, *Don Quixote,* courtesy of Jacob's Pillow archives and Ron Seymour

Starting with the popular Russian '*Giselle*' Svetlova and Canova portrayed the excerpt from the second act of the ballet with great creative achievement … Entirely different in style were Miss Svetlova and Mr. Canova interpreting … a series of dances dating from 1900. The Waltz, Polka, Tango, Charlston, Apache, Shirmmy and Lambeth Walk.[23]

The opening [of the Svetlova Dance Ensemble program] is an amusing skit of backstage life which introduces the artists and starts the program off on an amusing and friendly note. During the program that follows we have brilliant variations from the ballet repertoire … Miss Svetlova is in top dancing form and runs the gamut of techniques with amazing grace. Her sense of comedy is keen and delicious.[24]

One dance lover described on Facebook the impact produced by a performance she had attended of the Svetlova Dance Ensemble. This fan described how she vividly remembers Marina as a dynamic dancer who toured all over small-town America. She felt that the "Sugar Plum Fairy," danced by Miss Svetlova, showed great classical accomplishments from movement to movement and position to position. She stated that she found the pas de deux from "Bluebird" to be truly an enchanting moment.

Fiery with speed and precise movements the dancers engaged in great harmony of movement and proved with this performance their capture of pure classical technique as did that gentle flowing movements and port de bras in *La Traviata*. The sharp and fresh delivery of Miss Svetlova's Polka-coquette prove her ability in changing moods.[25]

It is rewarding to notice that Marina didn't dumb down her performances for American attendees.

Her community concert audiences are treated to the same Classic form with which Svetlova dance in Europe. She has dance in the four-act *Le Lac des Cygnes* of Saddler' Wells, with the Finnish National Ballet, and at Jacob's Pillow.[26]

Huge companies are limited by the expenses of traveling with costumes and sets expected by experienced ballet audiences in major halls found in large cities. The smaller traveling companies help to remediate the disappointment created by the absence of ballet performances by the mega companies, and tangentially, the presentations offered up by the itinerant ensembles provide greater artistic visibility for the performers.

> In America alone, Svetlova has danced for thousands more persons than could be crowd into the largest opera house in the world.[27]

Anyone who has ever attempted to sleep overnight while traveling on a train can relate to the trials faced by dancers who have just finished performing and are on their way to dance schools and the next out-of-town performance venue. First, there is the necessity of procuring a seat that will allow room enough for exhausted legs and overly stressed feet to respire. After a night not graced by the deepest of slumbers, the process of the morning ablution must be addressed. Before the performance, dancers are often expected to address civic organizations and possibly even visit local dance schools. Occasionally, it is necessary to offer up a white lie to effect a timely escape from tiresome social functions.

Just a small party after the program? … That's very hospitable, but our train leaves at 11:30 … yes, I know … trains are nearly all late these days, but when you least expect it, they can be annoyingly on time.[28]

A Dancer's Life of One-Night Stands

It is not uncommon for a dancers to become obliged to make a tour of one-night stands. This exists as an eventuality because he or she is doing something that does not conform with the predictable roster of events of an established theatre. One sacrifices the usual creature comforts of a private life in order to ensure that a performance will be as perfect in every detail as is within their power. These concerts come after months of daily rehearsals, combined with costume fittings and miscellaneous production rigors. These extraneous responsibilities include sessions with scene painters and makers of properties, which act as the preamble to a week of nerve-wracking strain during dress rehearsals and rehearsals for stage lighting. Many of these events begin as early as six in the evening and continue well into the night. Oftentimes, one has invested sums of their own money, which sometimes causes personal bankruptcy, necessitating the disaster of attempting to survive on loans or unemployment benefits. Eventually, dancers arrive at the typical American town, possibly having traveled all night on a Pullman. This drudgery may have had its inception immediately following the finale of that night's performance. The troupe is often greeted by a barrage of photographers determined to produce suitable material for impressive press releasees. After suffering through the importunities of the newspapermen, whom one dares not offend, the dancers check into their hotel, in anticipation of the day's rehearsal and the evening performance. The orchestra plays the overture. The curtain rises, and on cue, the dancers welcome the audience into a world of magic.

For the first time within twenty-four hours [the dancer] forgets the world of ugly actuality and lives within a world of magic beauty of her own creating. And from this fairyland she reaches out and invites the audience to join her.[29]

In Svetlova's and Shawn's wake have come hundreds of others, foreign and native, uniform only in caliber of performance.

So informed and discriminating has the mass audience become that he so-called provincial American stage presents nothing mediocre and, in general, only the best of the various genres. In quality, the very best is expected to have something more: it must, simply, be *special.*[30]

Olia lovingly remembers the visual effect generated by an endeavor that was truly a "family affair." The combined efforts of several cast members were evident:

By that time, Papa had the luggage loaded. The dancers and Mamma slipped into their fur coats, for the night was chilly … We went out too, in time to see the big car going down the street with its trailer swinging along behind.[31]

It would seem that the collective dedication of the Svetlova team did not go unnoticed:

One of the finest programs yet offered by the Community Concert Artists was presented Tuesday evening when Marina Svetlova, prima ballerina partnered by Jack Beaber … *Don Quixote* was a great favorite and proved a highlight of the evening. It was beautifully executed and must surely rank with the greatest.[32]

When a dancer has their own group, one can continue to create. You are your own boss, and the freedom to continue to create is built in. You can experiment and try out new ideas. With your own company, you have a ready means for testing the success or lack thereof with innovative concepts. One troupe leader opined that when directing your own show, you cannot be temperamental; that only leads to wasting energy. The impact of the performances of Marina Svetlova on the dance world is seen in the frequency with which her international accomplishments were cited in the press. On par with any of the other ballerinas of her time, the number of reports concerning her professional activities were frequent. Virtually all of the major dance writers/critics of the time offered their observations.

Marina Svetlova has probably been seen in person by more people than any other living artist.[33]

CHAPTER 18

Ballet on Television

Several good dancers were seen in recent weeks. Marina Svetlova was a rarely fine ballerina on the Firestone Hour of 7 October (ABC) [1957]. She danced to the *Pizzicato Polka* from Delibe's *Sylvia* with attractive freshness.[1]

Marina Svetlova, *Swan Lake, Dance Magazine,* November 1957

Marina was one of the first ballerinas to achieve enormous success through the medium of television. Some of these writers concurred in their assessment of the role television played in the effort to bring ballet into the homes of viewers who otherwise might not have had the opportunity to attend a dance concert. Some of the experts I have quoted offered opposing points of view. The advent of the televised ballet presentation was not unanimously well received.

"Looking at Television"
with
Ann Barzel

Barzel had a regular column in *Dance Magazine* about dance on television. Here are some excerpts from various issues of that magazine:

Neither Toumanova's great beauty nor her special dramatic quality come across. [1953] She frowned and stared into the camera as she perched on one toe and looked altogether ordinary. Any one of the girls in the regular ensemble has done better on occasion.[3]

Reports of skepticism about televised dance performances abound. In another article, "Looking at Dance," in *Dance Magazine*, Ann Barzel made the following observation:

For a while last month it seemed that dance was being brushed off the television screens. Snide remarks had been printed to the effect that 'ballet is poison.'[4]

As much as one touts the beneficial effects of television and ballet, it should never be viewed as a replacement for attending performances in the theatre. A viewer or listener must engage himself in the performance. Although televised dance concerts are useful for bringing dance into people's lives who might not otherwise have the opportunity to be part of a theater audience, televised dance concerts should never be accepted as a replacement for attendance at a show in the theater. Televised dance productions are a wonderful add-on but not an acceptable replacement.

The TV camera is a hard task master. It brings the foot-work and dramatic expression of dancers right into the living room ... It immediately spots slovenly rhythm, carelessly improvised movement ... the dancer must possess a special dramatic style to perform intimately, if he is to be successful on television.[5]

Looking at TV: Television dance is not the art it could be. In fact, today [1953], it is not nearly so interesting or imaginative as it was in the day of the seven-inch screen and the miniscule one-camera studio with its extravagantly experimental choreographers, unpaid dancers and accommodating cameramen.[6]

As the dancers whirled and spun in the exciting choreography of temptation and frustration, we who watched and listened could almost imagine the wind of their sweet swift bodies blowing across our faces. What is this—black magic? This is the newest and most universal scientific achievement ... This is television.[7]

This conversation about the role of television not only illustrates Marina's impressive success with the new media but also highlights her contribution to the popularity of this new medium. It was another aspect of the impact Marina had in spreading the word. Her televised appearances helped to create a new audience. Svetlova's lifelong efforts were to bring ballet to people who would not otherwise have the opportunity to see classical dance. The television performances began approximately halfway into her career. She had laid some of the ground work for bringing ballet to the masses through her itinerant performances with the Svetlova Dance Ensemble, but these were obviously to a limited audience. Television opened up a wider audience.

On June 27 the ballerina will dance with George Zoritch on television in Frankfurt, Germany when a one hour program will be presented.[8]

It is interesting to note that Marina was rather successful with her manifold televised appearances. In actuality, she said that she didn't enjoy performing on television because she missed the live feedback one experiences in front of a live audience. For me, television provided access to ballet for the first time in my life.

Marina Svetlova enjoyed extensive performing experience in Canada. She was popular not only on stage but also on the television.

Television has not made ballet popular in a mass sense in Canada, but it has done much to make it accessible.[9]

Although we lived in a relatively large Midwest state, touring ballet companies were not the norm. Given the fact that my father was a total sports addict, classical dance was not in the family vocabulary. By chance, I had just begun intermittent ballet lessons as a freshman in college. On one occasion when I was home for vacation, I casually turned on the television to watch one of the talent shows—*The Ed Sullivan Show* or the *Voice of Firestone*. As one of the seemingly random offerings, a classical ballet pas de deux was performed. Since I had recently begun studying ballet, my interest in the ballet portion of the show was piqued. The selection aired was the famous pas de deux from *Le Corsaire,* danced by Sonia Arova and Rudolf Nureyev. I didn't care for the music too much, but I found the dancing enthralling. Being a novice in the ballet world, I was fascinated by pointe shoes, so my attention was focused on Arova's feet. How do ballerinas point their feet encased by those boxes, anyway? My attention was eventually diverted to Nureyev. Wow! Such magnetism and almost animalistic power! Needless to say, I became mesmerized. The jumps, the strength, the artistry—the power was unavoidable!

Menotti's *Amahl and the Night Visitors* is an opera that was composed for the television. This is relevant to this discussion about dance for television because there is a significant dance portion of this one-act opera. Three major players in the dance profession took part in the creation of this dance created for the television screen. John Butler did the choreography, and one of the dancers was Glen Tetley, another choreographer of wide repute. Melissa Hayden was another of the solo dancers. Yes, the steps were simplistic and the presentation nonpretentious, but these dances were designed for intimate, close-up camera work.

Artistically, television presents dancers with new problems … and perhaps point the way toward dances created especially for the television—

call them teledances? …

Entertainment possibilities of television are so vast … We may hope that television will ultimately employ the thousands of dancers that vaudeville once accounted for.[10]

Even some of the most revered dancers did not always show themselves well on the screen.

Talks with scores of dancers who have worked for television have not yielded a single case of … complete despair … the reveling spirit is one of hope, offset by various degrees of dismay and frustration.[11]

By way of comparison, many viewers found a more optimistic confidence in the important influence that television was destined to have on the world of dance:

In television however, there *is,* to an amazing extent, the sense of actuality. You *know* there is a living performance actually taking place before your eyes at that very instant.[12]

Many observers have taken a more pragmatic approach while enumerating the positive contributions to the art of dance made by the television but also when evaluating the merits of the televised dance broadcast:

The new medium has given dancers more work, and consequently more money for food, doctors' bills and study. Economically, it is undoubtedly a good thing … The technical limitations of television dance and how to handle them are the subject of much conversation and experimentation among those working in it.[13]

Regardless of what it has done in its stages of infancy, television continues to explore methods with which to communicate with both the untutored and the cognoscenti. Television is a mode that has helped ballet seem like a medium reserved for the rich and famous.

In 1947 it appeared that the Lively Art of Dance would be a vital part of visual programming for the air … Today, with the exception of occasional airings of hour-long ballets such as NBC has presented in cooperation with the Ballet Theatre … dancing is only part of the picture …[14]

Here is an example of the struggles that some believers have endured to make dance be taken seriously as a part of the regular television programming:

A Time to Dance
by
Walter Terry

Walter Terry once painted a portrait of Martha Meyers, a diminutive associate professor and teacher of dance at Smith College. She knew that educational television programs tended to neglect dance. By outlining the tremendous growth of dance in America, Mrs. Meyers insisted on the inclusion of dance in the curriculum of many colleges and public schools. By drawing attention to the several commercial TV programs that have treated dance as a major art, she won her case. The National Educational Television Council, under the auspices of the Ford Foundation, provided WGBH with the funds to produce the series of nine half-hour programs called *A Time to Dance*. Then there arose the question of what should be covered? What artists should be engaged?

But it must be remembered that *A Time to Dance* was not designed for the professional. "Our special problem," said Mrs. Myers, "was to find a method for getting our subject across to the layman, to the general public, without over-simplifying it for those who might know something more about dance."

The Dance in Television

What the Newest Amusement Medium Means

Edward Padula
Department of Television, National Broadcasting Co.

With the advent of television, a new outlet is open to the dance, and a new field of exploration is open to the dancer. Resulting from the successful experiments made by the National Broadcasting Company during the past few months with almost every phase of dance, there is every indication that the popular and the serious types of dancing will comprise a great part of television programming in the future.

Dance and television have a great deal in common. Action is very suitable to the spontaneity and mobility of the cameras; beauty of movement and composition are visually interesting in its photography; and television's ability to select and emphasize the dexterity of the individual dancer by the use of close-ups adds to the appreciation of technique and enjoyment of the spectacle.[16]

Television has the possibility of adding another dimension to dance performances. Televised performances expanded the experience of balletgoers with the inclusion of material impossible to be witnessed by attendees in the theatre.

Before the ballet season began, balletomanes had a rare opportunity to observe the dancers at work on television. Two rehearsals were broadcast on June 28 [1937] with commentaries by Arnold Haskell, who described the rehearsal process and explained the ballet technicalities. By mid-1937 the quality of television transmission had improved considerably.[17]

The following article exemplifies one of the truly amazing benefits provided by television broadcasts: the prospect of seeing not only a complete ballet company but a performance of a full-length ballet.

Great Moments in Dance

One of the Greatest Moments in American Dance History Was the Nationwide
Broadcast Telecast of the Sadler's Wells Ballet in *The Sleeping Beauty*

In the nineteen-fifties, the inside of the back cover of an issue of *Dance Magazine* described the effect of a televised performance of the Sadler's Wells Company by recounting that no curtain will rise on the occasion and that no audience will greet the dancers with applause as they come on stage. The audience will be seated in their homes, allowing the television camera to act as the on-sight viewers. Tonight's audience sits in their homes across the viewing area. Fans around the world are moved by the magic of Margot Fonteyn's dancing. Their television screens have shown them that the drama, the beauty, the enjoyment of ballet, and all of dance belongs to everyone.

Eventually, New York's Metropolitan Opera took the use of televised broadcasts into its fold. The New York City Opera followed suit. Marina was a leading ballerina for both of these opera companies.

For some enthusiasts, a sort of hybrid art form emerged. It would seem that there developed a new form of dance expression:

But can it really report the dance? I say it *cannot*. What is picked up by the single … stationary camera will not coincide with what the spectator sees (and feels) in the theatre … It may be cruel to say this, but ballet today [1952]—*as movie and the television people see it*—is a fascinating novelty rather than a magnificent art form.[18]

Other advocates for the validity of televised dance performance put a different spin on the consideration. Another title was devised for the phenomenon of creating a new audience, or at least expanding an existent one, by broadcasting dance performance into people's homes.

Television: dancevision … Stand up and cheer! Two mediums have at last become one, and the new baby, teledance (admittedly still in its infancy) is thriving, healthy and beautiful. All this through the ground-breaking zeal of all connected with *Dance For Camera,* a series of three choreographed-for-television dance specials.[19]

After the occasional dance segment that was included in variety shows, such as the *Voice of Firestone*, one should be reminded of the gift that PBS has given to dancers, dance fans, and children in general. Early on, we got the *Live from Lincoln Center* series of special performances brought to us through the miracle of television. The yearly televised version of Baryshnikov's *Nutcracker* is also a perennial favorite, which gave birth to the annual televised broadcast of the *War of the Nutcrackers.*

Televised dance was inadvertently given another boost from the world of opera. Many operas contain substantial dance episodes, such as Bizet's *Carmen*, Gounod's *Faust*, and Giordano's *la Gioconda.*

Met 1951–2 Forecast Includes Television

Interesting plans to extend the scope of the Metropolitan Opera Associations functions were announced by Rudolf Bing, General manager … Mr. Bing announced that the Met has set up a television department, to put on special operatic productions for video.[20]

The seasoned male principal of the Diaghilev Ballets Russes, Adolf Bolm, described that on his first trip to the United States, there was no radio and no TV. He lamented that other artists apart from dancers, including singers, musicians, and painters, were capable of showing their skills in theatres, through personal appearances, on records, and eventually in the movies. With the advent of the radio, musicians and singers could reach a larger audience. Owing to the fact that they were working in a visual medium, dancers and choreographers were not supplied with a competitive resource. He found that television opened up a new world of unparalleled power, not only to the world of art but ultimately to people from every walk of life. He felt that dancers in 1942 should start preparations for their coming glory days on television.

CHAPTER 19

The Business of Ballet

A ballerina is created first by her own impetus and talent and is often fostered by commercial management which always needs prominent individuals on whom to focus publicity.[1]

Managers and agents certainly played a large role in the securing of concert dates and the promotion of Marina's solo career, as well as the Svetlova Dance Ensemble.

Dance Management of the Future

In the past, the manager has presumably had the choice of two methods in publicizing and handling a dance attraction. These were methods of exploitation or promotion. Exploitation is the easier of the two methods and its returns are immediate and bountiful.[2] Since the early 1940's, Marina Svetlova was always represented by a management for performing artists. Initially it was under the aegis of Columbia Artists. In 1958 she signed with National Concerts and Artist Management and stayed with that agency until 1962. One prominent artist manager during the Twentieth Century was Sol Hurok. He was "A Russian, with burning vision and a rock-like wisdom, he has sought to make a theatre and the concert hall, places for profound experience.[2]

Outstanding among the world's impresario of music, dance, and drama, S. Hurok has done more to bring glamour and novelty to the field of artistic entertainment than any other man. With uncanny judgment, he has imported, year after year, the best of foreign attractions, has fostered many careers in this country, and has been associated for a quarter of a century with the most significant artists of all lands.

A Russian with idea and a positive conviction that the American public can lend its appreciation to the finest of artists and organizations, he has left the small things to others and has devoted his boundless energy to the promotion of large-scale and often spectacular attractions. He fervently hopes that his efforts will bring about a renaissance of interest in the stage arts, surpassing that of European audiences. He is convinced that people in America need only be made aware of great art, and they will flock to it. Some years ago, the *New York Times* declared editorially that "S. Hurok has done more for the use of music than the invention of the phonograph."

Dancing Is a Business: To some dancing is an art, an expression, to others a exercise. To me, dancing is a business ... I found that for the public, ideas were far more important than intricate steps. (Statement by dance director Leroy Prinz)[3]

Mr. Hurok managed the last seasons of Anna Pavlova, Isadora Duncan, Fokine and Fokina, and Lois Fuller. He brought to this country the famous composers Richard Strauss and Alexander Glazounov. He presented many celebrated violinists, including Mischa Elman, Efrim Zimbalist, Eugen Tsaye, and Kubelik and scores of great singers, including Tetrazzini, Gluck, Schumann-Heink, and the immortal Chaliapin:

He introduced Mary Wigman to New York, kindling a future in the dance world that still continues, although interest has now turned to the brighter art of Ballet Russe. He also delivered for American delectation the fiery Flamenco dancer, Vincente Escudero, Uday Shan-Kar, and his Hindu Company Trudi Shoop and her Comic Ballet.[4]

Through depressions and prosperity, Mr. Hurok single-handedly continued to present large touring organizations of distinction. He managed the tours of the German Grand Opera, the Russian Grand Opera, the Habima Theatre, the Italian Piccoli Theatre, the Moscow Cathedral Choir, and the Vienna Choir Boys.

It has been said that stars are not born, not made, and that audiences, not managements, make stars. Both are true. And stars are useful as long as they are good dancers. [5]

That is perhaps a naïve notion. The importance of the role of management in the area of opportunity and success in the arts should not be overlooked. One should be reminded that authorities on the dance proffer that it was America who brought ballet to Hurok.

Ballet and Hurok have been linked by threads as shear as and indestructible as nylon. For it was Hurok who brought Ballet to America. [6]

We Are Discovering America
by
Sol Hurok

We liked to think of ourselves as a little more than just businessmen, just managers ... There is a big job to be done with American artists, especially dancers. They deserve all the attention and encouragement they can get, and we, on the business end of the profession, are going to give it to them. [7]

Twentieth Century ballet history attests to the fact that if there is any one individual to be recognized for having brought ballet to America, it must certainly be Sol Hurok. "When Mr. Hurok brought the original Russian Ballet of Colonel de Basil to New York in 1933, America had seen nothing comparable for seventeen years ... Mr. Hurok was the first to have introduced Russian ballet as well to the far East and Japan when he sent Anna Pavlova and her company there. [8]

Pavlova and Hurok

It is through her American manager, Sol Hurok, that we see Pavlova as a woman. "There can be no question that Hurok's relationship with Pavlova was as much inspired by personal attraction as by business … he found that the performances of Pavlova crystalized his to-date nebulous plans for sponsoring dance attractions[9]…

Dancers have much to say about impresarios. What does an impresario have to say about dancers?

An audience often takes the quality of its visiting performers for granted. They do not realize the amount of risk, judgment, and careful handling that go into the presentation of fine talent and especially dance talent.

A real impresario recognizes that the talent of an artist is part of his nature. He will encourage that talent till it enriches the world, knowing that the artist and impresario can only attain complete development one with the other.[10]

Many people will tell you that if you want to be an artist you must sacrifice everything to your art; but any artist will tell you that if it is a *sacrifice* you had better not try and be an artist.[11]

If you're not being offered the jobs you want, don't assume it is a reflection of your talent. Too frequently, the most gifted performers are defeated in their efforts by the ones who know how to work the industry better. Mistakes one doesn't even realize could be interfering with the intended success in auditions. It would be helpful to accept the fact that there is a difference between taking a class and auditioning. Dancers go to a lot more classes than they do auditions. But in an audition, you need to turn classwork into what might seem to be an extroverted performance. Many dancers aspire to be something they're not. It would be more productive to be cognizant of your place in the market and learn how to respect that. Does your agency have everything they possibly need to market you to the industry? If jobs aren't materializing, be proactive.

Have a meeting with your agent if you're frustrated. We always tell dancers that you have to control everything in your control … sometimes you just need to give it time. [12]

Volunteer Lawyers for the Arts

There is a misconception in the artistic community concerning funding for the Arts. Many dance companies have as their mantra: we don't have any money; but if we were tax-exempt, we would be eligible for all sorts of funding. Surely, if we operated as a non-profit organization, we'd get the money. "This notion is inaccurate. And Volunteer Lawyers for the Arts (VLA) works hard to explode this myth. Establishing financial need is one of the two criteria for receiving LVA's services.[13]

Endorsements

As is the case with sports, retailers are always looking for celebrities to help promote their merchandise. It is a business relationship that aids the sponsors with sales and the dancers financially and affords them additional public visibility.

Marina Svetlova was the poster girl for Selva dance shoes in *Dance Magazine*. One month, in an ad that included a full-length photo of her, the caption cited Marina Svetlova, premiere danseuse from Metropolitan Opera Association. "Miss Svetlova, internationally famous premiere ballerina, performs magnificently at the Metropolitan Opera House and on concert stages the world over, her feet graced by Selva toe shoes." Another month: "This Spring, internationally famous premiere danseuse will be performing on a small stage in a local recital. Give her the best equipment available for this important moment, give her Selva Dance footwear."

Philanthropy

But every ballet company has also a commercial side, not visible to the public but very, very important.[14]

Not only was Svetlova known for her donations in kind to various dance organizations, she also gave money and helped establish some of them. In Becket, Massachusetts, Marina established a scholarship for young dancers at Jacob's Pillow.

Patrons who sponsor the road appearances of dancers are very important people. Everyone in the dance world loves them and sincerely appreciates their toil on behalf of the arts industry. But more than social events are needed.

In fact, to make sure, you generally organize a delightful reception where the performers have the chance to get acquainted with the elite members of your society.[15]

The National Society of Arts and Letters is an organization that has existed for the purpose of supporting young talent in the performing, literary, and visual arts since 1944. Marina was a major donor.

On November 25, 1959, five major artists of the modern dance received awards of honor from an unexpected source. On that day, the Federation of Jewish Philanthropies of New York, at its Second International Festival of Dances, honored Martha Graham, Hanya Holm, Doris Humphrey, Helen Tamaris, and Charles Weidman. The Federation, a fundraising organization, is not basically concerned with art but has discovered that it is a wonderful ally. Earlier this year, it presented a gargantuan exhibit of painting and plastic art from around the world (which brought in $1,300,000). Last year, the Federation held its First International Festival of Art and honored John Martin of the *New York Times*. … The Federation supports 116 organizations, including the Ninety-Second Street Y and many other organizations. Its budget was $18 million for 1959. Its aim is always to use funds for healing, educating, and constructive purposes.

It is this kind of enlightened attitude that has also created the idea of the Federation's dance festival and its dance awards. All of the prominent dancers who appeared, as well as musicians and stage crew, did so on a volunteer basis, offering their efforts to the work of the Federation.

But what is the meaning and purpose of all of this? John Martin, in his introductory speech, put it succinctly:

If you check the meaning of the word "philanthropy" in Webster's Dictionary, you may be surprised to find that it is not only, as many people believe, a matter of charity, but rather it is a 'love for mankind: good will to all men.[16]

The Ballet Theatre Foundation is a non-profit organization, contributions to which have been ruled tax-exempt. Its purpose is to further, as a recognized American art medium, which combines the already sponsored arts of music, painting and drama. A hearty and earnest invitation is extended to all lovers of ballet to become members of the Foundation. [17]

"If you want to make art public, you have to treat it like a business. Successful businesses rely on careful money management as well as excellently planned production. Fundraising is a year-round effort—both for maintenance and for special programming."[18]

'Sponsoring dance,' reports one sponsor, 'can be the most exciting, fulfilling, enjoyable thing in life.'[19]

At Indiana University, Marina endowed scholarships for young dancers.

In 1913, Pavlova reappeared at the Metropolitan Opera House with her own company, had a return engagement in 1914, toured the country in 1914–1915, and in 1916 joined forces with the Boston Opera Company, in which she invested a considerable share of her own means to keep the company from collapse.[20]

Provocative is the word for Lincoln Kirstein's *American glossary,* with which the new quarterly *Dance Prospective* has launched its career. For this is quite the most remarkable glossary that I have ever encountered. Many of its entries remind me of Dr. Johnson's immortal definition of the word 'patron' in his dictionary."[21]

Ted Shawn believed that Olga Maynard was proud of her national theatre but was well aware of the fact that something more must be done if American dance was to reach its full potential. He felt that she gave us insight into the artistic quality of our dance theatre but continued to point out that "in Ballet there are aspects of promoting excellence in Ballet which many writers neglect, such as the economic conditions which effect the artistic quality of performance, and the attitudes from the stage and street which effect theatre dancing."[22]

Jacob's Pillow

Marina was named a major donor in perpetuum.

Message to Congress
More Than Luxury

Theatre, to the Russians, has always been far more than a luxury. It has been, and still is, a mirror of the hearts and souls, of their achievements and of their aspirations. The arts in general, and the theatre in particular, have always served as props to the Russian ethos. What began under the Romanoffs has been perfected into a precision instrument by the Soviets. The Czars were right. The esteem that, from the time of Peter the Great, Russia has craved has come through its arts. But it was far more than glory that they loved their theatre arts. Although recognition of it is limited, the artistic resources of dance in the United States are among our great national treasures.

A Direct Route

It is no good to bury the talents of our choreographers, composers, artists in an artistic Fort Knox. Show them, gentlemen of Congress. It is worth a try (and a few million dollars) to see what effect … both on the masses and on the Kremlin hierarchy—our best efforts can have. Would it not be a hard-working business venture to spend money on a ballet company? It would be money so well spent …[23]

Sergei Diaghilev
Looking Back

A passionate worshipper of physical beauty, he realized his visions in creating a complete union of the arts—of color, sound, and movement. All this meant a heavy pull on whatever funds were available, but Diaghilev never cared what his lavish productions cost, and money was poured out extravagantly to achieve perfection. Beauty was his obsession.[24]

Portrait of the Patron

Is not a patron, my lord, one who looks with
Unconcern on a man struggling for life in the water, and
When he has reached ground encumbers him with help?
—Samuel Johnson,1755

Patronage of the arts, either by states or individuals, once meant the provision of money toward certain creative ends. The Roman Catholic Church, the Medicis, Louis XIV, and Ida Rubinstein derived pleasure in the production of painting, sculpture, architecture, music, or stage—works for which they paid, for a variety of public and private reasons. Some delighted in a product in which they themselves had no part, except the capacious achievement of beauty. Others preferred to participate, and still others to pay for a frame in which they could themselves shine or could be illuminated by reflected glory.

Polignac, Mesdames de Euphrussy, Otto Kahn, Sir Basil Zaharov, Lord Rothermere, Mesdames de Euphrussy, Chanel, Misiaert, the Marchioness of Ripon and D'etienne de Beaumont—most of these influential but cultivated people genuinely loved the ballet. It was their opulent pleasure to permit Diaghilev to employ their money as he desired. There were few conditions attached. Frequently, these patrons would detest the results that their money made possible. The givers were his devoted personal friends; the gifts, mostly genuine expressions of their affection or admiration. When *Union Pacific* was in consideration, that benevolent despot Colonel de Basil implored a committee of American ladies

175

to subvention this new ballet, which was to be *their* new ballet, as a private and personal enterprise. This was an efficient system and eventually on subsequent works … White Russians.

The great mystery as to why America does not have a more state-supported system for the development and sustaining of the arts persists until this day. Comparison between America and Russia has been the cantus firmus seemingly forever.

You can beat water until it foams, but even so it's never cream. The top is off the Russian Bottle. Now it is up to us to whip our own cream. What can we do? First of all we can make ourselves conscious of the economic situation as it actually is. We can realistically marshal and inspect our own forces and feel our power. [25]

A plea to the local sponsoring committee:

You kind ladies and gentlemen who sponsor the road appearances of dancers, are Very Important People. Every in the dance world loves you and sincerely appreciates your toil in their behalf. You always do our best to give your visiting celebrities a warm greeting and to make their stay in your city a happy and memorable one.[26]

And what, Mr. Martin pointed out, could be more appropriate for those interested in humankind than a concern for the arts? Does it not make good sense that the artistic and spiritual contributions of the arts be considered a basic part of philanthropy? Does it not make good sense that members of the Federation turn to the dance for its stimulation, its revelation, its beauty? "For philanthropy is not just a matter of giving from the pocketbook—although that is essential, too—but also of respecting and appreciating the things of the spirit, for that is a part of love for mankind goodwill to all men."[27]

The Ballet Theatre Foundation is a non-profit organization, contributions to which have been ruled tax-exempt. Its purpose is to further, as a recognized American art medium, which combines the already sponsored arts of music, painting and drama … A hearty and earnest invitation is extended to all lovers of ballet to become members of the Foundation.[28]

Ballet Associates in America

This group is a New York membership corporation organized to foster the appreciation of ballet as a form of American art. Its program is to cover all activities in connection with the ballet. By sponsoring new ballets, it hopes to encourage and develop choreographers, musicians, and scenes and costume designers. All ballets will be owned by the association, and royalties earned from them will be used for the production of new ballets.

OUR FIRST BALLET 'On Stage' was one of the highlights of the 1945 season. Our second will be the production in October 1946 at the Metropolitan Opera House of '*Camille*' with choreography by John Taras, music by Franz Schubert, arranged for the ballet by Vittorio Rieti, costumes and scenery design by Cecil Beaton. THE CORPORATION has been informed by the United Sates Treasury Department that contributions made to it may be taken as deductions in the income tax returns of contributors. FURTHER INFORMATION may be procured by addressing the corporation at room 1115, 119 West 57th Street, New York 19, New York."[29]

"Ballet Theatre is proud to be able to frequently announce the presentation of newly created works by both established and promising young choreographers. For example, in times gone by, ABT was capable of announcing events such as the premiere of *The Harvest According* by Agnes de Mille, who last winter increased her reputation as a creative artist. Instances of the ability of this company to promote new choreographers was witnessed when it proudly added a new work by William Dollar and, as a product of its embryonic choreographers' workshop, it produced Edward Caton's *Triptych*. This company also excels in presenting revivals such as a new production of David Lichine's most enduring ballet, *Graduation Ball*. These events are made possible through loyal support. "Ballet Theatre continues to be grateful to members of the Ballet Theatre Foundation, without whose contributions it could not create new ballets, develop new stars, and continue to make ballet an integral part of the artistic life of communities throughout the country."[30]

Marina believed not only in supporting and encouraging students, but she also was a patron for dance companies. In the 2010 spring season of the American Ballet Theatre at the Metropolitan Opera House, the estate/trust provided significant financial support for an all-classical program.

But every ballet company has also a commercial side, not visible to the public but very, very important.

Svetlova Dance Center

Upon entering the estate of the Svetlova Dance Center, one was aware that magical things were afoot and that something extraordinary was about to transpire. Permeating the environs was a sense of tranquility coupled with a sincere sense of purpose. It became immediately apparent that although the order of the day was to focus on intense ballet training, there was also time reserved for the exploration of related disciplines in the arts.

The Svetlova Dance Center was founded in 1965 in Dorset, Vermont. Although she had garnered great acclaim for her superb dance performances, it was perhaps her endeavors at the Svetlova Dance Center, surrounded by young, enthusiastic girls, that were the accomplishments of which she was most proud. I knew Marina in NYC, Bloomington, and Dorset, and it seemed to me that when she was at the Svetlova Dance Center, her demeanor became more relaxed and perhaps more gregarious. Her face exhibited a calmer state, and it was obvious that, although she had a great amount of responsibility running her own dance camp, she was far more composed, and she managed to present a countenance of a caring individual rather than that of an astute businesswoman. Noticeable tension was dispelled from her demeanor.

The front gate first opened to a smallish front yard and a curious log cabin–type house. Over the door was a sign that read "Marinated." For the longest time, I thought it was some sort of joke referring to the quasi-rustic atmosphere emanating from the house, accompanied by the intimation of flavorful, marinated steaks for epicurean dining. Eventually, I came to realize that her name was Marina, and her husband's was Ted; hence the elision of the two first names became the "Marinated" House. This was not only their home but Marina's office. (Occasionally, when there was an overflow of students, some lived in the attic of Marinated, and it was dubbed the "Doll House.")

Marinated was also the site of what Marina called "cocktail hour," when all of her faculty were invited to assemble for drinks and relaxing socializing just before dinner. After several cocktail hours over a period of several years, I never saw Marina have a single drink. Eventually she came to allow herself one glass of red wine with dinner. Marina did not encourage discussions about the students. Cocktail hour was a time for faculty to sit back, put up their feet, and relax, not to think about work. She made regular inquiries to us concerning our satisfaction with our accommodations, the maintenance thereof, and the quality of the food being provided for us. Of course, she was curious as to whether or not our classes were progressing favorably, but she was determined to allow her faculty to disengage from duties in the studio so that we might enjoy some relaxed, personal moments for ourselves. She reserved discussion about student accomplishments for working hours. Marina advocated for a separation and provided for an enviable balance between work and relaxation.

Personal collection of Marina Svetlova, Indiana University Archives

Within walking distance of the Svetlova Dance Center is a well-known and widely respected arts establishment, the Dorset Playhouse. This was one of the cultural opportunities available in Dorset. Another local distinction was that Dorset is the seat of a famous and widely respected antique show that takes place during a few weeks of the summer, in the center of town. There was also a sophisticated country store that was a short walk up the main road in Dorset. The real thrill was when the older girls were allowed to walk down to this store, named Peltiers. The store was located directly across the street from the Dorset Inn, a typical Vermont downtown gathering place for locals and visitors alike. Some of Marina's teachers and pianists were occasionally boarded there.

Marina told me that her mother had always wanted her daughter to settle down and have her own ballet school. Marina said that as they were shopping for an appropriate location, they came across this absolutely gorgeous property in Dorset, Vermont. Marina described how her mother instantaneously opened a carpet bag and—just like in the movies—pulled out bundles of cash for a down payment on the property.

Marina shared with me her feelings about what she had experienced with the de Basil company. The events she witnessed had grown into a resentment toward the intensive rivalry and extreme completion among the ballerinas within the Original Ballet Russe. She told me how certain dancers had resorted to secretly putting glass slivers into pointe shoes of rival ballerinas. This helps explain Marina's desire to move on from the Original Ballet Russe in search of more congenial environs.

In his book *The Ballets Russes,* Vincent Garcia-Marques remarks that jealousy and rivalry were common in the theatre. He describes how one solo ballerina had a strap cut on her costume before she went on stage. The ballerina was stupefied, and the audience was scandalized.

My own experiences can attest to the professionalism of Marina Svetlova and the excellence of her dance center. One summer, I was working in Cleveland, Ohio, as a pianist for the Cleveland Ballet and the Cleveland Civic Ballet. One afternoon, I received a telephone call from Marina, whom I had not seen or heard from for several years. Needless to say, I was quite surprised when she identified herself. She asked me if I would consider coming to Vermont that summer to be a piano accompanist at her dance center. Realizing that I had never been to her summer academy, she immediately began describing to me the essence of the institution and its programs. Without having been asked, she explained to me the terms of the employment: free room and board, Olympic-size swimming pool, enough free time to attend performances at the Dorset Playhouse or travel to the Southern Vermont Arts Center or Manchester for shopping. She described the situation as a working vacation. When it came to the topic of financial remuneration, she informed me of the salary. She stated that she knew me and the quality of my work and that she wanted me to strongly consider the offer. She went on to say that she was paying me exactly the same amount of money as she was the teachers. When I expressed my surprise, she said to me, "Ballet teachers are a dime a dozen. A good ballet pianist is worth their weight in gold." She told me that I would be greeted at the airport and driven to Dorset. The very next day, I received via special delivery a round-trip ticket from Cleveland to Manchester, Vermont. I was met at the plane by her husband and driven to Dorset. This experience introduced me to the efficiency and professionalism that were her hallmarks. It made me understand how she managed to survive all those years on the road, running her own touring ensemble. Everything about the dance center was as she had described it. It was a tasteful New England estate, complete with a large white manor surrounded by lush green lawns and trees—everything one could expect from a large estate in a small, upscale New England town.

The students received lectures and demonstrations in other areas, such as costume making and stage makeup. A bonus added to the Svetlova summer dance experience was that she occasionally brought guests other than dancers to work with the students. Dance critics, visual artists, and historians were frequent guest lecturers.

There was also time reserved for relaxation and for friendly summer camp comradery. The dance center had an Olympic-size, heated swimming pool and an attentive lifeguard.

In reference to the bonding that takes place among the campers at the Svetlova Dance Center, in order that the campers might stay in contact with one another, the girls created a Facebook group for alumnae of the Svetlova Summer Camp experience.

Marina arranged weekly attendance at performances of the New York City Ballet at the Saratoga Performing Arts Center. During one return trip, Marina got a huge smile on her face and took a deep breath. She opined that one notices a change in the air as soon as one crosses the state line between New York and Vermont.

I Want to Be a Ballerina

I want to be a ballerina and dance until I can no longer dance ... Just daydreaming about a ballerina won't make me one.[1]

The success of the Svetlova phenomenon is inextricably interwoven with that of a few other major dancers, past and current. Photos of Edward Villella and Jacques d'Amboise adorned the walls of the lobby to her main studio. Most prominent was a picture of Anna Pavlova.

Sir Anton Dolin and Anna Pavlova

Owing to the fact that he was a ballet partner for both Anna Pavlova and Marina Svetlova, Pavlova was an idol and a role model for Marina. My friend, mentor, and coach, Sir Anton Dolin, described how he believed that a well-rounded education influences the development of the artist inside the dancer. He described Anna Pavlova as being a remarkable human being. He shared that at dinner, their conversation rarely contained remarks about dance. He reported that she conversed with wit and charm about a host of topics, from international affairs to a recent contemporary novel. He stated that although dancers must engross themselves in their chosen art form, they must occasionally find ways to get away from it, in order to effect a balance between work and usual human existence.

Pavlova was one of Marina's idols and proved to be a tremendous inspiration. The touring Svetlova Dance Ensemble grew out of Marina's great respect for Anna Pavlova and her touring troupe. Marina admired Pavlova for having brought ballet to many people in the world that never otherwise would have had the opportunity see it. Marina was a replication of Dolin's description of Pavlova's, in that she, as was the case with Pavlova, sought a healthy balance between her art and other human activities. In addition to being a ballerina, a teacher, and a choreographer, Marina was a poet and an avid reader.

What Constitutes an Effective Studio Parent?

Mothers are not always objective, and in the dance world particularly, there are many examples of the overprotective and overambitious mothers. In almost all cases, they hinder more than they help. The moment you become a studio mother, you may become prone to exhibiting characteristics of what is known as a stage mama. Mothers often believe that their child is not being given enough attention in ballet class. Oh, and when it comes to casting, their child is being ignominiously overlooked. "This year, it is my daughter's turn to be cast as the Dew Drop Fairy. After all, she was stuck with being only a Mirliton last year!" Or, "My son was the Nutcracker Prince for several years. Isn't it time for him to assume a more grown-up role?"

Fathers can even be worse. Often, they are convinced that their daughter is a rare find and an extraordinary talent. When the father accompanies his daughter to a college visit, for example, the father raves about his daughter's unique abilities. After all, "She even dances on pointe!"

Marina Svetlova with student, courtesy of the Indiana University Archives

Bill Como, a highly respected dance critic who wrote extensively for the *New York Times,* wrote an article about the Svetlova Dance Center and dubbed it "Only the Best." He opined that Dorset, Vermont, is a small but precious jewel mounted in a glorious setting. This tiny and old New England town is snuggled down in a valley surrounded by the famous Green Mountains. In recent years, he acknowledged that the dimensions of this town expanded as it grew as a haven for artists of every kind. He pointed out that for six years, Marina directed her own summer ballet school at the Southern Vermont Arts Center. Customarily, at the end of each season, she staged a full-length classical ballet, bringing in famed stars to dance with her students. Marina made it clear that hers was a dance center and not a camp. She insisted that she was determined to keep the center small enough to give each girl a great deal of personal attention.

The ratio of teachers to students is very high. Dancing every day means that the girls must have fine food to keep up their energy. In every respect I'm following Anton Dolin's advice. "You must give them the best, Ducky …' He's right, but the *best* is always more expensive than the average.[2]

Dolin occasionally comes all the way from Monte Carlo to lecture and give guest classes at Svetlova's Dance center. It's part of my program of providing the best. I'll have several visiting lectures and choreographers, too. One member of the local artistic community is the famed pianist, Claudio Arrau. He occasionally teaches Music classes at the Svetlova Dance Center. Art Appreciation classes are offered by artists Luigi Rucioni and dean Fausett.

I also met another well-known dance critic, Clive Barnes, who had come to Dorset at Marina's bidding. He gave an inspiring overview of dance in America, claiming that it had become the hub of the world's dance community. This is another example of the variety of offerings Marina worked at providing for her students.

Weekly visits were planned to museums, concerts at Tanglewood and Marlboro, and the various summer theaters close by. Marina believed that one of the wonderful things about New England in the summer was that there were multiple major artistic institutions scattered throughout the vicinity. Not far from the Svetlova Dance Center, for example, was Jacob's Pillow dance oasis and the Williamstown art museum.

In addition to dance training, the center offered tutoring in French, Russian, Spanish, and other academic subjects. Ballet, modern, jazz, flamenco, and ballroom were all taught. Marina wanted her girls to acquire grace, poise, self-assurance, and an appreciation of all the arts. It would enrich their whole lives, whether or not they continued to dance.

Bill Como from *Dance Magazine* asserted that if anyone had the self-assurance to run a center of this kind, and with poise to spare, it was this tiny, graceful woman who was for seven ears the prima ballerina of the Metropolitan Opera.

Nothing, nothing in the world … has ever been as exciting as teaching young girls. All artists want immortality and my idea of immortality is not just having my name in some dance books and in "Who's Who," It's passing on what I have learned to others, some of whom will pass it on to others later. That's rewarding![3]

In 1959, *Dance Magazine* announced an exciting development in the curriculum of the Southern Vermont Art Center. Located in Manchester, Vermont, the Southern Vermont Art Center had been offering a sophisticated program of study in music, drama, and visual arts since 1950. The art center was a nonprofit institution that had as a mission the bringing together of graphic arts and the various forms of the theatre and concert stage in southern Vermont. Proof of the fact that the center had been able to accomplish its initial goals was its plans to incorporate a school of ballet into its already productive program. A unique addition to the art center's already prestigious catalogue of class offerings came with the addition of the study of ballet. Marina Svetlova was invited to become the director of the school of ballet and taught intermediate, advanced, and professional classes. Of special interest is that students of promise were featured with Miss Svetlova's concert group in performances of *Les Sylphides* and excerpts from *Swan Lake*.

Vermont Life

An edition of *Vermont Life* offered its own take on the Svetlova Dance Center. It reported that Marina's students learned the rewards of discipline and hard work and had fun at her Dorset ballet school. Approximately eighty girls each summer visit her school, where they swap shorts for leotards and abandon more carefree pursuits for the disciplined life of ballet dancers. Girls between the ages of eight and eighteen from all over the country, from as far away as California, Kansas.

One might say however, that teaching is this tiny dancer's first love, but Svetlova directs her dance school like a tightly-run ship. Each student is given her personal attention … Classroom work, of necessity, is all business.[4]

The roster of dancers and musicians at the Svetlova Dance Center varied from summer to summer. Some of the professionals Marina engaged one summer included the following:

Ballet

- Nathalie Krassovska, former leading ballerina with many leading ballet companies, including London's Festival Ballet, Massine's Ballet Russe de Monte Carlo, and Ballet Theatre
- Denise Warner, former dancer and assistant ballet mistress, American Ballet Theatre; ballet mistress, Minnesota Dance Theatre
- Nancy Dow, Smith College; The Walden School
- Zina Hoppenstand, former dancer, Warsaw Ballet; teacher, the Neubert School at Carnegie Hall
- Chantal Brenot-Linval, former Paris Opera; Academie de Danse Classique, Paris, France
- Edmond Linval, former Paris Opera Ballet; president de la Federation National de la Danse Educative et Professionelle
- Frank Ohman, former soloist, NYC Ballet Company; owns own school in Long Island
- Alexis Rassine, former leading dancer with the Royal Ballet London, England

Modern Dance

- Nathan Montoya, Graham technique
- Annette Montoya, Graham technique
- Jessica Sayre, leading dancer in Alwin Nickolas Company

Jazz

- Georgia Deane, Academie in Mendon, Massachusetts, formerly president of the Boston Teacher's Association
- Kim Duddy, Luigi School, NYC
- Jeff Hendrix, Luigi School, NYC
- John Schenz, Cincinnati, Ohio

Spanish

- Jose Barrera, Spain's Escudero Company, Svetlova Dance Ensemble

Character Dance

- Andrew Buleza, former leading dancer, Tambouritzen Company

Piano Accompanists

- Michael Limoli, accompanist for American Ballet Theatre, Pacific Northwest Ballet Company, Cincinnati Ballet Company, Cleveland/San Jose Ballet Company, Ballet Hispanico Company,

Nevada Dance Theatre Company, NY School of Ballet, Joffrey School (American Dance Center), New York School of Ballet, David Howard Studio, Youskevitch School of Ballet, Ballet Arts school

- Stella Walstein, distinguished Russian ballet pianist, trained in Russia as a ballet accompanist

At the Svetlova Dance Center, I had the honor of making the acquaintance of Nathalie Krassovska, one of the prominent stars of the ballet world. She was a star of the Ballet Russe and London's Festival Ballet. She was born in Petrograd, Russia, on June 1, 1918. At her birth, she was given her father's family name, Leslie, and she became Natasha Leslie. She began her career using the name Leslie and resumed using that name toward the end of her career. She is one of the four ballerinas, along with Alicia Markova, Alexandra Danilova, and Mia Slavenska, in the famous early Ballet Russe photo of *Pas de Quartre.* She made her official stage debut in 1932 with the Theatre de Dance. This company was still in its infancy and was formed by Bronslava Nijinska, the sister of the widely accomplished and acclaimed dancer Vaslav Nijinsky. In 1933, Krassovska continued her rise to stardom when George Balanchine invited her to join his new company, Les Ballets 1933. In this company, she brushed shoulders with other famous ballerinas, the likes of Felia Doubrovska, and she was in the cast of some of Balanchine's early creations, another legacy that Svetlova and Krassovska have in common.

I worked as a pianist for each of these ballerinas. Svetlova had a more refined and natural sense of music. Krassovska effused more with the essence of the stereotypical classical ballerina. I never saw her without her hair in a ballerina bun, looking and behaving like a romantic ballerina. Krassovska and Svetlova were very good friends, and it was wonderful watching the interaction between two such successful artists. They spoke together in French and Russian and giggled together about incidences that had taken place in their lives, both personal and professional. Their respective careers had taken different paths, but they seemed to respect each other's choices and accomplishments.

I distinctly remember one moment that transpired during my professional association with Krassovska. She expressed to me a desire to travel from Dorset, Vermont, to have dinner with me in Saratoga Springs, New York. It was a drive of about one hour, and on the way to Saratoga, I witnessed one of the events that I will never forget. It demonstrated the unpretentious sort of kindness that even a truly great world-renowned ballerina could possess. It was fairly dark at night en route to Saratoga when Krassovska spotted a victim and became deeply distressed. She asked me if we might stop the car. She stated that she might wrap her shawl around the suffering animal. It was a spontaneous and generous reaction from this world star, and I was truly speechless and moved. At that time, I did not know Saratoga Springs at all, not realizing that I would one day become a resident. She directed me toward a restaurant that she remembered and called the Firehouse (now known as Forno Tuscano). We spent a delightful evening sharing each other's histories and adventures. She was not at all engrossed in her own stories and seemed genuinely pleased to hear about mine. She was excited to hear my stories about having accompanied classes for her former colleagues (e.g., George Zoritch and Sir Anton Dolin). She was somewhat astounded when I shared with her my professional interactions with Sir Anton Dolin, and she was amazed to learn that at one point in my life, I had been a performing ballet dancer. It was at that time that she confided in me, somewhat coyly and at the same time childlike, that her real name was Nathalie Leslie. She told me about a former marriage she had had with an Austrian diplomat. She made a point of informing me that she had been prima ballerina in the Ballet Russe, second only to Danilova.

Every summer, Svetlova bussed her students to Saratoga Springs so that they might attend a performance of the New York City Ballet, and at the end of the summer session, Marina had the girls at the Svetlova Dance Center participate in a talent show. At this event, the students presented original creations, most of which were hysterical comedy skits. This encouraged the students to make fast friends, many of whom became regulars at the dance center.

Beyond the Ballet Classroom
The Mother of a Ballet Student Advocates Broader Training for Young Dancers

One ballet mom asserted that, unlike at the Svetlova Dance Center, while training children for dancing, too often insufficient attention is given to mental development. Ballet teachers can suggest subjects and sources for reading and study, but the parents of youthful dance students are in a better position to encourage children to expand upon the technical ballet training they receive in the ballet studio. Dance students can be encouraged to learn more about the history of the dance and to keep up with current developments through reading dance magazines and newspaper reviews and notices. The mother went on to proclaim that much can be done along this line with results that are gratifying to mother, daughter, and teacher. As was the case at the Svetlova Dance Center, the knowledge her daughter had attained of the history of dancing led naturally to a keen nearest in the history of music, opera, painting, drama, and other fields.

Think what appreciative dance audiences this would make for the future. May I appeal to teachers all over the country, in towns, large and small, to encourage their students to read more, to start a dance library, and perhaps to organize parent-teacher groups to encourage the cooperation of mothers …[5]

If Your Daughter Wants to Be a Dancer

by Marina Svetlova

The very foundation of American philosophy of education for the last century has been the doctrine of generalization … In the Soviet Union, on the other hand, I found when I was coaching at the Kirov that in the performing arts, the opposite theory, early specialization prevails. From the very beginning, someone who wants to have a career as a dancer is permitted to concentrate on dancing. The emphasis was placed on the unique art form. Each approach could probably benefit from an assimilation of some of the other's method. In the United States, earlier and greater specialization in the performing arts could substantially improve the quality and number of American artists. On the other hand, a more conscientious effort at a wider range of education for Soviet artists would encourage intellectual diversity and create a climate which would allow for true freedom of thought and perhaps encourage the creation more inventive forms of choreography. More study of a variety of subjects might also lead to a less inhibited display of emotion in their performances.[6]

Marina Svetlova was definitely a class act.

CHAPTER 21

Honors

"First American Ballerina of the World Today"

Marina Svetlova: Popular Favorite
by Paul Rawlings

Marina Svetlova Honored in Boston

Prima ballerina Marina Svetlova received another honor on Tuesday evening when she was named International Ambassadress of the dance by the Dance Teachers Club of Boston. The award was presented to Miss Svetlova before a large and enthusiastic audience of professional dancers, teachers and guests. 'To Marina Svetlova, International Ambassadress of the Dance, whose grace and artistry have been an inspiration to ballet lovers.' In her acceptance, Miss Svetlova stressed the joy of teaching and the opportunity it gives her to inspire and guide new young talent … The choice of Miss Svetlova for the award was timely in light of her most recent triumph in Italy. Just two months ago the important Rome newspaper proclaimed her the 'first American ballerina of the world today.

A letter addressed to Marina Svetlova:

The Board of Trustees of the French Federation of the Dance have expressed the wish to award you with the title of *Docteur Honoris Causa.* This recognition is offered to only a very small number of distinguished professors that have contributed, thanks to their high competence and their devotion in favor of the Dance, toward the development and the improvement of the quality of this art in France. [2]

- honorary member: Arts & Letters Society, AGMA, Southern Vermont Art Center
- Marquis *Who's Who in the World*
- has been awarded the title of Doctor Honoris Causa from the board of trustees of the French Federation of the Dance through the minister of culture
- citation: Federation Internationale de Danse, Championnat de Monde de las Danse, Premiere Prix avec Medaille d'Or pour la danse pure Classique, 1931, 1932, 1933
- citation: Council of Performing Arts, Sydney, Australia, May 1941

- citation: certificate and gold medal presented by Prime Minister Jawaharlal Nehru in Delhi, September 15, 1953
- certificate and silver medal "in recognition of her extraordinary contribution to the artistic climate of this capital," Lima, Peru—June 20, 1946
- 1953 citation: testimonial and plaque presented by Princess Margaret Rose: "In gratitude to the great Prima Ballerina, Marina Svetlova, for honoring our London Festival Ballet during the coronation season ..."
- citation: Award of the International Festival of the Arts, Cook, Ireland, October 1, 1958
- citation: Honored Artist of the Teatro Colon, Buenos Aires, July 4, 1962
- citation: gold medal and *diplome*, Maestros de Baile de Puerto Rico, "with gratitude for her Master Classes whose benefits will continue ..."
- citation: Dance Masters of America
- "International Ambassadress of Dance whose grace and artistry have been an inspiration to Ballet lovers," June 1962
- beginning in 1959, taught master classes for Dance Masters of America and Dance Educators of America
- designed curricula for dance schools throughout America.
- national chairman of dance for National Arts and Letters Society, 1980–1982

Dance Magazine usually prints a calendar for the coming year:

All New 1946 Calendars

The 1946 All-Ballet Calendar features famous ballet duos in glamorous action photos. A collector's item for yourself, an appropriate gift for your ballet-loving friends ...

The ballet duos represented are Alicia Alonso with Kriza, Muriel Bentley with Leonid Massine, Ruthanna Boris with Leon Danielian, Alexandra Danilova with Frederick Franklin, Nana Gollner with Paul Petroff, Rosella Hightower with Andre Eglevsky, Nora Kaye with Hugh Lang, Nathalie Krassovska with George Zorich, Marie-Jeanne with William Dollar, Alicia Markova with Anton Dolin, Janet Reed with Jerome Robbins, and Marina Svetlova with Alexis Dolinoff.

Every one of the dancers included with Marina in this calendar is a major, international star of the ballet world. One critic summed Marina's accomplishments up by asserting that she has a big name, an enviable reputation built up through many years in which she has unfailingly given the public unadulterated beauty combined with superlative showmanship.

Another example of the stature to which Marina had risen is exemplified by the following statement. It also demonstrates an awareness of her position in the Ballet Russe phenomenon. Her presence was duly acknowledged.

Along with having enjoyed many years as a guest artist through performances around the world, Marina was also skillful at arranging performances where she would be the producer arranging for guest appearances by other luminaries in the dance world.

John F. Kennedy

An example of Madame Svetlova's skill at producing performances and her sense of personal generosity was made evident when she organized and produced a tribute in dance to President John F. Kennedy. She was quoted In *Vermont Life* as having said that of all the dancing, directing, producing, and choreography she had done in her life, nothing moved her more than the *Tribute in Dance to President John F. Kennedy,* which she organized on the anniversary of his death.

Knowing his passion for excellence, she capitalized on her extensive contacts throughout the dance world and called on the best dancers from all over the world: Melissa Hayden, Jacques d'Amboise, and Maria Tallchief from New York, Carla Fracci from Milan, Yvette Chauvire from the Paris Opera, Antonio Gades from Spain, Nadia Nerina from the Royal Ballet, and Carmen de Lavellade. At the invitation of Madame Svetlova, they all came to pay homage to Mr. Kennedy. Marina stated that nothing written about her in *Who's Who in America* has meant more to her or made her more proud of her colleagues and of the entire ballet world.

CHAPTER 22

Madame Professor

Dancers need a good education in order to meet society on its own level.[1]

The future of adult education in dance rests in the inclination and dedication of institutions of higher education. Colleges and universities must recognize that dance should not be considered part of the athletic or physical education. The existence of college dance has done more harm than good to the development and promotion of performance dance. However, dance as a scholarly and scientific discipline has become a viable and valuable course of study. Of course, governmental assistance would help in the development and promotion of each of these programs.

A wise and informed national leader might, within a decade, transform the very spirit of a people through the medium of dance ...[2]

Madame Svetlova was approached by the *New York Times* to express her opinion about dance in the college setting. When she wrote the following article, she had recently begun teaching at Indiana University, Bloomington. She found that a young dancer of college age who has sufficient talent and ability is tempted to join a professional company. However, she wrote:

The dancer's career is short enough anyway—but there are, I believe, also arguments to consider going to college first. The primary one is that a dancer is a human being as well as an artist and will presumably want, during the balance of his life, to understand more of the world than pirouettes and pas de deux.[3]

Are Dancers Dumb?

Frequently, it is thought and verbalized that dancers are dumb. Generally, it is believed that they educate their bodies and not their minds. They may be regarded as such because they find it difficult to express their ideas fluently through speech or the written word. Nevertheless, a dancer's method of expressing feelings and ideas usually becomes apparent through their dancing, which is their most practiced medium of expression. Most professionals in any endeavor subscribe to the notion that learning by doing is often the best means of educating one's self. This the dancer often accomplishes through extensive travel. Just because a dancer is not a brilliant historian or a famous scientist is no indication that he or she is dumb.

No dancer is dumb … if she is able by bodily motion to convey an emotion to her audience … It is safe to say that when a dancer communicates she is using her mind as well as her body in order to do so. [4]

Some people think dancers are dumb because they are show-offs and are consumed with physical appearance. A dancer who participates in the lifelong art of the theatre lives in a small world of their own. Often, they forget that they are also living in an ordinary world. Some dancers are intelligent, some dull; some are quick, some slow. Some are as good at math as they are at *fouettes;* others may not be versatile.

All dancers aren't dumb, neither are they brilliant. Most dancers are just a bunch of hard-working people who use their feet as well as their heads in order to earn their living by dancing because it is the thing that they love best in the whole world. [5]

Some dancers are extremely dumb, some not-so dumb … There are plenty of stupid musicians, plumbers, painters, prize-fighters and sculptors around. As for the 'Irmas', the 'Miss Brooks' and 'Lucy,' beloved wife and mother, who could be dumber than they are—or better loved? … Dancers dumb? Like foxes! Like people! Like you and me![6]

Anthony Tudor Responds to the Question, "Are Dancers Dumb?"

In an interview with Anthony Tudor, dancer, choreographer par excellence, director of the Ballet Theatre and Metropolitan Opera Ballet School, teacher at the Juilliard School of music, Mr. Tudor was asked if dancers are dumb. He replied, "Of course not. In most cases, you will find dancers are usually smarter than other people with similar high school educations." It was his opinion that dancers manage to learn a great deal by reading and by conversation and that there are many opportunities during rehearsal and on trains and boats and airplanes to engage in such learning processes. He believed that one must distinguish between intelligence and intellect. The intellectual approach does not deal in the physical; therefore, it is not so important to a ballet dancer, but native intelligence is essential. However, the dancer who wants to choreograph a ballet suddenly finds that the intellect has become very important. In preparation for his ballet *Undertow,* Mr. Tudor had to read many books about psychiatry. As a final word, he added that a dancer must have imagination. "Imagination fosters curiosity which in turn fosters."[7]

Marina believed that the end of a dance performance career was "just the beginning of new joys." She felt that "life is the best school."

Part One: Exploration

When I arrived at Indiana University, Bloomington in 1966 as a music major, I was presented with the proposition of fulfilling my freshman year's physical education requirement by enrolling in Beginning Ballet. It was an intriguing consideration but not one that had previously crossed my mind. My knowledge of the ballet profession was quite limited at that time, but I quickly learned that ballerinas wore a bizarre thing called a tutu. Men wore something called a jerkin.

My first ballet classes took place in a strange studio in what might be considered the subbasement of the Indiana University School of Music. It seemed as if one were descending into a pit, the likes of which one might find in an Edgar Allen Poe tale. This descent issued into the loge of the Ballet Department, which consisted of one peculiar studio with a tiny room off to the side, which functioned as the office designate. The studio itself, although it boasted of a nice-looking wooden floor, was of a bizarre, small trapezoidal space. It had a mirror on one wall and a huge post right in the center of the studio. There were meagre dressing rooms that consisted of a few benches and lockers.

The first effort at improving upon the unfortunate space in the subbasement of the Music School was when an abandoned, rectangular, old dining hall space was appropriated for the expansion of the Ballet Department. It was somewhat of a distance from the Music School building (but the previous trapezoid-studio continued to be part of the ballet real estate). A fine ballet floor was installed in the abandoned dining hall studio, and the space acquired a sort of magic all to itself. The long studio, with a fairly high ceiling, was surrounded on three sides with windows, which were adorned by deciduous trees that gave the unlikely space a boost. Granted, it had the aura of a makeshift summer camp building, but this novel studio space was like moving into Valhalla after having dwelt in Albrecht's subterranean pitstop.

Undoubtedly owing to the fact that I was a male recruit, I was offered an automatic A in the ballet technique class, should I choose to participate in a ballet partnering class. I really had no idea what that would entail, but curiosity got the better of me. Upon arrival in the ballet studio for the first pas de deux class, I became intoxicated by the girls who had just returned to school that fall after having spent the summer enjoying the rays. Their suntanned bodies were in stark contrast to the various shades of brightly colored leotards. (Looking back, I don't remember a single black leotard.) I was bowled over, watching them as they engaged in what seemed to me to be superhuman feats of bending and stretching, which included placing one foot on the ground and the other in the opposite corner of the overhead doorjamb. Who ever heard of such a thing? And the beat goes on … It quickly became apparent to me that these warm-up antics were part of a natural and oft-repeated ritual. These Therpsichorean goddesses were found calmly sliding down into splits, which seemed to me a feat limited to only the most gifted rubber persons. These miraculous humanoids were even bending in several directions while maintaining that curious position on the floor. I had never seen the likes of this, and it seemed like some sort of otherworldly gathering of celestial spirits. I became intoxicated.

Like most beginning male dancers, I became infatuated with my first ballet teacher. Not surprisingly, she had been one of those exotic creatures who had displayed some of the superhuman physical feats while warming up in the pas de deux class I had recently attended. She was a petite, exquisitely put together female specimen who had danced professionally and who continued her career in ballet by performing with the Indiana University Ballet Theatre dance ensemble, while getting a degree in psychology after returning from New York City. Eventually I was blessed with the opportunity to perform with her in certain ballet and opera productions.

After a few months of sporadic ballet classes, I was invited to perform in the university's annual *Nutcracker* presentation. I was dumbstruck and found it an honor to appear in performances with the beautiful, fabulous Danish ballerina Toni Lander and her virile American cavalier, Bruce Marks. (Little did I know that the following year I would find myself in the orchestral pit, performing the principal clarinet part in the *Nutcracker* orchestra.) Later during that first year of college, I found myself dancing a solo part in Smetana's opera, *The Bartered Bride*. Apparently, I was considered a balletic "find" and was encouraged to continue dancing. When it was later discovered that I was an accomplished pianist, I was soon invited to accompany ballet classes in which I was not dancing.

While still only a novice dancer, I became keenly interested in everything balletic. My fascination with ballet increased when I saw my first professional ballet performance, the Royal Ballet performing Fokine's *Les Sylphides*—breathtaking! Next, I saw Antoinette Sibley and Anthony Dowell perform *Swan Lake*, and I was enthralled. Then I saw Fonteyn with Nureyev, and there was no turning back!

I would secretly, late in the night, take my tiny portable record player into an empty studio and revel in the music and in the excitement of practicing the movement I had learned that day in class. I had a favorite ballet class recording with which I was delighted. The pianist was Gladys Celeste. Much to my surprise and delight, a few years later, our careers converged, and we became good friends. She joked with me and declared that my profession was that of a clarinetist/dancer/pianist, and occasionally we shared pianist duties for the same ballet companies and ballet schools. Of course, my clarinet teachers were appalled that I was being enticed into dividing my time between ballet and clarinet (and piano?). Conversely, my ballet pedagogues were always insisting on additional evening rehearsals, although they acknowledged that they were forcing me to steal time from my clarinet. These various activities in the arts culminated in the inevitable conflict of interest. At one point, I found myself scheduled to be in Philharmonic Orchestral rehearsal, band rehearsal, and a ballet rehearsal for a performance in which I was cast in various solo roles. I finally went to the dean and said to him, "Now what?" Needless to say, I chose to go to the ballet rehearsal. After four years at Indiana University, I managed to earn separate degrees, one in music and the other in ballet. Upon the completion of my master's degree, I was off to the races.

I was soon invited to become a private student by the esteemed ballet pedagogue Edward Caton. I later learned that he had also been one of Madame's main teachers in the US, and this realization prompted me to wonder just how much I had in common with her. Eventually, Caton sent me off to the Harkness Ballet in New York City, where I was offered a contract to become a Harkness Ballet trainee. A year later, I found myself in Salzburg, Austria, where I was dancing with the *Salzburger Ballett*, while seeking an orchestral clarinet post in various European orchestras. (I began to remember the movie *The Three Faces of Eve,* in which Joanne Woodward portrayed a schizophrenic woman with multiple personalities.)

Svetlova and Dolin: Indiana and Vermont

During the 1971–72 season at Indiana University School of Music, full-scale productions include *Les Noces, l'Histoire du Soldat, Nutcracker* and *Giselle.* The university's ballet department, under the direction of chairman Marina Svetlova, offers a Bachelor and Master of Science in Ballet, in order to prepare students for careers in ballet as dancers, teachers, choreographers, and historians. The faculty includes Marina Svetlova, Anton Dolin, John Kriza, Kenneth Melville, Jurgens Pagels. Anton Dolin, co-chairman of Indiana's ballet department taught students in a master class at the Svetlova Summer Dance Camp at Dorset, Vermont, concluding the season in a performance of *Coppelius* in which Svetlova danced Swanilda and Dolin danced Dr. Coppelius.[8]

Sir Anton Dolin and Marina Svetlova.
Photo: William G. Sargent
in the Indiana University Archives.

For some students—myself, having been there, done that—the first obstacle is to realize that putting ballet into the college setting is analogous to attempting to put a square into a round hole. It's a great notion but one that is not easily implemented. The first consideration is the distribution of time and the delegation of responsibilities. The second one is scheduling. Marina was enormously sympathetic to all of these considerations. I watched her bend over backward to helps students finalize their schedules and find ways in which they could reserve sufficient time to engage in ballet rehearsal. At times, to fit performances into their complicated lives was a gargantuan task. Marina was not anti-academia, nor was she antiestablishment, but she was very much pro-student. She wielded her power and knack for persuasion to encourage the administration of the university at times to bend their policies and to accommodate the unique complications presented by life in the arts in the university setting—emphasizing the extraordinary rigors presented in the pursuit of excellence in the world of ballet. She referred to herself as "the mother superior" of the IU Ballet Department. I was a ballet student in the Indiana University School of Music from the very beginning of the Svetlova takeover and throughout most of its duration.

Part Two: Discovery

After a few years in the ballet world, I was intensely interested in the history of formal training in ballet. Sometime after her arrival in Bloomington, I learned that Madame Svetlova had been a student in Paris during the time in which pedagogy was being offered by the renowned former dancers from the Russian Imperial Ballet. Svetlova had been described as having been trained by "a galaxy of outstanding ballet teachers in Paris." [9]

After coming across this statement describing Madame Svetlova's early training in ballet, I became further intrigued. Owing to her sharp brain and enviable memory, I suspected that Marina would be capable of supplying me with keen details surrounding the various training techniques and unique personalities of the ballet teachers who had immigrated to France in the early part of the twentieth century. I was expecting to hear anecdotes concerning the hallowed trinity about whom I had already heard, those being Olga Preobrajenska, Mathilde Kchessinska, and Lubov Egorova. It was through Marina that I learned of Vera Trefilova, another Russian Imperial ballerina who had settled on Paris but whose name was often omitted from mention when discussing the list of renowned Russian ballet pedagogues who had settled in Paris around the time of the Russian revolution of 1917.

Eventually, I learned that there were more than these former ballerinas from the Russian Imperial Ballet tradition who had become renowned teachers in Paris. There were also male teachers, such as Gorsky and Vilsak, both of whom had been Madame Svetlova's teachers.

A few years later, while I was a staff ballet pianist at the North Carolina School of the Arts, I stumbled upon a book entitled *The American Ballet,* written by the esteemed dance historian Olga Maynard. Not only did I find it to be an interesting and comprehensive volume about dance in America, but it contained a beautiful full-page photo of Madame Svetlova—one of only a handful of such photos in the book. That picture certainly caught my attention, and I was anxious to read the accompanying entry. Maynard's book had a significant impact on me.

Ted Shawn—generally regarded as the dean of American dance—wrote about Maynard:

She has a trained and observant eye, a retentive mind, and scrupulous impartiality ... she gives us the results with unique insight into the artistic values of our dance theatre ...[10]

Shawn goes on to describe Maynard as a major talent in the constellation of dance journalists. He endorses the book, hoping that it will stimulate a greater understanding of dance, which he identifies as "the oldest and noblest and most cogent of the arts."[11]

This description of Olga Maynard illustrates how the conclusions she shares about the professional life of Madame Svetlova are based on thoughts and observations that emanate from the eyes and mind of a knowledgeable professional. In the world of dance, one couldn't wish for a more powerful recommendation and validation than that coming from the pen of Ted Shawn.

In her acknowledgments at the beginning of her book, Olga Maynard points to some of the other established and revered dance writers who helped catapult her into the major league of dance scholars. There is an oft-repeated phrase, "the ballet world is a small world," implying that it is probably no coincidence that each of the dance persons referenced at the outset of Maynard's volume, at some time or other, had written articles about Marina during her long and elective career in dance.

For example, Maynard specifically credits William Como, who was a leading dance critic during much of the twentieth century, as being the guiding force behind the creation and organization of her book.

He regularly wrote articles for *Dance Magazine* and the *New York Times.* For *Dance Magazine*, he wrote a long article that praised Marina's work as a teacher in her own ballet academy. The article presented a laudatory account of Madame Svetlova's pedagogical work, especially with young dancers. In his piece, he not only points out Svetlova's concern for quality dance training for her charges, but the article praises her organization skills as well. He also commends her great concern for providing a comprehensive artistic and cultural experience for her students at the Svetlova Dance Academy in Dorset, Vermont.

Maynard points to other dance experts, each of whom wrote articles about Marina. These writers include Ann Barzel, who wrote glowing reviews of Marina's work in *Dance Magazine.* Also referenced is Doris Herring, who in the book *25 Years of American Dance* makes mention of Marina's contribution to the world of opera ballet. This entry is accompanied by a flattering picture of Marina in *La Traviata.* Maynard also credits Edwin Denby, who describes extensively the work of Marina Svetlova in his book *Looking at the Dance.* Included in Maynard's list of dance journalists is P. W. Manchester, who compiled and edited *The Dance Encyclopedia,* in which is included a beautiful photo of Madame Svetlova in *Don Quixote.*

After reading the Maynard book, it seemed as though the lid had been lifted from a valuable treasure chest of remarkable and important knowledge. It seemed as though I was an archeologist who had suddenly stumbled upon a valuable treasure chest of remarkable and important knowledge. I was encouraged to do more research into the career of Madame Svetlova. Up until that point, I had only general knowledge about Svetlova's career, not much beyond the fact that she had been a member of the Metropolitan Opera Ballet. Since Indiana University School of Music was primarily an opera haven, the emphasis on Madame Svetlova's connection with the Met was only natural. Come to find out, she had previously been a member of the Original Ballet Russe. It was the Serge Diaghilev Ballets Russes with which most young dancers and the public at large were familiar. Diaghilev's ballet company had produced some international stars. Some knew the name Nijinsky, and many were familiar with the legend and the stature of the dancer Anna Pavlova, whose name had become nearly synonymous with the word "ballet." Like many, if not most, I had assumed that "Original Ballet Russe" referred to the first Ballet Russe, the astounding company headed by Serge Diaghilev. In researching the Diaghilev company, I found no mention of Marina, so I thought the Ballets Russes connection was a myth. I eventually learned that she had been an important artist in the legitimate company called the de Basil Original Ballet Russe, not the Diaghilev Ballets Russes. This realization constituted for me one of the largest components in the process of discovery.

Once I realized that the Ballet Russe quandary was due to a lack of knowledge on my part, as was the case with virtually all of my college ballet colleagues, I was amenable to giving Madame Svetlova a fair shake. There existed some problems beyond my ken, which she would generally be obliged to overcome before she would realize success in Bloomington.

Inherent Obstacles to Success with Ballet in Bloomington

Indiana University is a Big Ten university in America's Midwest. It achieved great fame from its spectacular championship basketball team and Bobby Knight. It also became famous as the hometown setting in the movie *Breaking Away.* This film accurately depicts a huge divide between the somewhat backwater mentality of the locals, as opposed to the pseudo-sophisticated academic community of the university. Yes, there truly was this geo-cultural dichotomy that existed. It was not make-believe material to become fodder for the movie and television reports. After Madame Svetlova assimilated into the university atmosphere in Bloomington, she made it a mission to embrace the locals and make ballet interesting to them. This was a tricky proposition because the rest of the student body at the university felt rather superior to the "stonies," so named because the city of Bloomington relied heavily upon an industry that capitalized on the natural limestone deposits found in the environs. The university students were not anxious to have their ballet performances "dumbed down."

Butler School

Another unfortunate situation that presented itself to Madame Svetlova as she assumed the chairmanship of the IU Ballet Department was the existence of the Butler University Ballet Department located in Indianapolis, Indiana—only a few miles from Bloomington. Until Marina's arrival in Bloomington, the Indiana University Ballet Department faculty and staff were aware of Butler's reputation for excellence in ballet and its close proximity to Bloomington but refused to acknowledge Butler's importance, relevance, and accomplishments. The Indiana University Ballet Department had always assumed that IU was superior, and they ignored the existence of Butler. After all, Butler had an impressive track record, having produced successful dance professionals, including the likes of Ian Horwath, who had a respectable career in American Ballet Theatre and went on to become associate director of the Cleveland Ballet Company, and Joan Kunsch, who directed the Burmingham Ballet Company, became a revered codirector of the Nutmeg Ballet, and became an internationally revered guest teacher. Another accomplished Butler graduate was Richard Camack, who went on to become a dancer in American Ballet Theatre. After retiring from performing, he moved to California, where he opened his own ballet school. Butler also boasted an outstanding faculty, which included Margaret Dorsey and George Verdak, a former dancer from the Massine Ballet Russe.

Butler became a formidable threat to Indiana University because Butler became the home of Indianapolis Ballet Theatre. When Marina arrived in Bloomington, rather than ignore Butler and the Indianapolis Ballet, Marina embraced the prospect of having a much-respected ballet school as a neighbor. She decided that it was more productive to recognize its existence and perhaps even enter into cooperative ventures.

War of the Worlds, Balletic Style

Once it was understood that Madame Svetlova was coming to take over the directing of the IU ballet program, which was already in a state of turmoil, curiosity about her career and academic certification became intense. The scuttlebutt was that yes, for whatever reason, this former ballerina from Texas had been invited to become a faculty member of the IU ballet program and, perhaps, its top administrator. This was very confusing because the students were under the impression that the prior year, Kent Stowell had been invited to become cochair with Gilbert Reed. Many students felt as though they owed an allegiance to Gilbert Reed. He had trained many of them and had composed many ballets for them. Several students had embraced the new teaching style of Kent Stowell and were excited about his involvement in the IU Ballet Department. With the appointment of Madame Svetlova, it seemed that now there were actually three chairpersons of the department.

Why Svetlova over Reed? Why Svetlova over Stowell?

Why another abrupt change in leadership and focus? Who was she, anyway? Needless to say, the transfer of power was truly chaotic. Here follows a thumbnail of the major players enveloped in the struggle for survival in the Indiana University School of Music, Ballet Department:

Gilbert Reed

Reed had been a member of the Denham Ballet Russe de Monte Carlo and then a dancer at the Metropolitan Opera. He was recognized as a gifted ballet teacher and was the official chairperson of the IU Ballet Department upon my arrival in Bloomington. He certainly was also an inspired choreographer. However, he was not a people person and made no bones about it. Academia was not his thing, although he had chaired the department for several years. His training was firmly ensconced in the Cecchetti syllabus, as had been presented to him by Margaret Craske. He continually created fascinating ballets directly in the Anthony Tudor psycho-melodramatic mold. More importantly, from a commercial point of view, he managed annually to present a beautiful *Nutcracker*, which was a highlight of the year—both for the university and the locals. He also made no bones about criticizing and mocking the NYC Ballet style. He frequently criticized the students with comments like "We don't want those New York City Ballet arms."

Nancy Reed

Nancy Reed was a rather accomplished dancer. She had realized a modest career in the Metropolitan Opera Ballet and could more than hold her own in her husband's ballets. She was not a particularly engaging ballerina, but she was a work horse and undertook any choreographic assignment as prescribed by her husband. She was in charge of the children's training program and had proven herself to be a successful teacher and director of the very young students. Her unequivocal gift, however, was that she was a highly accomplished costumer. She built truly magnificent tutus and other costumes as needed. She assembled some wonderful costumes for me in several of Gilbert's ballets. One of my ballerina partners often stated that she, as the Dew Drop Fairy, had a more beautiful tutu (built by Nancy Reed) than the Sugar Plum Fairy.

Mattlyn Gavers

Gavers had been a ballet mistress at the Metropolitan Opera from 1950 to 1965, where she also did some choreography. She taught in the dance program at Juilliard School and was assistant director at the Vienna State Opera. She was a visiting faculty in the Dance Department at Indiana University, Bloomington.

Kent Stowell

Kent had been a major dancer with the New York City Ballet Company. He arrived at Indiana University as an exponent of a type of ballet dancing that was anathema to the Cecchetti method in which we had all been raised as ballet students at Indiana University under Gilbert Reed and his disciples. Although foreign to me at the start and very challenging, I eventually found it to be a highly liberating way of approaching dance. He took me under his wing and brought me to New York, where I was permitted to take classes taught by Stanley Williams. For Kent, academia had been as much of a new prospect as it was to be for Marina. He had been trained out west by Lew Christiansen, a well-respected ballet teacher and ballet master from the San Francisco Ballet and Utah University. Kent, too, was a brilliant teacher, and his method was strongly influenced by his years of dancing in the New York City Ballet and the teaching of Stanley Williams at the School of American Ballet.

Francia Russell

Francia had also been a dancer in the New York City Ballet Company. She was brilliant at everything having to do with ballet. Although she had been a part-time college student at Fordham University while she was in New York, dancing in the New York City Ballet, when she came to Indiana University to take over the directorship of the children's training program, she was the proverbial fish out of water. The children's program had been directed by Nancy Reed, the wife of Gilbert Reed. Francia was still a ballet mistress for NYC Ballet and at times needed to be in New York.

Marina Svetlova

One of the highlights in Marina's résumé was that she had been a baby ballerina with the de Basil Original Ballet Russe and prima ballerina of the Metropolitan Opera of New York City. That is about all the information that had been provided to the ballet students at Indiana University. Owing to the fact that the music faculty of the Indiana University School of Music consisted of many former singers and conductors from the Metropolitan Opera, Madame Svetlova's appointment to the ballet faculty at the IU School of Music seemed like a natural. It was anticipated that Marina would bring a significant amount of international experience and had been brought in to right the ship.

Here are some of Marina's colleagues from the Met who also joined the faculty of the Indiana University School of Music:

Zinka Milanov

Milanov was one of the foremost divas of the Metropolitan Opera. On February 2, 1944, Milanov sang the title role in Giuseppe Verdi's *Aida*. On that occasion, Marina danced in the ballet.

Margaret Harshaw

Harshaw was another major star at the Met, having started out as a mezzo soprano, eventually becoming a successful soprano. Along with sharing the stage with Harshaw in performances of several complete operas, Marina also danced at some of the traditional Metropolitan Opera galas in which Harshaw sang excerpts from various operas. These performances included the following:

- December 9, 1945: Harshaw sang "Voce di Donna"; Marina danced in the Hindu Dances from *Lakme* by Leo Delibes
- December 9, 1945: voce di donna; Marina presented the solo in "Dance of the Hours" from *la Gioconda,* by Giordano.
- December 10, 1944: Harshaw sang "Condotta Ell'era in Ceppi" from Verdi's *Il Trovatore*; Marina performed the dances from *Aida*, *Lakme*, and repeated "Dance of the Hours"
- December 21, 1945: Favorita

Charles Kullman

Charles Kullman had enjoyed a stellar career with the Metropolitan as one of its leading tenors. He and Marina performed together in complete opera performances as well as on opera gala performances.

On January 13, 1946, two Indiana University School of Music faculty singers performed on the same show. Charles Kullman sang "Il mi Tesoro" from Mozart's *The Magic Flute;* Margaret Harshaw sang "O Mio Fernando" from Donizetti's *La Favorita*.

Martha Lipton

Lipton was one of the Met's foremost mezzo soprano stars. She performed frequently with Marina during several opera galas.

On the gala of January 21, 1945, Lipton sang arias from Donizetti's *La Favorita, Faust*; Marina performed dances from George Bizet's *Carmen*.

On January 6, 1946, Lipton performed "Lakme," Viens Milika from *Lakme*; Marina presented her solo in "Dance of the Hours" from *La Gioconda* and the dance of the veil from *Bayadere*.

Tibor Kozma

Conductor at the Metropolitan Opera from 1948 to 1957. Conducted operas starring several IU voice teachers, including Zinka Milanov, Margaret Harshaw, and Martha Lipton.

A stroke of genius on the part of Svetlova was that she had arranged for the ballet tuition income to stay in the coffers of the School of Music rather than being added to the university funds. This was a coup that certainly further ingratiated her to the dean of the School of Music and was a tribute to her prowess as negotiator/organizer/producer/promoter. Previously, all the tuition from ballet classes went into the University General Fund.

Thoughts about Being a Dancer or Choreographer

My good friend Sir Anton Dolin was asked if he was more interested in dancing than in choreography.

Dolin replied, "I am interested in both." He went on to say that he loves to dance, but he also enjoys producing classical ballets and recreating old ballets. When the opportunity to choreograph arises, he can't resist it. Dolin cautions that it is difficult for a dancer to choreograph, rehearse a ballet all day, and then dance at night. A classical dancer is obliged to conserve energy for performances, or it isn't fair to the audience or to the ballerina who is your partner. Dolin went on to cite a few examples of his favorite ballet productions:

He felt that *Noces* as choreographed by Nyjinska is one of the finest things one can see anywhere. And if I could think of higher praise, I would write it. He went on to praise the choreographic genius he saw displayed in the creations of Marius Petipa. He claimed that in *Sleeping Beauty* of Petipa, the solo dances performed by the Good Fairies in the middle of the ballet were a lovely string of solos that reflected the light evocation of the natural graces of nature one hears in the Tchaikovsky score. Also, the Rose Adagio, danced by Princess Aurora and her cavaliers, has a story of its own, which gives its formal bravura an amiable overtone. Dolin felt that it is proof of Petipa's great power as a choreographer that even out of their context in the full-length ballet, in Petipa's dances we can see created a wonderful spell.

College Choreography

Apart from teaching ballet classes to the ballet students at Indiana University, the faculty was expected to create original ballets and devise choreography for use in the opera productions. The divergent approaches to composing choreography displayed by Reed, Stowell, and Svetlova produced another parameter that could be used to differentiate among the relative merits and weaknesses exhibited by the major players in the IU Ballet Department debacle. Quite simply put:

Gilbert Reed came to rehearsal with a libretto.
Kent Stowell came to rehearsal with a music score.
Marina came to rehearsal with classical tradition, a legacy.

Gilbert Reed was a gifted choreographer in the Anthony Tudor tradition. Most of his ballets were conceived around one or more intense emotional conceits. Reed came into the studio with a psychological/emotionally wrought scenario in his mind that was to be acted/danced out through his choreographic plan. The choreography of Agnes de Mille also had a great influence on Reed's work. One of Reed's ballets of which I was quite fond and in which I danced one of the principal roles was entitled *My Sister*. It was the story about a woman who was jealous that her sister was having a baby. The first had thrown her own concerns about having a child on her sister. Come to find out that it was she herself, not her sister, who was having a baby.

Kent Stowell, who had enjoyed considerable success as a leading dancer with the New York City Ballet, produced some choreography for the Indiana University Opera Theatre. However, it was in the creation of choreography for original ballets that his talents were most evident. I was fortunate to have had a leading role in a ballet that was set on me and others by Stowell called *Out of the Blue*, which was his crowning achievement at Indiana University. As a demonstration of his devotion to his guru, George Balanchine, Stowell came into the studio with a music score. In some ways, his analytic approach to creating an abstract work seemed a bit cerebral, but the result was spectacular.

Marina came into the studio with tradition and a legacy. She had actually lived the ballet history of the first half of the twentieth century, beginning with her rehearsals and performances with Ida Rubinstein's company and de Basil's Original Ballet Russe Ballet. This accumulation of ballet history continued through her years with the ballet of the Metropolitan Opera. It was Marina who brought Dolin to Indiana University. When addressing the issue of a balletic legacy, one could hardly outdo Anton Dolin. He actually did some original choreography in Bloomington, including a ballet named *Defile vers la Danse,* in which I performed the principal role. He also set his *Pas de Quatre* on the students and set and coached me in the solo male role in *Les Sylphides.* It was no coincidence that Madame Svetlova had performed every role in Dolin's *Pas de Quatre* and had received considerable acclaim for her performances in *Les Sylphides.*

This author with an I. U. ballerina
in performance of *Les Sylphides.*
Photo: Richard Pflum.

Although I had officially stopped dancing, Marina invited me to perform in *Les Sylphides.* I agreed to do the role but was secretly panicking because I knew I was not in top shape, especially for such a demanding role. During vacation days, when the school buildings were open but the ballet studios were locked, I found myself slipping into the Music School building, turning a stairway railing into a barre, and giving myself a barre in secret. (How many dancers have not done plies or battements tendus on the subway on the way to class or standing in Barnes and Noble, secretly squeezing in some ballet warm-up steps?) I remember years later, when discussing the demanding *Sylphides* role with Frank Augustyn, the marvelous star of the Royal Canadian Ballet, he opined, "And all those soft plies!"

While in Bloomington, Madame Svetlova supervised a large number of productions. Some of the ballets included *Autumn Leaves, Pas de Quatre, Jazz Concerto, Coppelia, Saloma, l'Histoire du Soldat, Moods, Nutcracker, Les Sylphides, Concertette, Faust, Don Giovani, Giselle, Impressions, As Vengeance Strikes, Graduation Ball, Carmen, Story of Judith, Firebird, Be Jubilant My Feet, Faerie Queen*, and *Sangre Negra*. She also provided the choreography for operas such as *Dr. Faust, Eugene Onegin, Romeo and Juliet*, and *Rigoletto*.

After Madame Svetlova had been in Bloomington a couple of years, one of the longstanding scenic designers (Mario Cristini) said to me that he was delighted that she had come to Bloomington (where there was also a Modern Dance Department in the Physical Education Department). He was thrilled that Madame had brought some classical white ballets to Bloomington so that we no longer were obliged to watch dancers constantly rolling around on the floor in darkness. It sounds like an oxymoron, but Madame Svetlova had brought something new to the Indiana University Ballet by bringing in something old.

The Svetlova Era Had Begun

I don't believe that initially any of the students were aware that Madame Svetlova was bringing her own selection/collection of teachers along with her. They were all men, and Madame Svetlova referred to them collectively as her gestapo. Having had very little experience as a ballet dancer, I had little awareness of the international stature and enormous prestige most of these men had achieved in the dance world.

Faculty: "Gestapo"
Sir Anton Dolin

To begin with, Madame Svetlova promised to bring Sir Anton Dolin to Bloomington to be the cochairman. It was rumored that she had been offered the job because she promised that she would bring Dolin with her.

When it comes to Dolin, where does one begin? Dolin exerted an enormous influence in the development and promotion of the career of Madame Svetlova. He was Irish by birth, and his given name was Patrick Healy. He enjoyed a career in terms of accomplishment, success, and longevity that was beyond the imagination of most mortals. He danced with Diaghilev's Ballets Russes, the de Basil Original Ballet Russe, the Massine Ballet Russe, London Festival Ballet, the Markova-Dolin Ballet, and the list goes on …

As a widely celebrated danceur noble, he had created leading male roles in many of the early masterpieces of the twentieth-century ballet repertoire, such as Nijinska's *Le Train Blue* and Fokine's *Les Sylphides*. He performed with every leading ballerina of his day, including Markova, Spessivtseva, Svetlova, and Krassovska. He also had partnered Marina Svetlova in her touring troupe before going on to found London's Festival Ballet, a company with which Marina Svetlova was also to perform as a guest artist.

He was invited to Bloomington, at the invitation of Maria Svetlova, to teach and be her cochairman of the Ballet Department. He taught ballet technique and pas de deux. I had the privilege of taking each of these classes with him. I also was piano accompanist for some of his classes. He coached me in some of his own roles, including that of the Poet in *Les Sylphides*. He also worked with me on my role of the North Wind in a Pavlova ballet, *Autumn Leaves*, which had been set by Madame Svetlova. Needless to say, owing to his international obligations, Dolin was in and out of Bloomington (more out than in).

John Kriza

Kriza was an extremely well-known and much-loved star dancer, especially with American Ballet Theatre. Although he occasionally appeared as premiere danceur in the classics, he was not everyone's idea of the dancer noble. He is remembered in the more classical role, especially for his balletic partnership with the petite Ruth Ann Koesen. He excelled in the more rugged roles, like one of the Sailors in Jerome Robbins's *Fancy Free*. He is best remembered for having been the epitome of the machismo lead role in Eugene Loring's *Billy the Kid*. At Indiana University, he was in and out as a ballet class teacher. Sometimes he taught Partnering class. His presence was sporadic, so one never knew when he would show up or when he would leave. The same was true with Dolin. Kriza occasionally coached students in performance roles. Although not one of his signature roles, he at least once coached me for my performance as the Poet in *Les Sylphides*. He was somewhat mischievous, and he always ended his ballet technique class by saying, "Okay, it's fancy dance time." He would proceed with the grand allegro combination and bring the class to a close. One of his more mischievous actions was that he once staged Jerome Robbins's famous ballet *Interplay* for all girls. Because that is not the original conception of Robbins's choreography, I once asked him about his alteration of the casting, which of course altered the idea of the ballet, resulting in his staging of Jerome Robbins's *Interplay*—a ballet that was one of his prize roles—for a complete cast of all women. When I confronted him about this alteration in the casting of the ballet, Kriza glibly responded with, "Oh, Jerry's such a nice guy. He won't care." Unfortunately, Kriza's presence in Bloomington was rather sporadic.

Kenneth Melville

Another new faculty member Marina brought to Indiana University was Kenneth Melville. His career included having been a principal dancer in London's Festival Ballet. He had also occasionally been Svetlova's partner—as had Dolin—in the Svetlova Ballet Ensemble. Although a bit shy, he carried himself with quite a regal gait. He had extremely supple feet, the envy of any ballerina. He once told me that when the other boys in the school of the Royal Ballet where he trained would show off their turn-out, he would simply point his foot, which would shut them right up. He had rather buck teeth, so one Halloween, a couple of the girls supplied all the students in one of his classes with those wax monster teeth. He also confided in me that at times Svetlova seemed ruthless in her classroom demure, especially during rehearsals, but he opined that she knew she was being a bit extreme, but she had to be, and that she knew she was being rather demanding, so one should overlook the abrasive manner.

205

Jurgen Pagels

The other member of the new Svetlova faculty Marina had assembled was Jurgen Pagels. There never lived a kinder and more generous man than Jurgen Pagels. He was the essence of humility. He was born in Lubock, West Germany, in 1925. I used to joke with him about his hometown being the birthplace of marzipan. He also studied with Preobrajenska in Paris, but his major claim was to have been a student of Legat. He was a dancer in various opera houses throughout Germany and had a great love for music as well as dance. I was so excited when, while accompanying his ballet class, I played an obscure piece from a German operetta. He came to the piano and was excited and thanked me for playing that piece. He knew the name of the piece and the operetta from which it came. I also remember once playing the Chopin Barcarolle, and he came to the piano and shared with me how it reminded him of his first ballerina, his first love. He, under the sponsorship of Dame Margot Fonteyn, appeared as guest artist and guest teacher in several countries around the world, especially in Western Europe. Under the sponsorship of Dame Margot Fonteyn, he taught extensively in South America. He was a dancer in the Metropolitan Opera and opened his own school in Dallas, Texas. His was particularly interesting and fun because of his love for and knowledge of character dance. He was fun because he could share his expertise with certain dances like the *krokriat* and the Schublaten.

There were other important ballet personalities Marina brought to the Indiana University School of Music Ballet Department. These artists came as guest faculty members.

Nicolas Beriosoff

Beriosoff was a particularly special guest in the Indiana University Ballet Department because he was still very active in the professional dance world. His specialty was staging Fokine ballets, especially lessor known works. He had staged *Firebird* for American Ballet Theatre, for example, but one of his projects at the time was to help the Joffrey Ballet become the holder of as many as possible of the old ballets he remembered, especially the Fokine works. When he first came to IU, I was the pianist for ballet technique classes he taught, and he came to consider me an outstanding piano accompanist. So, when he came to stage in the Pagodas, he insisted that I be his pianist. He was actually using the IU time for working the choreography back into his memory, but it was an honor for the students to have the opportunity to work with such a giant in the ballet world. Coincidentally, he was the father of the illustrious ballerina in London's Royal Ballet, Svetlana Beriosoff.

Dean Crane

He had been a circus performer for many years—a tumbler, an acrobat, a trapeze artist, and a bareback rider. Born in Logan, Iowa, he later danced in operas in Central City, Colorado. In NYC at Ballet Arts, he was a student of Edward Caton, Anthony Tudor, and others. He danced solo parts in several shows at Radio City Music Hall and appeared in many TV shows, industrials, and commercials. To add another dimension to his already varied résumé, he studied drama with Uta Hagen. He makes masks and designs theatrical jewelry and does some photography. He became a visible faculty member of the Ballet Arts Academy at Carnegie Hall.

Vladmir Oukatomsky

Oukatomsky enjoyed a successful career in ballet, mostly in Europe. He was perhaps most successful and recognized as a regular partner of Tamara Toumanova. He toured with her extensively. Owing to the fact that Toumonova never lost the allure of the baby ballerina identity, coupled with the fact that she enjoyed such visibility in Hollywood, Oukatomsky's position in the hierarchy of ballet personages was considerable. Madame Svetlova brought him to Bloomington especially to be her cavalier when she danced the Sugar Plum Fairy in one season's production of their annual performances of *The Nutcracker*. This man had been Toumonova's partner, and now he was Svetlova's.

Colin Russel

Colin Russel began his career in dance as a dancer with the Irish National Ballet. He eventually moved on to being a member of Canada's Winnipeg Ballet. After retiring from dancing, Russel became a ballet master for London's Sadler's Well Opera Ballet.

Victor Upshaw
Stroke of Genius

Madame Svetlova's decision in 1970 to bring Victor Upshaw as a visiting ballet faculty member was inspired. Up until that time, the ballet program at IU had little or no instruction in jazz dance. Here is a perfect example of Madame Svetlova's genius as director, as well as a demonstration of her genuine efforts to enhance the dance experience for the dancers in the IU Ballet Department. Upshaw directed his own company in Paris, where he was rather successful. He taught some classes in jazz and was featured at IU as a guest choreographer. He was a tall, slender African American and performed the leading male role in his new ballet. At that time, there was a particularly striking, tall, well-built blond girl in the Ballet Department—a perfect foil to Upshaw in appearance. He cast her to be his partner in a rather sensual pas de deux, which was choreographed to exist as the central focus in his ballet, and this it certainly achieved. Needless to say, the effect was breathtaking!

Dudley Davis

Davis came to IU as a cover for Dolin. I knew nothing about him. He was a friend of Dolin, who apparently had arranged for him to direct a ballet company in Iran. Subsequently, Dolin recommended him to be Dolin's substitute for a year of absence. I knew little or nothing about Davis, other than the fact that he taught an outstanding men's class in ballet.

The Building of an Empire

Shortly after Svetlova's arrival at IU, the Music School had its facilities renovated to include a performing arts center called the IUMAC. This building boasted a stage large enough to rival that of New York's Metropolitan Opera House at Lincoln Center. Marina oversaw the inclusion of a ballet wing, complete with extremely large ballet studios. At last, the Ballet Department was recognized as a force to be reckoned with. During the consecration week celebrating the first performances in the new music edifice, an entire evening was devoted to the presentation of a ballet gala.

This is the facet of her career I think Svetlova sensed as her ultimate accomplishment. This tenure represented the combination and culmination of the various Svetlova skills exhibited heretofore. In the Bloomington dance program, she was chairperson, organizer, developer, choreographer, and performer.

Little by little, Madame Svetlova called upon her organization skills and her experience with the implementation of plans and ideas. She certainly can be credited for reorganizing and revitalizing of the Indiana University Ballet Department. Much to the delight of the dean of the music school and the university at large, Madame Svetlova accomplished a large increase in ballet enrollment.

Marina Svetlova has been appointed tenured faculty at Indiana U-Bloomington. Since assuming leadership of the department in 1969, enrollment in dance courses has gone from 100 to 700. She continues to operate her summer dance center in Dorset.[12]

Marina was very appreciative of being invited to join the ballet faculty at Indiana University. She did not take the honor for granted and even discussed her surprise at the prospect. She contended that for a girl with no schooling after the age of seventeen and no college degree, it was quite amazing to find that only on the merits of an extensive performing career, she found herself being appointed the position of full professor at Indiana University. She later jokingly quipped that "that should give all people hope." After years at her job in Bloomington and listening over the years to all the problems of so many students, she began to refer to herself as the mother superior of the Ballet Department.

All Good Things Must Come to an End
Madame Chairman Steps Down

After many years as chairman of the IU Ballet Department, the tide began to turn. It could be said that Marina Svetlova was the most effective and successful chairman of the Ballet Department in the history of the Indiana University School of Music. Her accomplishments are legion. However, partially owing to sabbatical and professional leaves of absence, a crew of ambitious temporary substitutes began to hallucinate themselves into thinking that they should run the department. Especially when Svetlova was away, unrest among the students was initiated and even fueled by them. The students banded together and approached the dean of the school of music to convince him of their unhappiness with the ballet program. They pointed to Marina as the cause of their malcontent and worked to have Svetlova replaced. Notice how in the following quote, other directors of dance programs expressed the realizations to which they came while leading a group of dancers:

The Experience of a Young Choreographer in Working with a Group …
by Jo Taylor

(choreographer 1950,51, 52 Buck's Rock, New Milford, Ct., Director Jo Taylor Dance Company, So far, I have found no way to please everyone, or even the majority … I have tried my best to be fair. There have been times, however, that things have not worked out as I wished. Artists, especially young struggling ones, can become horribly emotionally upset.[13]

One of the biggest complaints was that they alleged was that Madame Svetlova played favorites, which resulted in unfair casting for the performance ballets. Anyone familiar with ballet schools and ballet companies understands that casting is always the cause of much resentment. Practically every dancer resents it when a role that they coveted has been assigned to someone else. It is the ballet human condition. This phenomenon occurs most especially with *Nutcracker* casting. Why *Nutcracker*? Because this ballet is so widely performed, in small schools, small companies, large schools, and large companies. Students come to experience the college dance experience, often with a weakness in training with which they themselves were not aware. Almost every dance student has danced in a local or regional presentation of *The Nutcracker*. They have their favorite role, their coveted roles, and the roles they had previously been promised or performed in their hometown organization. There is usually an unspoken hierarchy of roles in which a student expects to rise. For instance, if a young girl had performed as the Sugar Plum Fairy in her home school, she becomes quite resentful when she is assigned only the role of Dew Drop Fairy, for instance. Or if a student has already performed in a second act divertissement, the expectation is that the next step is that of a more featured soloist role. The student becomes resentful, occasionally extremely bitter. Apparently, one of the main sources of discontent with which the students were presented revolved around the casting of the Indiana University production of *The Nutcracker*.

Svetlova Resigns from Ballet Post

The Administration of the I. U. School of Music thought that the Chairman of the I. U. ballet department reacted as though the resignation of Madame Svetlova was totally unexpected. I. U. Music School Dean Charles Webb said that her resignation was not immediately accepted or rejected … Thursday's rehearsal of the 'Nutcracker Suite'—[]here again we revisit the *Nutcracker* casting debacle—was canceled after an emergency meeting between Webb, the Ballet faculty and the students. The meeting produced nothing but 'emotionally-based, personal attacks,' according to persons attending … Discontent with casting procedures … Svetlova has too much power in departmental matters … 'Madame controls everything around her—in my opinion she has control-itis. She couldn't stand to have anyone above her' … The ballet Department has no secretaries to handle departmental matters, forcing Madame Svetlova to be obliged to address all correspondence herself, including the applications sent to the office … She had been building the department. Since Svetlova came to head the department in 1969, the number of ballet majors increased from 11 to 48. At the point of her resignation, there were 382 ballet elective students as compared with 112 seven years ago. Marina Svetlova was also is the only faculty member of the school to be listed in the 1976 edition of *Who's Who in the World*." According to Anna Paskevska, visiting lecturer in Music, and Jurgen Pagels, associate professor of ballet, "the student outburst was unexpected and unfortunate. I was shocked by the whole thing. It was such an emotional meeting. It was not good for the department.' … there was no petition of grievances presented to the faculty or the Dean.[14]

It seemed as though students had not talked to Madame Svetlova about their unhappiness. Thus the problem was exacerbated by the lack of communication, and there was no record of earlier complaints.

Contrary to the reports that the ballet students at Indiana University, Bloomington, were unhappy with the directing of the Ballet Department, this student unrest was not an exclusive proposition. One example of support for Marina Svetlova, which stands in opposition to the reports of widespread animosity toward Svetlova, is evidenced by the realization that at least one student, Kathy Lee Morgan, funded the Marina Svetlova scholarships that were awarded to particularly gifted ballet students.

Svetlova's Resignation as Chairman Accepted

Svetlova asserted that one faculty member cannot 'undermine the respect for their teachers by brainwashing students into believing that one person's method of teaching dance is correct and that others are wrong … These issues of student discontent included casting complaints with the "Nutcracker Suite" ballet.[15]

Did I just hear reference to *Nutcracker* casting protocol? The casting of this ballet has probably caused more headaches in the ballet world than any other item.

Svetlova Steps Down

Marina Svetlova, chairperson of the IU Ballet department, suddenly resigned this year, shocking many persons … An explanation for her resignation, written by Svetlova, said, 'Because the climate of support (on the part of administrators, faculty and students) has, for the moment, disappeared[16]

Madame Svetlova and I had already discussed the prospect of me writing a book about her career and her teachers. Although she found the idea flattering, initially she was a bit reticent—almost shy about the recounting of her life story. I found that a bit unusual because most everyone with whom I had spoken, who had not been immediate professional colleagues, viewed her as a sort of prima donna rather than prima ballerina. This is an example of how she was actually a very shy person. She put on a good front, but she never portrayed herself in grandiose fashion, nor did she inflate her position in the dance. After we began collaborating on this book, she said one day said to me, with a devilish smile on her face and mischievous twinkle in her eye, "Let's wait until they're all dead, and then I will tell all." I was armed with an ever-increasing number of questions and a growing curiosity. I rather gingerly began searching for answers. While acting as the piano accompanist for her classes, she would occasionally find herself making a particularly noteworthy statement, and as an aside to me, she would whisper, "Write that down and put it in the book."

At the time of her retirement, Madame Svetlova wanted a short letter of appreciation, which I wrote to be read her retirement ceremony at Indiana University. Here are excerpts of that article:

As Marina Svetlova eases into retirement this Spring after twenty-two years as Professor of Ballet at Bloomington's world-famous School of Music, is ballet witnessing the passing of an era? … Svetlova's is a career with few. If any parallels in the annuls of Ballet History. Not only did she transform herself from one of the Paris Opera Ballet's "little rats" into one of the leading ballerinas of her day, but she went from the life of Russian immigrants to being named *Docteur Honoris Causa* by the *Board of Trustees of the French Federation of the Danse* … This writer knows Svetlova not only as a consummate artist and an inspiring colleague, but as a vivacious and fun-loving human being. She possesses an extremely engaging smile and is one of the most photogenic persons imaginable. She is well-loved not only by her 13-year old students who attend classes at the Svetlova Dance Center, but by Dance Majors and elective Adult Ballet students which she has graciously taught at the University. When I was in Paris years ago, there were billboards sporting the titles of a show that Roland Petit had just choreographed for his wife which read *Zizi, je t'aime.* I will close this letter with the words, "Marina, je t'aime."

Courtesy of the Indiana University Archives

"All artists want immortality and my idea of immortality is not just having my name in some dance books and in *Who's Who*. It's passing on what I have learned to others, some of whom will pass it on to others later. That's rewarding!" —Marina Svetlova

Courtesy of the Indiana University Archives

ENDNOTES

Chapter 2
Ballet Pedagogy

1. Katherine Sorley Walker, *De Basil's Ballets Russes* (Alton: Dance Books, 1982), 97.
2. Selma Jeanne Cohen, vol. 1 of *International Encyclopedia of Dance* (London: Oxford Press, 1998), 191.
3. Lucille Marsh as quoted in *Dance Magazine* (October 1944): 27.

Chapter 3
Baby Ballerinas

1. Katherine Sorley Walker, *De Basill's Ballets Russes* (Alton: Dance Books, 1982), 180.
2. Lincoln Kirstein, *Ballet: Bias & Belief* (New York: Dance Horizons, 1983), 176.
3. Caryl Brahms, *Footnotes to the Ballet* (London: Peter Davies, 1936), 70.
4. Ibid., 59.
5. Rosalyn Krokov, *The Dance* (October 15, 1947).
6. Walker, 188.
7. Ibid., 8.
8. Kirstein, 305.
9. Vincente Garcia-Marquez, *The Ballets Russes* (New York: Alfred A. Knopf, 1990), 49.
10. 10.Walker, 7–8.
11. Ibid., 16.
12. Ibid., 190.
13. Sol Hurok, *The World of Ballet* (London: Robert Hale, 1955), 167–169.
14. Arnold Haskell, *Balletomania* (London: Victor Gollancz, 1934), 240.
15. P. Cohen, *International Encyclopedia of Dance* (Sydney, Australia: 1940), 313.
16. Anatole Chujoy, *Dance Magazine* (January 1941): 4.
17. Olia Philippoff, *Marina Svetlova* (New York: Camereon & Bulkley, 1942), foreword.
18. Ibid.
19. Olga Philippoff, *International Favorite of Four Continents* (New York: Prospect Printing, 1942).
20. Ibid., foreword.
21. Carlos Jose Costa, "Ernesto De Quesada," as quoted in *La Historia del Teatro Colon* (Lima:1908–1968), 168.
22. Olga Maynard, *The American Ballet* (Philadelphia: Macrae Smith, 1959), 154.
23. Anatole Chujoy, as quoted in *Dance Magazine* (December 1940): 2–5.
24. Caryl Brahms, *Footnotes to the Ballet* (London: Peter Davies, 1936), 43.
25. Francis Mason, "What is a Ballerina?" *Dance Magazine* (November 1953): 16.
26. "The Original Russia Ballet to Return to the United States," *Dance Magazine* (February 1940): 42.
27. Anatole Chujoy, "Original Ballet Russe," *Dance Magazine* (December 1940, 3.
28. Walker, 89.

Chapter 4
Ballerina

1. Francis Mason, "What is a Ballerina?" *Dance Magazine* (November 1953): 14.
2. Caryl Brahms, *Footnotes on the Ballet* (London: Peter Davis London, 1936), 6–8.
3. Ibid., 61.
4. Ibid.
5. Ibid., 262. R. C. Jenkinson, "The Ballet from the Front of the House."
6. *American Ballet Theatre Souvenir Program, 1944–45.*
7. *Indiana University News Bureau* 4 (1960): 28.
8. Olga Maynard, *The American Ballet* (Philadelphia: Macrae Smith, 1959), 154.
9. Ibid.
10. Ohia Philippoff, *Marina Svetlova* (1942).
11. Ibid.
12. *Ballet Today* (March 1960): 13.
13. L. Whitelock in *Telegraph Brisbane,* as quoted in Philippoff.
14. S. M. Powell in the *Star, Montreal,* as quoted in Philippoff.
15. Ibid.
16. Roger Duhamel in *Le Canada Montreal.*
17. Marcel Valois in *La Presse Montreal.*
18. M. R. De Coteret in *La Patria Montreal.*
19. Morgan-Powell in *Star Montreal.*
20. C. Armstrong, *Evening Citizen, Ottawa.*
21. H. R. Rudkin Montreal.
22. Anatole Chujoy, *Dance Magazine* (1940): 3–4.
23. B. Burdett in the *Herald, Melbourne,* as quoted in Philippoff.
24. *National Magazine Australia.*
25. Chujoy, *Dance Magazine* (October 1941): 22.
26. R. J. in *Sun Sydney,* as quoted in Philippoff.
27. A. Briddle, Washington, DC.
28. C. E. C, the *Telegraph,* Brisbane.
29. ABT 1944–45.
30. Jean Cocteau in Arnold Haskell, *Balletomania* (London: Victor Gallancz, 1954), 85.
31. Anatole Chujoy, *American Ballet Theatre Souvenir Program, 1944–45.*
32. Brahms, 9.
33. Edwin Denby, *Dance Writings* (New York: Borzoi Book, 1980), 7
34. "Vera Zorina," *Dance Magazine* (December 1959): 69.
35. Brahms, 10, 14.
36. Doris Herring, *Dance Magazine* (December 1959): 92.
37. Haskell, 57.
38. *Dance Magazine* (April 1958): 11.
39. Haskell, 25.
40. Ibid., 63–64.
41. Denby, 252.
42. Ibid., 7.
43. Lincoln Kirstein, *Ballet: Bias and Belief* (New York: Dance Horizons, 1986), 392.
44. Edwin Denby, *Dance Writings and Poetry,* 133.
45. *Reading Dance,* 705.
46. Michael Pye, "GEOconversation," *Geo* (August 1983)": 13.
47. Gottlieb, 705.

48. Pye, *Geo* 8 (1983): 13.

49. Dorothy Alexander, *Dance Magazine* (September 1944): 17.

50. D'Archy Marsh in Philippoff.

51. Ted Shawn, *How Beautiful Upon the Mountain* (Lee: Kissinger, 1948), chapter 7.

52. Lorca Peress, "New York Theatre," http://adaumbelles.squarespace.com/interviews2011/12/15/temple-of-the-souls interview.

Chapter 5
Balletomania

1. L. J., "A Balletromane's Scrapbook," *Dance Magazine* (September 1959): 22.

2. Arnold Haskell, *Balletomania* (London: Victor Gallancz, 1954), 36.

3. Esquire (July 1949): 39.

4. Edward W. Wodson, Toronto as quoted in Olia Philippoff, *Marina Svetlova* (New York, Cameron & Bulkley, 1942).

5. Lincoln Kirstein, *Ballet: Bias & Belief* (New York: Horizon Books, 1983), 307.

6. Vera Zorina, *Dance Magazine* (December 1959): 69.

7. Dance Magazine (September 1959): 23.

8. Caryl Brahms, *Footnotes to the Ballet* (London: Peter Davies, 1941), 182, 185.

9. Haskell, 61.

10. Haskell, 59.

11. Jack Anderson, *Ballet & Modern Dance* (Pennington: Princeton Books, 1995), 102.

12. Ibid., 113.

13. Haskell, 35.

14. Ibid., 61.

15. R. C. Jenkinson, "Ballet from the Front of the House." as quoted in Brahms, 256, 263.

16. Ibid., 71.

17. Lincoln Kirstein, *Dance: A Short History* (New York: Dance Horizons, 1977), 254–55.

18. Emily Coleman, *Dance Magazine* (November 1941): 17, 23.

19. Haskell, 41,

20. Olia Philippoff, *Marina Svetlova* (New York: Cameron & Bulkley, 1942).

21. Diana Daniels, *Dance Magazine* (September 1959): 44, 83.

22. John Chapman, *Dance Magazine* (September 1946): 37.

23. (May 1944): 4–5.

24. Selma Jeanne Cohen, *Dance Magazine* (July 1976): 51.

Chapter 6
Sleeping Beauty

1. Olga Maynard, *The American Ballet* (Philadelphia: McCrae Smith, 1959), 154.

2. Anatole Chujoy, "The Sleeping Beauty Is Fifty Years Young," *Dance Magazine* (January 1940): 11.

3. Chujoy "Ballet Theatre Opens Third Season," Ibid. (December 1941), 17.

4. R. H., *Montreal Matin,* as quoted in Olia Philippoff, *Marina Svetlova* (New York: Cameron & Bulkley, 1942).

5. Arnold Haskell, *Balletomania* (London: Victor Gollancz, 1954), 56.

6. Ibid., 54.

7. Ibid., 59.

8. Caryl Brahms, *Footnotes to the Ballet* (London: Peter Davies, 1941), 12.

9. Haskell, 22.

10. Roger Buchmel, *Le Canada, Montreal,* as quoted in Philippoff.

11. H. Wittaker, the *Gazette, Montreal.*
12. Marcel Valois, *La Presse Montreal.*
13. De Cuteret, *La Paytrie, Montreal.*
14. S. M. P., the *Star, Montreal.*
15. *Dance Magazine* (April 1963): 34–38.
16. Akim Volynsky, "Olga Spessivtseva" Gottlieb (New York:Pantheon Book, 2008) 456–458.
17. Sir Anton Dolin, "Olga Spessivtseva," Ibid. 1122–1123.

Chapter 7
Guest Appearances

1. *Dance Magazine* (August 1950): 4.
2. John Gilpin, *A Dance with Life* (London: William Kimber 1982), 92.
3. Ted Shawn, *How Beautiful Upon the Mountain* (USA: Kessinger Legacy Reprints, 1947).
4. *Dance Magazine* (February 1945): 22.
5. *I. U. News Bureau* (April 28, 1970).
6. *Dancer's Notebook* 12, no. 1 (1966): 2.
7. *Dance Magazine* (January 1968): 14.
8. "Successful Toranto," *Dance Magazine* (August 1945).
9. Gilpin, 90.
10. Eva Maze, *With Ballet in My Soul* (Sarasota: Moonstone Press, 2017), 65–70.
11. Ibid.
12. *Esquire* (July 1949): 39.
13. *Dance Magazine* (October 1953): 3.
14. Ibid.
15. *Esquire* (July 1949): 39.

Chapter 8
Col. W. de Basil's Original Ballet Russe

1. Vicente Garcia-Marquez, *Ballets Russes* (London: *Daily Express,* 8/21/29), 3.
2. Edwin Evans as quoted in *Col. W. de Basil Ballets Russes 1934–35 Souvenir Program.*
3. Valerian Svetloff, "Westward Ho the Dance!" as quoted in *Twenty-Five Years of American Dance,* ed. Doris Herring (New York: Rudolf Orthwine, 1954), 21.
4. Arnold Haskell, *Balletomania* (London: Victor Gallancz, 1954), 90.
5. *Original Ballet Russe Souvenir Program 1936–1937.*
6. Katherine Sorley Walker, *de Basil's Ballets Russes* (Alton: Dance Books, 1982), 4.
7. Arnold Haskell as quoted in *Ballet Russe Souvenir Program 1936–37.*
8. Arnold Haskell as quoted in Walker, 236.
9. *Original Ballet Russe Souvenir Program 1936–1937.*
10. Lincoln Kirstein, *Ballet: Bias & Belief* (New York: Dance Horizons, 1983), 176.
11. Haskell, 243.
12. Garcia-Marquez, xii.
13. Walker, 237.
14. Caryl Brahms, *Footnotes on the Ballet* (London: Peter Davies, 1936), xv, xvi.
15. *Original Ballet Russe Souvenir Program 1935–1936.*
16. Ibid., 1934–35.
17. Ibid., 1935–36.
18. Garcia-Marquez, 139.

19. *Ballet Russe Souvenir Program 1934–35.*

20. Walker, 238.

21. Sono Osato, *Distant Dances* (New York: Alfred A. Knopf, 1980), 147.

22. Edward Denby, *Looking at the Dance* (Terre Haute: Popular Library, 1949), 191.

23. Garcia, 247–48.

24. Ibid., 5.

25. Dance. March 1939): 2.

26. Ann Barzel as quoted in *Dance Magazine* (December 1940): 5.

27. Walker, 97.

28. *Dance Magazine* (November 1941): 14.

29. Garcia-Marquez, 269.

30. *Dance Magazine* (December 1940): 3.

31. Ibid., 43–47.

32. B. Burdett, the *Melbourne Herald Tribune,* quoted in Olia Philippoff, *Marina Svetlova* (Cameron & Bulkley, 1942).

33. *Dance Magazine* (November 1939): 7.

34. *Dance Magazine* (February 1940): 47.

35. *Dance Magazine* (December 1940): 8.

36. *Dance Magazine* (February 1940): 46.

37. *Dance Magazine* (December 1940): 8

38. *Dance Magazine* (January 1937): 16.

39. Walker, 179.

40. Ibid., 238.

41. *Original Ballet Russe Souvenir booklet 1934–1935.*

42. *Ballets Russes de Monte Carlo, Direction W. de Basil 1935–36 Souvenir Book.*

43. Osato, 179.

Chapter 9
La Lutte Eternelle

1. Olia Philippoff, *Marina Svetlova* (New York: Cameron & Bulkley, 1942).

2. Ibid., October 1940, 22–23.

3. Igor Schwezoff as quoted in Ibid., June 1940, 3.

4. Katherine Sorely Walker, *de Basil's Ballets Russes* (Alton: Dance Books, 1982), 100.

5. Edwin Denby, *Dance Writings* (New York: Alfred A. Knopf, 1986), 70.

6. Walker, 103.

7. *Dance Magazine* (June 1940): 2.

8. *Dance Magazine* (December 1946): 32, 43, 44.

9. J. J., *Montreal Star,* as quoted in Philippoff.

10. J. D. Callagham. *Detroit Free Press as quoted in ibid.*

Chapter 10
Graduation Ball

1. Vicente Garcia-Marquez, *The Ballets Russes* (New York: Alfred A. Knopf, 1990), 310.

2. Ibid., 264.

3. Edwin Denby, *Dance Writings* (New York: Alfred A. Knopf, 1986), 68.

4. Garcia-Marquez, 247.

5. Denby, 172.

6. Ibid., 68.

7. Garcia-Marquez, 238.

8. Arnold Haskell. *Dancing Times,* as quoted in Garcia-Marquez, 242.

9. Garcia-Marquez, 188.

10. Arnold Haskell, as quoted in Garcia-Marquez, 242.

11. Katherine Sorley Walker, *De Basil's Ballets Russes* (Alton: Dance Books, 1982), 102.

12. Ibid., 103.

13. Garcia-Marquez, 239.

14. Ibid., 239.

15. S. M. Powell in *Montreal Morning Star,* as quoted in Philippoff.

16. Olia Philippoff, *Marina Svetlova* (New York: Cameron & Bulkley, 1942).

17. Walker, 99.

18. Ibid., 216.

19. Garcia-Marquez, 270.

20. Walker, 145.

Chapter 11
Balustrade

1. Vicente Garcia-Marquez, *The Ballets Russes* (New York: Alfred A. Knopf, 1990), 280.

2. Katherine Sorley Walker, *de Basil's Ballets Russes* (New York, Dance Books, 1982), 104–05.

3. Garcia-Marquez, 278.

4. Ibid., 277.

5. Robert Gottlieb, ed., D*ance Readings* (New York: Simon & Schuster, 1967), 824–825.

6. Edwin Denby, *Looking at the Dance* (Terre Haute: Popular Library, 1949), 208.

7. Edwin Denby, *Dance Writings* (New York: Alfred A. Knopf, 1986), 413.

8. John Martin as quoted in Garcia-Marquez, 277.

9. Ibid., 277.

10. Edwin Denby, *Dance Writings* (New York: Alfred A. Knopf, 1986), 413.

11. Walker, 104.

12. Ibid., 105.

13. Garcia-Marquez, 280.

14. Walker, 104.

15. Ibid., 281.

16. Denby, 412–13.

17. Walker, 104.

18. Ibid., 105.

19. Ibid., 105.

20. Lillian Moore, "*Ballustrade* the New Balanchine" as quoted in *Dancing Time*, 383–84.

21. Garcia-Marquez, 277.

22. Ibid., 278.

23. Edwin Denby, "A Note on Balanchine's Style" in *Dance Index,* ed. Ronald Windam (New York: Dance Index-Ballet Caravan, March 1945), 38.

24. Denby, 204.

25. Ibid., 205.

26. Lillian Moore, *Dancing Times* (April 1941): 382–385.

27. Gottlieb, *Reading Dance.*

28. Moore Lillian, *Dancing Times* (April 1941): 382–385.

29. Sono Osata, *Distant Dances* (New York: Alfred A. Knopf, 1980), 178.

30. Francis Mason in *Reading Dance*, 824–25.

31. www.cmi.university.frmescouhe/danse/*Balustrade*.htlml-Emily Cohen, Elizabeth Lynch, Sandy Kurz, Suzie Snyder Via.

32. Garcia-Mendez, 280.

33. Walker, 103–104.

34. Ibid., Lillian Moore, 102–105.

35. Edwin Denby, *Looking at the Dance* (Terre Haute: Popular Library, 1949), 205.

36. Ibid., 204–05.

37. Denby, 108.

38. Ibid., 204.

39. Anatl Chujoy as quoted in Garcia-Marquez, 280–281.

40. Garcia- Marquez, 278–80.

41. Denby, 205–206.

42. Ibid., 205.

43. Garcia-Marquez, 280.

44. Ibid., 280.

45. Ibid., 280.

46. Walker, 105.

47. Denby, 413.

48. Garcia-Marquez, 278.

49. Garcia-Marquez, 281.

50. Denby, *Looking*, 208.

51. Walker, 105.

52. Ibid., 105.

Chapter 12
Battle of the Ballets Russes-es

1. *Dance Magazine* (May 1944), 4–5.

2. *Col. W. de Basil Original Ballet Russe* souvenir program,1946–47.

3. Olga Maynard, *The American Ballet* (Philadelphia: Macrae Smith, 1959), 41.

4. *Col. W. de Basil Original Ballet Russe* souvenir program, 1946–47.

5. *Ballet Russe* flyer.

6. Arnold Haskell, *Balletomania* (London: Victor Gallancz, 1954), 229.

7. Walker Sorely Katherine, *De Basil's Ballets Russes* (Alton: Dance Books, 1982), 81.

8. Ibid., 101–102.

9. Lincoln Kirstein, *Ballet Bias & Belief* (New York: Dance Horizons, 1983), 217.

10. *Dance Magazine* (November 1941): 14.

11. Vicente Garcia-Marquez, *The Ballets Russes* (New York: Alfred A. Knopf, 1990), 209.

12. Maynard, 87.

13. Garcia-Marquez, 274.

14. Edwin Denby, *Dance Writings* (New York: Alfred A. Knopf, 1986), 68.

15. Garcia-Marquez, 215.

16. Ibid., 268–269.

17. *Dance Magazine* (November 1941): 12–13.

18. Ibid., 15.

19. *Dance Magazine* (December 1940): 8–12.

20. Ibid., 3–4.

21. Garcia-Marquez, xii.

22. Paul R. Milton in *Dance Magazine* (March 1939): 2.

23. *New York Times,* November 7, 1940, as quoted in Garcia-Marquez, 269.

24. Ibid.

25. *Metropolitan Opera House,* October 12, 1944, 24.

26. *Dance Magazine* (May 1944): 2.

27. *Dance Magazine* (October 1940): 12.

28. Richard Pleasant, Alexander Kahn in *Dance Magazine* (February 1940): 32.

29. Anatole Chujoy as quoted in *Dance Magazine* (February 1940): 33–34.

30. Rudolf Orthwine, *Dance Magazine* (August 1946): 7.

31. Denby, 121.

32. *Dance Magazine* (December 1941): 15.

33. Anton Dolin as quoted in *Ballet Theatre 1940 Souvenir Program.*

34. *Dance Magazine* (May 1944).

35. *Met Ballet Program,* October 12, 1944, 3.

36. Denby, 123–34.

Chapter 13

The Great Migration

1. Valerian Svetloff, "Westard Ho The Dance," as quoted in Doris Hering, *Twenty-Five Years of American Dance* (New York: Rudolf Orthwine, 1954), 10.

2. John Gruen in *Dance Magazine* (October 1976): 48.

3. Anton Dolin, "Ballet Takes Sanctuary—in America," *Ballet Theatre* 1940 program book, (New York: Artcraft Lithograph and Printing, 1940).

4. John Briggs in *Dance Magazine* (December 1946): 48–49.

5. *Dance Magazine* (June 1940): 3.

6. Moira Hodgson, "After Diaghilev," as quoted in the *New Criterion* 9 (March 1931).

7. Lincoln Kirstein, *Ballet Bias & Belief* (New York: Dance Horizons, 1983), 54.

8. Ibid., 167.

9. *Dance Magazine* (October 1940): 9.

10. *Dance Magazine* (March 1939): 2–29.

11. Eugene Loring, "A Heritage for Ballet in America," as quoted in *Ballet Theatre 1940.*

12. Anatole Chujoy in *Dance Magazine* (March 1941): 4.

13. *Ballet Russe 1937–1938 Souvenir Program Book.*

14. *Dance Magazine* (February 1940): 43.

15. Sono Osato, *Distant Dances* (New York: Alfred A. Knopf, Barzoi Book, 1980), 179.

17. *Ballet Russe de Monte Carlo Souvenir Program Book 1945–46.*

18. *Dance Magazine* (October 1940): 9.

19. L. T. Carr in *Dance Magazine* (October 1941): 24.

20. Loring.

21. Kirstein, 213.

22. *Metropolitan Opera Program,* August 12, 1944, 3.

23. *Dance Magazine* (April 1939): 9.

24. Garcia-Marquez, 269.

25. Michel Fokine, "The American Ballet Today" as quoted in Hering,11.

26. *Ballet Russe de Monte Carlo 1945–1946 Souvenir Program Book.*

27. Anatole Chujoy in *Dance Magazine* (March 1941): 4.

28. John Briggs in *Dance Magazine* (December 1946): 49.

29. L. T. Carr, "Dance World," as quoted in *Dance Magazine* (October 1941): 2410, 41.

30. Kirstein, 169.

31. Edwin Denby, *Looking at the Dance* (New York: Popular Library, 1943), 53.

32. Dance Magazine (February 1941): 22, 41.

33. Kirstein, 57.

34. Ibid., 205.

35. Dance Magazine (December 1939): 7.

36. Edward Denby, *Dance Writings* (New York: Alfred A. Knopf, 1986), 121.

37. Walter Terry in *Dance Magazine* (February 1940): 31, 56.

38. Denby, *Looking at the Dance*, 46–50.

39. Kirstein, 67.

40. Ibid., 45.

41. Dance Magazine (February 1940): 6.

42. Dance Magazine (October 1941): 22.

43. Met Program, October 12, 1944, 24.

Chapter 14
Jacob's Pillow

1. Ted Shawn, *How Beautiful Upon the Mountain* (Ted Shawn, Kessinger Legacy Reprints, 1948).

2. Ibid.

3. Rachel Strauss, *Jacob's Pillow Dance Festival: A Dance Heritage Collection.*

4. Sharry Traver Underwood, *No Daughter of Mine Is Going to Be a Dancer!* (Sharry Traver Underwood, 2012), 41.

5. Ibid., 25–26.

6. Dance Screen and Stage (February 1948): 18–20.

7. La Meri as quoted in *Dance Magazine* (September 1952): 22.

8. Shawn, *Mountain.*

9. Ibid., chapter 7.

10. Ibid., chapter 8.

11. Ibid.

12. Ibid.

13. Ibid.

14. Strauss.

15. Michelle Potter, *On Dancing* (www.broadwayworld.com, Michelle Potter).

16. Ibid.

17. New York, December 19, 1948.

18. Dance Magazine (May 1944): 28.

19. Harry Wagstaff Gribble as quoted in *Dance Magazine* (February 1940): 41.

Chapter 15
Opera Ballet

1. Caryl Brahms, *Footnotes to the Dance* (London: Peter Davies, 1941), 38.

2. Edwin Denby, *Dance Writings* (New York: Alfred A. Knopf, 1986), 189.

3. Maya Kulkarni as quoted in *Dance Magazine* (January 1976): 82.

4. Ibid., (November 1942): 11.

5. Ibid., Anatole Chujoy (April 1939): 16.

6. Dance Magazine (June 1943): 8, 9, 32.

7. Cohen, *Ballet Dictionary* IV, 388.

8. John Rosenfeld in *Dallas Morning News,* April 23, 1949.

9. Denby, 189.

10. *Dance Screen and Stage*, ed. Doris Herring (February 1948): 47.

11. Elizabeth Eulass in *Opera News,* December 1945, 28–30.

12. *Dance Magazine* (December 1951): 22, 23, 36–38.

13. George Kearny in *Dance Magazine* (January 1946).

14. *Dance Magazine* (February 1953): 34.

15. *Dallas Morning News,* April 13, 1970, 15A.

16. *Saturday Evening Post,* January 24, 1970.

17. *Irving Daily News*, Irving, Texas, "Opera," February 1965, 34.

18. *Dance Magazine* (April 1946): 52.

19. *Dance Magazine* (November 1945): 5–6.

20. *Opera News,* November 1945, 4–6.

21. *New York Sun,* as printed in *International Favorite of Four Continents* (Prospect Printing Co., 1944).

22. *New York Herald Tribune,* as quoted in Ibid.

23. Eugene H. Palatsky in *Opera News,* April 1965, 13.

24. *Dance Magazine* (January 1951): 21.

25. *International Favorite on Four Continents.*

26. *Musical Courier,* April 1951, 3.

27. Press release, NYC Opera, 1950.

28. *Musical Courier,* April 1951.

29. *Manchester, Vt., Journal,* August 23, 1962.

Chapter 16
Choreography

1. *Evening Recorder, Amsterdam, MNY,* January 17, 1958, 12.

2. Caryl Brahms, *Footnotes to the Ballet* (London: Peter Davies, 1941), 4.

3. Arnold Haskell, *Balletomania* (London: Victor Gollancz, 1954), 129.

4. George Balanchine as quoted in *Dance Index* IV, nos. 2, 3 (March 1945): 20.

5. Edwin Denby, *Looking at the Dance* (New York: Popular Library, 1949), 47.

6. Susan Reiter as quoted in (April 2011): 27.

7. George Kearny as quoted in *Dance Magazine* (April 1946).

8. Metropolitan Opera House Ballet Theatre program pamphlet, October 12, 1944, 3.

9. Lincoln Kirstein, *Ballet: Bias and Belief* (New York: Dance Horizons, 1983), 255.

10. Ibid., 306.

11. *Dance Magazine* (November 1940): 11.

12. *Evening Recorder Amsterdam*, January 23, 1958.

13. An Barzel as quoted in *Dance Magazine* (January 1955): 7.

14. Sol Hurok, *Sol Hurok Presents* (New York: Hermitage House,1953), 146.

15. Brahms, 48.

16. Ibid., 98.

17. Eva Desca as quoted in *Dance Magazine*, 30.

18. Gilbert Reed as quoted in *IU News Bureau Archives,* November 21, 1969.

19. John Ardoin as quoted in *Dallas Morning News,* November 23, 1967.

21. *Dance Encyclopedia,* ed. Anatole & P. W. Manchester (New York: Simon and Schuster, 1967), 72.

22. *Dance Magazine* (November 1942): 11.

23. Denby, 217–218.

24. Kirstein, 311.

25. Bill T. Jones as quoted in (1976): 16.

26. Ibid., (January 1959): 34–35.

27. Roland Wingfield as quoted in *Dance Magazine* (January 1959): 34–35.

28. Edward Allen Jewell as quoted in *Ballet Russe de Monte Carlo Souvenir Program Book.*

29. Lincoln Kirstein as quoted in *Reading Dance,* 1300–01.

30. Frederick Ashton as quoted in Ibid., 2–3.

31. Michal Pye as quoted in *Geo* (August 1983): 12.

32. Brahms, 83.

33. Denby, 165.

34. Daniel Nagrin as quoted in *Dance Magazine* (September 1951).

35. Ibid., (March 1959): 44, 45, 84, 85.

36. Brahms, 73.

37. Joan Kunsch, *Playing with Gravity* (Simsbury: Atrim House, 2007), 29.

38. Kirstein, 397.

39. Brahms, 11.

40. Kirstein, 423.

41. Denby, 81.

42. *Dance Magazine* (February 1940): 8.

43. Denby, 153.

44. Ibid., 129.

45. Brahms, 129–130.

46. Ibid., 8.

47. George Clark Leslie as quoted in *Original Ballet Russe 1946–47.*

48. Brahms, 345.

49. Kirstein, 422.

50. Ibid.

51. Ibid., 423.

52. Kirstein, 422

53. Kirstein, 423

54. Dance Magazine (June, 1959): 44

Chapter 17

Touring

1. *Evening Recorder,* Amsterdam, NY, January 17, 1958.

2. Olga Maynard, *The American Ballet* (Philadelphia: Macrae Smith, 1959), 147.

3. Ibid., 156.

4. Saul Cohen as quoted in *Dance Magazine* (May 1953).

5. Ibid., (November 1944): 14.

6. Ibid., (October 1939): 14.

7. Maynard, 155–56.

8. Vicente Garcia-Marquez, *The Ballets Russes* (New York: Alfred A. Knopf, 1990), 4.

9. Pierre Vladimiroff in *Dance Magazine* (January 1941): 14.

10. John Gruen in *Dance Magazine* (October 1976): 48.

11. Maynard, 154.

12. *Twenty-Five Years of American Dance,* ed. Rudolf Orthwine (New York: Rudolf Orthwine, 1954), 36–37.

13. Maynard, 154.

14. Dorothy Alexander in *Dance Magazine* (September 1944): 9.

15. Maynard, 156.

16. John Gilpin, *A Dance with Life* (London: William Kimber, 1982), 91.

17. Dorothy Alexander in *Dance Magazine* (September 1944): 17.

18. *Chicago Sunday Tribune*, April 20, 1947, 15.

19. *Dance Magazine* (October 1940): 15.

20. Maynard, 154.

21. Ibid.

22. *Kingport News*, October 21, 1945.

23. Victoria Kelly, *Dance Magazine* (November 1944): 14.

24. Maynard, 154.

25. D. Med as quoted in the *Daily News*, October 1957, 4.

26. *Dance Magazine* (November 1944): 14.

27. Letter from Svetlova fan found on Facebook.

28. Maynard, 154–56.

29. Ibid., 154.

30. Miriam Marmein in *Twenty-Five Years of American Dance,* 135.

31. Ted Shawn in *Twenty-Five Years of American Dance,* 132–34.

32. Maynard, 156.

33. *Chicago Sunday Tribune,* Marge Sunrise Mountain Farm, April 20, 1947, 1, 11.

34. *Valley News,* Van Nuys, California, June 3, 1955.

35. *Dance Magazine* (December 1960): 37–38.

Chapter 18
Television

1. Ann Barzel as quoted in *Dance Magazine* (November 1957): 8.

2. Ibid., 84.

3. *Dance Magazine* (November 1953): 7.

4. Ann Barzel in *Dance Magazine* (May 1955).

5. *Twenty-Five Years of American Dance,* ed. Doris Hering (NY: Rudolf Orthwine, 1954), 192.

6. *Dance News* (September 1958).

7. Nathan Cohen in *Dance Magazine* (August 1957): 43.

8. *Dance News,* September 1958.

9. Nathan Cohen in *Dance Magazine* (August 1957): 43.

10. Louise Kloepper in *Dance Magazine* (October 1939): 10.

11. Barbara Frost in *Dance Magazine* (May 1952): 18, 19, 26.

12. Ibid., (November 1942): 24.

13. Ibid., (May 1952): 18–19, 36–37.

14. *Twenty-Five Years of American Dance,* ed. Doris Hering (New York: Rudolf Orthwine, 1954), 188–196.

15. *Dance Magazine* (August 1959): 36–39.

16. *Dance Magazine* (October 1939): 10.

17. Vicente Garcia-Marquez, *The Ballets Russes* (New York: Alfred A. Knopf, 1990), 178.

18. Julius Postal in *Dance Magazine* (September 1952): 4.

19. Norma Mclain Stoop in *Dance Magazine* (September 1976): 95.

20. *Musical Courier* (April 4, 1951): 5.

Chapter 19
The Business of Ballet

1. Lincoln Kirstein, *Ballet: Bias & Belief* (New York: Dance Horizons, 1983), 304.

2. Francis Hawkins, "The Future of Dance Management," *Dance Magazine* (April 1939): 10.

3. Ibid., (May 1944): 13, 28.

4. *Ballet Russe de Monte Carlo, Gen. Director: de Basil, 1933 Souvenir Program.*
5. Constantine in *Dance Magazine* (September 1944): 8.
6. *Col. W. de Basil Souvenir Program 1936–1937.*
7. Kirstein, 393.
8. *Metropolitan Opera Program,* "A decade Plus One" (August 1944): 3.
9. *Dance Magazine* (April 1939): 9.
10. Ibid., (October 1940): 13.
11. K. R. N. Swamy, "Pavlova and Hurok," *Dance Magazine* (January 1976): 62.
12. John Dougharty, "West Coast Impresario speaks out about Dancers," *Dance Magazine* (February 1960): 14–15, 76–77.
13. La Meri in *Dance Magazine* (October 1941): 19.
14. Ibid., (May 2015): 35.
15. Bruce V. Bordelon in *Dance Magazine* (February 1976): 24.
16. Ibid., (February 1940), 55.
17. Ibid., (January 1959), 67.
18. Ibid., 54.
19. *Ballet Theatre Souvenir Booklet, 1953.*
20. *Dance Magazine* (August 1976): 84.
21. Bruce V. Bordelon in *Dance Magazine* (July 1976): 92.
22. Winthrop Palmer, *Theatrical Dancing in America* (New York: A. S. Barnes, 1978), 183.
23. Robert Savin "The Bookshelf," *Dance Magazine* (March 1959): 21.
24. Ted Shawn, Olga Maynard's *Ballet in America* (Philadelphia: MaCrae Smith, 1959), foreword
25. *Dance Magazine* (August 1959): 46, 68, 69.
26. Ibid., 40–41.
27. Arnold Haskell, *Balletomania* (London: Victor Gallancz, 1934), 221–223.
28. Maynard, 248.
29. Ibid., 241–243, 248, 263.
30. Kirstein, 213, 251.
31. *Dance Magazine* (January 1959): 67.

Chapter 20
The Svetlova Dance Center

1. Edith Allard, *Dance Magazine* (October 1940): 23.
2. Bill Como in *Dance Magazine* (February 1966): 74, 75.
3. Ibid.
4. Nancy H. Otis as quoted in *Vermont Life* XXII (summer 1968): 44–46.
5. Frances M. Thomas as quoted in *Dance Magazine* (November 1941): 21.
6. *New York Times,* August 1972.

Chapter 21
Honors

1. *Manchester, Vt., Journal,* August 23, 1962, 23.
2. Philippe Canet, *French Federation of the Dance,* December 12, 1988.
3. *Dance Magazine* (August 1946): 7.
4. *Dance Magazine* (June 1962).
5. *Dance Magazine* (February 1943): 3.
6. *Dance Magazine* (January 1945): inside back cover.

Chapter 22
Madame Professor

1. Anthony Tudor in *Dance Magazine* (May 1953): 41.
2. *Dance Magazine* (April 1939): 12.
3. *New York Times*, August 1972.
4. Roberta Bernard in *Dance Magazine* (March 1953): 40.
5. Judy Chazin in *Dance Magazine* (March 1953): 40–41.
6. Jo Taylor in *Dance Magazine* (May 1953): 41.
7. Lloyd Katz in *Dance Magazine* (March 1953): 41.
8. Judith Brin in *Dance Magazine* (October 1971): 4.
9. Katherine Sorely Walker, *De Basil's Ballets Russes* (Alton: Dance Books, 1982), 97.
10. Ted Shawn in Maynard, *The American Ballet* (Philadelphia: Macrae Smith, 1959), foreword.
11. Ibid.
12. Heidi Obenhauer as quoted in *Dance Magazine* (August 1976): 88.
13. *Dance Magazine* (March 1953): 38.
14. Scott Dever in *Indiana Daily Student,* November 15, 1976.
15. Ibid., 16.
16. *Arbutus* (Bloomington: IU Press, 1977).

Marina Svetlova's performances of complete operas with the Metropolitan Opera Ballet:

1943

The Bartered Bride 12/12/1943; Carmen. 12/23/1943; Cavalleria Rusticana/Pagliacci, 12/25/1943

1944

Carmen 1/22/1944; *Cavaleria Rusticana/Pagliacci* 1/29/1944; *Aida* 2/4/44; Zinka Milanovas *Aida; Mignon* 2/5/44; *Aida* 2/4/44; *Cav/Pag.* 2/23/44; *Aida* 2/29/44; *Carmen* 3/3/44; *Aida* 3/7/44; *Mignon* 3/16/44; *Aida* 3/23/44; *Carmen* 3/24/44; *Mignon* 3/31/1944; *Aida* 4/3/1944; *Carmen* 4/5/1944; *Mignon* 4/6/1944; *Carmen* 4/12/1944; *Aida* 4/14/1944; *Aida,* in Manhasset 4/20/1944; *Mignon* 4/21/1944; *Carmen* 4/22/1944; *Aida* 4/27/1944; *Mignon* 5/4/1944; *Tanhausser* 5/5/1944; *Carmen* 5/6/1944; *Aida* 11/30/1944; *Carmen* 12/7/1944; *Aida* 12/15/1944; *Aida* 12/16/1944; *Carmen* 12/25/1944

1945

Aida 1/1/1945; *Carmen* 1/6/1945; *le Coq d'Or.; Aida* 1/31/1945; *Gioconda* 2/5/1945; *Carmen* 2/7/1945; *Mignon* 2/9/1945; *Aida* 2/16/1945; *Mignon* 2/19/1945; *Gioconda* 2/21/1945; *Mignon* 2/27/1945; *le Coq d'Or.* 3/1/1945; *Gioconda* 3/3/1945; *Mignon* 3/3/1945; *le Coq d'Or* 3/19/1945; *Aida* 3/23/1945; *Carmen* 3/24/1945; *Tannhauser* 12/14/1945; *Traviata* 12/15/1945; *Tannhauser* 12/18/1945; *Gioconda* 12/21/1945; *Tannhauser* 12/27/1945; *Traviata* 12/31/1945

1946

Gioconda 1/2/1946; *La Gioconda* 1/19/1946; *Tannhauser* 1/21/1946; *Traviata* 1/23/1946; *Tannhauser* 2/27/1946; *Gioconda* 2/28/1946; *Traviata* 3/7/1946; *Gioconda* 3/16/1946; *Traviata* 3/23/1946; *Tannhauser* 3/23/1946; *Gioconda* 3/25/1946; *Gioconda* 4/1/1946; *Tannhauser* 4/2/1946; *Tannhauser* 4/4/1946; *Traviata* 4/6/1946; *Traviata* 4/15/1946; *Tannhauser* 4/23/1946; *Tannhauser* 4/29/1946; *Tannhauser* 5/2/1946; *Traviata* 5/3/1946; *Tannhauser* 5/6/1946; *Traviata* 5/7/1946; *Gioconda* 5/8/1946; *Tannhauser* 5/13/1946; *Lakme* 11/11/1946; *Aida* 11/12/1946; *Aida* 11/18/1946; *Lakme* 11/23/1946; *Traviata* 11/23/1946; *Aida* 12/4/1946; *Lakme* 12/6/1946; *La*

Traviata 12/10/1946; *Lakme* 12/17/1946; *La Traviata* 12/21/1946; *Lakme* 12/25/1946; *Hansel und Gretel/Walpurgis Nacht premiere* 12/25/1946;
Walpurgis Nacht/Hansel und Gretel 12/27/1946; *Aida* 12/28/1946

1947

Tannhauser 11/13/1947; *Mignon* 11/24/1947; *La Traviata* 11/29/47; *Tannhauser* 12/1/1947; *Aida* 12/5/47; *La Traviata* 12/8/47; *Manon* 12/9/1947; *Louise* 12/12/47; *La Gioconda* 12/18/47; *Manon* 12/20/47; *Louise* 12/22/47; *Hansel und Gretel/a Midsummer Night's Dream* 12/26/47; *Tannhauser* 12/27/47; *Hansel/Midsummer Night's* 12/28/47; *Aida* 12/30/47

1948

Manon 1/1/48; *Gioconda* 1/2/48; *Traviata* 1/4/48; *Louise* 1/6/48; *Louise* 1/10/48; *Aida* 1/12/48; *Traviata* 1/14/48; *Gioconda* 1/17/48; *Tannhauser* 1/30/48; *Manon* 1/31/48; *Manon* 3/27/48; *Traviata* 3/31/48; *Aida* 4/5/48; *Traviata* 4/7/48; *Manon* 4/9/48; *Traviata* 4/11/1948; *Aida* 4/18/48; *Manon* 4/20/48; *Traviata* 4/24/48; *Aida* 4/26/48; *Traviata* 5/1/48; *Traviata* 5/5/48; *Manon* 5/10/48; Enzio Pinzo, *Count des Grieux; Rigoletto* 12/4/48; Martha Lipton, Madelena; *Mignon* 12/8/48; *Louise* 12/10/48; *Mignon* 12/23/48; *Aida* 12/24/48; *Louise* 12/27/48; *Traviata* 12/31/48

1949

Mignon 1/4/49; *Aida* 1/8/49; *Louise* 1/12/49; *Mignon* 1/17/49; *Louise* 1/21/1949; *Traviata* 1/22/1949; Eleanor Steber as Violetta; *Aida* 1/24/49; *Aida* 3/20/49; Margaret Harshaw as Amneris; *Traviata* 3/23/49; *Mignon* 3/26/49; *Aida* 3/26/49; *Mignon* 4/5/1949; *Traviata* 4/6/49; *Traviata* 4/12/49; *Mignon* 4/19 49; *Traviata* 4/20/49; *Mignon* 4/23/49; *Aida* 4/24/49; Margaret Harshaw, Amneris; *Traviata* 4/30/49, Bidu Sayoa as Violetta; *Traviata* 5/7/49, Richard Tucker as Alfredo; *Manon* 5/10/49; *Mignon* 5/13/49; *Carmen* 5/17/49, Bloomington; *Carmen* 5/20/49, St. Louis, Missouri; *Carmen* 12/19/49; *Traviata* 4/6/49; *Traviata* 4/12/49; *Mignon* 4/19 49; *Traviata* 4/20/49; *Mignon* 4/23/49; *Aida* 4/24/49, Margaret Harshaw as Amneris; *Traviata* 4/30/49; Bidu Sayoa as Violetta; *Traviata* 5/7/49; Richard Tucker as Alfredo; *Manon* 5/10/49; *Mignon* 5/13/49; *Carmen* 5/17/49, Bloomington; *Carmen* 5/20/49, St. Louis, Missouri; *Carmen* 12/19/49, Martha Lipton as Mercedes

1950
Traviata 1/24/1950, Ferruccio Tagliavini as Alfredo; *Carmen* 3/25/1950, Jean Madeira as Carmen; *Aida* 3/25/1950, Jerome Heines as Ramfis, Lubja Welitch as Aida; *Aida* 4/1/50 in Boston, Massachusetts; *Aida* 4/4/50, Jean Maeira, Amneris; *Traviata*. 4/6/50, Dorothy Kirstin as Violetta; Jan Peerce as Alfredo, Robert Merrill as Giorgio Germont; *Samson et Dalila* 4/10/50; *Aida* 4/14/50; *Carmen* 4/15/50; *Samson* 4/18/50, Bloomington; *Aida* 4/19/50; *Samson* 4/22/50; *Samson* 4/30/50; *Traviata* 5/1/50

BIBLIOGRAPHY

Alexander, Dorothy. *Dance Magazine* (September 1941).

Ardoin, John. *Dallas Morning News.* November 23, 1967.

Ballet Today (March 1960).

Barzel, Ann. "Dance in Review." *Dance Magazine* (December 1940).

Brahms, Caryl. *Footnotes to the Ballet.* London: Peter Davis, 1936.

Briggs, John. *Dance Magazine* (December 1976).

Chujoy, Anatole, Manchester, P. W. *The Dance Encyclopedia Revised and Enlarged Edition.* New York: Simon and Shuster, 1967.

Chujoy, Anatole. "The Sleeping Princess is Fifty Years Young." *Dance Magazine* (January 1940).

———. "Dance in Review." (February 1940).

———. "Dance in Review." (December 1940).

———. "Dance in Review." (January 1941).

———. "Dance in Review." (March 1941).

———. "Dance in Review." (October 1941).

———. "Dance in Review." (November 1941).

———. "Dance in Review." (April 1963).

———. "Dance in Review." (February 1945).

———. "Dance in Review." (January 1968).

———. "Original Ballet Russe." (December 1940).

———. *American Ballet Theatre 1944–45 Program Book.*

Carr, L. T. *Dance World* (October 1941).

Chapman, John. *Dance Magazine* (September 1941).

Cohen, Selma Jeanne. *Dance Magazine* (July 1976).

Coleman, Emily. *Dance Magazine* (November 1941).

Dance Magazine (January 1937; March, April, November, December 1939; January, June, October, November, December 1940; January, March, April, October, November, December 1941; October, November 1942; June 1943; May, October 1944; November 1945; February, April, December 1946; January, December 1951; January 1955; January, March 1959; April, January 1968).

Dallas Morning News, April 13, 1970.

Dance Stage and Screen (February 1948).

Daniels, Diana. *Dance Magazine* (September 1959).

Denby, Edwin. *Looking at the Dance.* New York: Popular Library, 1936; *Dance Writings.* New York: Alfred A. Knopf, 1986.

Desca, Eva. *Dance Magazine.*

Esquire magazine (July 1949).

Evening Recorder, Amsterdam, New York, January 1958.

Haskell, Arnold. *Balletomania.* London: Victor Gollancz, 1934.

Garcia-Marquez, Vincent. *The Ballets Russes.* New York: Alfred A. Knopf, 1990.

Gottlieb, Robert. *Reading Dance.* New York: Pantheon Books, 2008.

Gribble, Harry. *Dance Magazine* (February 1940).

Grout, Donald J. *A Short History of Opera, One-Volume Edition.* New York: Columbia University Press, 1947.

Gruen, John. *Dance Magazine* (October 1976).

Herald-Telephone Bloomington, May 2, 1986.

Hering, Doris, ed. *25 Years of American Dance,* Revised and Enlarged Edition. New York: Rudolf Orthwine, 1954.

Hurok, S. *Presents.* New York: Hermitage House, 1953.

———. *The World of Ballet.* London: Merritt and Hatcher, 1955.

Indiana Daily Student, November 16, 1976.

Jewell, Edward Allen. *Original Ballet Russe Pram Book.*

Jones, Bill T. *Dance Magazine* (May 1976).

Kearny, George. *Dance Magazine* (January 1946).

———. (April 1946).

Kirstein, Lincoln. *Ballet: Bias & Belief.* New York: Dance Horizons, 1983.

———. *Dance.* New York: Dance Horizons, 1935.

Krokov, Rosalyn. *The Dance* (October 1949).

Kulkarine, Maya. *Dance Magazine* (January 1976).

Kunsch, Joan. *Playing With Gravity.* Simsbury: Antrim House, 2007.

Manchester, Vermont, Journal (August 1962).

Limoli, Denise Warner. *Dance in Saratoga Springs.* Charleston: History Press, 2013.

Maynard, Olga. *The American Ballet.* Philadelphia: Macrae Smith Company, 1959.

Maze, Eva. *With Ballet in My Soul.* Sarasota: Moonstone Press, 2017.

Mitchell, Jack. *Dance Scene U.S.A.,* Cleveland: The World Publishing Company, 1967.

Musical Courrier, April 15, 1951.

Nagrin, Daniel. *Dance Magazine* (September 23, 1951).

New York Times, November 1940.

"Opera." *Irving Daily News,* February 1965.

Opera News, November 1945.

Opera News, March 11, 1946.

Original Ballet Russe Program, 1933–34, 1934–35, 1935–36, 1936–37, 1937–38, 1940–41, 1946–47.

Orthwine, Rudolf. *Dance Magazine* (August 1946).

Osato, Sono. *Distant Voices.* New York: Alfred A. Knopf, 1980.

Palatsky, Eugene H. *Opera News,* April 1965.

Palmer, Winthrop. *Theatrical Dancing in America,* Second Revised Version. London: A. S. Barnes & Company, 1978.

Philippoff, Olia. *Marina Svetlova.* New York: Cameron & Bulkley, 1942.

Pleasant, Richard. *Dance Magazine* (February 1940).

Reed, Gilbert. *I. U. News Bureau,* November 23, 1969.

Reiter, Susan. *Dance Magazine* (April 2011).

Rosenfield, John. *Dallas Morning News,* April 23, 1949.

Saturday Evening Post, January 1970.

Shawn, Ted. *How Beautiful Upon the Mountain,* 3rd edition. New York: Kessinger Legacy Reprints,1947.

Siegmeister, Elie. *The Music Lover's Handbook.* London: William Morrow & Company, 1943.

Simon, Henry W. *100 Great Operas and Their Stories.* New York: Anchor Books, Random House Books, 1957.

Linda Thomas. *Sunday Herald-Times Bloomington*, January 22, 1989.

Vermont Life XXII, no. 4 (summer 1968).

Walker, Katherine Sorley. Alton: Dance Books, 1982.

Wingfield, Roland. *Dance Magazine* (January 1959).

ABOUT THE AUTHOR

"Not only does he have a fine eye for dance, but his expert training in Ballet manifests itself in the way he is able to encourage dancers to realize more of their potential … An added bonus which Mr. Limoli possesses is that he is a fine musician which amplifies the range of his work in Dance." These words were written by Vassili Sulich, a well-known dancer and founder of the Nevada Dance Theatre. Limoli has enjoyed a life totally immersed in the performing arts. While still in high school, he was a Martha Holdings Jennings Award recipient in music, which sponsored his participation in the Oberlin College program at New York's Chautauqua Institute. He won a competition at the Cleveland Institute of Music, which sponsored his studies in clarinet under the principal clarinetist of the Cleveland Orchestra, Robert Marcellus. Limoli matriculated to Indiana University, Bloomington, where he earned separate degrees in clarinet and ballet and eventually received a doctorate, with a major in clarinet and a minor in ballet. As a Fulbright Scholar, Limoli earned a diploma in clarinet from Salzburg's Mozarteum.

The *New York Times* wrote that his clarinet playing "was intimate and imaginative with gently tapered phrases and subtle interpretive strokes," and although the *Cleveland Press* declared that "Michael Limoli seems to have been born to the clarinet," for Limoli, dance had become a passion. *Indiana University: The Bain Regime* reported that Limoli was constantly torn between his great desires to make music and to dance and that "fortunately he was able to perform at a high level in both fields." In Austria, Limoli's dance performances were also greeted with great enthusiasm. The *Salzburger Nachtrichtung* wrote that between ballets, "there was long applause and 'bravo' calls for soloists Dusanka Duricanin and Michael Limoli." The *Bloomington Herald Tribune* reported that: "Principals Nancy Reed and Michael Limoli were particularly affective … Limoli is first clarinetist of the I. U. Philharmonic Orchestra." He was a ballet protégé of Edward Caton and studied under David Howard as a Harkness Ballet trainee.

Currently, Limoli is in high demand as a ballet pianist. He has been an accompanist in most of the foremost dance schools in NYC and has been a pianist for many professional ballet companies, including American Ballet Theatre, New York City Ballet, Pacific Northwest Ballet, the Cleveland/San Jose Ballet, the Cincinnati Ballet Company, and Ballet Hispanico.

He has been on the music faculty at Skidmore College, Empire State College, University of Nevada, Las Vegas, the College of Saint Rose, Albany, and the Nutmeg Conservatory for the Arts in Torrington, Connecticut. He has been on the dance faculty at Indiana University, Skidmore's University without Walls, and Adelphi University, Garden City.